Leopold I of Austria

JOHN P. SPIELMAN

Leopold I of Austria

with 44 illustrations

Rutgers University Press
New Brunswick, New Jersey
1977

For my parents
Jack and Lewanna Spielman

© *1977 Thames and Hudson Ltd, London*

Printed in Great Britain by
Cox & Wyman Ltd, London, Fakenham and Reading

Library of Congress Catalog Card
Number 76-41057

ISBN *0-8135-0836-3*

Contents

Preface

A substantial historical investigation of the rise of the Habsburg monarchy in central Europe remains a major piece of unfinished historical business. This study does not pretend even to begin such an ambitious undertaking; but the series 'Men in Office' offers a welcome occasion to examine the monarch who, by dynastic accident, stood in so crucial a spot on the chessboard of European power politics in the late seventeenth century, forced by circumstances to match his play against the most astute and colourful personalities of his age: Louis XIV, John Sobieski, Innocent XI, Kara Mustafa, and a host of enthusiastic Hungarian insurgents like Peter Zrinyi, Imre Thököly and Ferenc II Rákóczy.

Readers who are familiar with this period will recognize at once how much I have relied on the work of such great Austrian scholars as Oswald Redlich, Alfred Francis Pribram and others. What I have attempted to do here is order the events of this tempestuous epoch chronologically, as they were experienced by the men in power in Vienna, and then to show how these men responded to them and thereby displayed their assumptions and prejudices, their abilities and inadequacies.

The stage for this very baroque drama is mainly central and eastern Europe, an eddy of nationalities that has for centuries swirled around the Alps and eastwards into the Danubian plains. The shifting of political boundaries since the collapse of the Austrian empire has endowed many cities with two or even three names in different languages. The seventeenth-century capital of royal Hungary, known as Pressburg to the Germans and Pószony to the Magyars, is today the Czecho-slovakian city of Bratislava. I have dealt with place-names arbitrarily, using the contemporary name by preference. I have been equally arbitrary in using what I suspect to be the most familiar spelling of proper names (Lobkowitz rather than Lobcović) to spare the reader having to refer to an appendix on the pronunciation of Slavic, Turkish or Magyar names.

One of the great pleasures of working in Austrian history in any period is the courteous, skilful support one receives from archivists and librarians in Vienna, scholars rather than custodians whose patient assistance to a foreign scholar is evident on every page of this book. I am particularly grateful to Dr Anna Benna who introduced me some years ago to the riches of the Haus- Hof- und Staatsarchiv, and to her many colleagues who over the years have always been willing to help decipher a messy passage or unravel a troublesome question of provenance. For this particular project I am indebted to the staff of the Bildsammlung of the Austrian National Library who helped me locate and reproduce many of the illustrations, and to that of the Musiksammlung of the Albertina where I was able to examine Leopold's musical compositions.

The administration of Haverford College generously provided a grant from Ford Foundation funds to assist in gathering illustrative material for this book and for my courses. The staff of the Haverford College Library deserve a monument rather than this brief word of thanks for their unstinting effort to transform a fine undergraduate library into an excellent research facility. The very efficient staff of the Archivo Historico of Simancas, Spain, helped me deal with several small but vexing questions in a most expeditious manner.

No one could be more fortunate than I have been in the wise council and careful comments of the editor. Ragnhild Hatton's detailed comments have improved every page. Derek McKay also read the manuscript and caught a number of errors. Those that remain are, needless to say, entirely my own responsibility. In preparing the manuscript I have enjoyed at every step of the way the encouragement and expert criticism of my wife Danila. The delay this has caused in her own research projects makes my debt all the greater.

Haverford College, 1975

I

The Habsburg Family Enterprise

One of his earliest biographers called him 'Leopold the Great',[1] but the tag never took hold. Even though it is generally agreed that the long reign of Emperor Leopold I brought into being a great new world power, a multi-national empire comprising his dynastic possessions in the middle of Europe, the character of the monarch himself has remained obscure. The lack of historical interest in him may reflect his own rather bland temperament and his preference for allowing circumstances to produce decisions for him. It also reflects the prejudices of generations of historians who have either despised or foolishly romanticized the Habsburg monarchy.

For much of Europe the seventeenth century saw the highest development of the notion of personal sovereignty. The fates of provinces, kingdoms and empires depended upon vital statistics: the marriages, births and deaths within and among a few families. Of these families none represented more perfectly the dynastic aspect of European politics than the house of Habsburg, hereditary dukes of Austria since the thirteenth century.

The *Casa de Austria*, the 'August House' as it was universally known, was unlike any other European dynasty. For nearly four centuries it had preserved unbroken descent through one branch or another from 'the Ancestor' Emperor Rudolf I (1273–91). By comparison the Bourbons, Stuarts, Vasas and Romanovs were recent upstarts. In the fifteenth century Frederick III (1457–93) and Maximilian I (1493–1519) used the prestige of the elective office of Holy Roman Emperor to unite their house by marriage to the heiresses of the rich Burgundian counties in the Netherlands and of the throne of Castile. In Maximilian's lifetime the extinction of these related ruling houses made Spain and the Netherlands a part of the Habsburg patrimony.

Maximilian's grandson Charles I of Spain (1516–56), Charles V of the Empire (1519–56), inherited the rich fruits of this dynastic good fortune, presenting Europe with the danger of a universal monarchy built from hereditary sovereignties and supported by the riches of Castile and its expanding empire in the new world. The problems that arose out of this inheritance were of a magnitude proportional to its size and complex diversity. Charles and his counsellors realized quickly that a single monarch could not hope to manage the whole empire. Geography and the difficulties of long-distance communication prevented that.

As head of the family by right of primogeniture, Charles held for himself the Imperial title, the Burgundian states of the Netherlands, and the crowns of Spain with their colonial and Italian possessions. To his younger brother Ferdinand, who had been brought up in Spain, he transferred the family's original base, the Austrian duchies, and along with them the vexing problems of the eastern frontier against the Turks. Ferdinand's own portion increased suddenly after 1526 when Ladislas, last heir to the united crowns of Bohemia and Hungary, fell in battle against the Turks at Mohács. Ferdinand's marriage with Anne of Hungary, sister of the ill-fated Ladislas (son of the last Jagellon king of Bohemia and Hungary) who had married Ferdinand's sister Mary, gave him claims to both crowns which he managed to make good by election within a few years.

Upon his abdication in 1556 Charles V confirmed this division of the dynasty into two more or less equal branches, passing the Imperial crown along with the eastern possessions to Ferdinand, and the Netherlands and Spain to his own son Philip II. In spite of this practical separation of its parts, however, the family remained a unit. This living 'society of tradition', as Adam Wandruszka has termed it,[2] resembled in many ways a modern family business corporation, a holding company directing at the highest levels the policies of a great variety of subsidiary enterprises. Whenever it could, the family kept its quarrels to itself. The two centres of direction, Madrid in the west and Vienna or Prague in the east, maintained close ties with each other, usually supported each other against the enemies of either or both, and for the most part accepted the primacy of dynastic interests over those of any one part of the whole enterprise.

Everyone born into the family, women as well as men, had a role to play in holding things together and helping to manage the family's affairs through marriage, service as viceroys or by holding important offices in the Church. Most of the Habsburgs did their jobs well and without argument, retaining a voice in the family councils but accepting the duties assigned them.

Preserving the conglomerate whole was not an easy matter. It had, of course, to be defended in battle against its many enemies, but military power alone could not preserve hereditary rights. Biological good fortune had built the family enterprise, and the failure to produce the necessary male heirs in each generation could destroy it by allowing other families to claim all or parts of it through marriage with daughters. Since most of what the family held had been acquired in this fashion, it was not difficult to see how it could also be lost in the same way. Habsburg marital politics had to be defensive as well as aggressive. The commonest means of defence was intermarriage among the branches of the family itself.

The Church had traditionally guarded European society from the supposed moral dangers of incestuous unions, but dispensations could be bought when political necessity seemed to recommend a forbidden marriage. The seventeenth century saw the problem not in terms of modern genetics but as an issue of conscience. For the Habsburgs intermarriage well within the prohibited degrees often made good sense from the proprietary point of view, for it provided a measure of insurance against the dynastic failure of either branch. Within a few generations, however, at least by the middle of the seventeenth century, the genetic dangers of this policy were manifest. The Spanish line suffered most dramatically.

Philip II of Spain married four times; only his last wife, Anna, was a Habsburg. She was, however, his own niece, the daughter of his sister Maria, wife of his first cousin Maximilian II. It was this last union that produced the surviving male heir, Philip III (1598–1621), who in his turn married his cousin Margaret of Styria, sister of the future Emperor Ferdinand II. Their son Philip IV (1621–65) first married Isabella of Bourbon, then after her death the daughter of his own sister, Maria Anna, wife of his cousin Ferdinand III. Again, as in his grandfather's case, it was this late union of uncle and niece that produced the surviving heir to the throne: the half-imbecile, sexually impotent Charles II (1665–1700), in whom the Spanish descendants of Emperor Charles V found a pitiful end.

The Austrian Habsburgs fared somewhat better. Ferdinand I had three sons: the eldest, Maximilian II (1564–76) married his first cousin Maria, the sister of Philip II. In accord with the family by-laws, the *Hausordnung*, he inherited the Austrian duchies and the claims to Bohemia and Hungary by right of primogeniture. Ferdinand I could not resist the temptation to provide for his younger sons, however, and he invested Maximilian's brothers Ferdinand and Karl with states of their own: the Tyrol and Styria (or 'Inner Austria') respectively. Maximilian II had five children who survived infancy: Anna, the fourth wife of Philip II; Rudolf and Mathias, the ill-starred brothers who succeeded in turn to the royal and Imperial dignities and whose wars with each other nearly destroyed the hereditary lands; Elisabeth, wife of Charles IX of France; and Albrecht, who married Philip II's daughter Isabella Clara Eugenia. None of the three sons provided a male heir.

Rudolf and Mathias both showed signs of mental disturbance and physical weakness. Their quarrels over Hungary, Bohemia and the Imperial crown could easily have fragmented the dynastic enterprise in eastern Europe. This did not happen because their cousin Ferdinand, the vigorous duke of Styria, intervened firmly and ultimately won recognition as the single heir to all the hereditary dominions in the east and in 1619 election as Holy Roman Emperor. Ferdinand of Styria, the scion of a prolific cadet line, took his own bride from the Bavarian electoral family with whom the Styrian dukes were tied by generations of friendship and common dedication to the work of the Catholic counter-reformation. Once he was at the head of the Austrian branch of his family, however, Ferdinand II returned to family custom and married his heir, the archduke (later Emperor Ferdinand III), to Maria Anna of Spain, daughter of Philip III, husband of his own sister Margaret. Their younger son, Leopold I of Austria, was the last Habsburg to produce male heirs who survived childhood.

Ferdinand II restored the family fortunes in eastern Europe for a time at least, but his election as king of Bohemia in 1617 provoked a rebellion of his Protestant subjects that plunged the Empire and ultimately all of Europe into a generation of violence, the Thirty Years War. This was in an important sense a Habsburg war, a conflict between the house of Austria and those rivals in Europe who envied, feared or coveted its might or hated its attachment to the Church of Rome. In the beginning it seemed to be a religious war; for the Habsburgs it remained so to the end, so deeply had the confessional differences become symbolic of the underlying political and social issues that separated the Habsburgs from their powerful neighbours and rebellious subjects.

The house of Austria found itself in the centre of passions stirred by the Reformation from the moment Luther challenged the Imperial Diet in Charles's presence in 1521. Both Protestant and Catholic historians have since viewed the Habsburgs as the single-minded, fanatic (or pious) defenders of the papal cause against the forces set loose by Luther and his followers. Such a view, satisfyingly over-simple, distorts both the role the dynasty played in the religious controversies and its own peculiar kind of family piety.

Charles V and Ferdinand I were both men of moderate temperament, though Ferdinand's Spanish education had made him perhaps less willing to compromise in questions of belief. Both had been influenced, more or less subtly, by Erasmian criticism of ecclesiastical malpractice and by the prevailing gentle scepticism of Italian and northern humanism. They rejected completely the political and social radicalism that often accompanied the more extreme doctrines of the reformers, seeing clearly that the secularization of church property in Germany would strike a devastating blow at the Emperor's waning authority. Although they deplored the unsettling consequences of the reform movement, they were compelled to come to terms with it. In the religious peace of Augsburg in 1555 Charles V acquiesced and let his brother recognize the Lutheran princes' right to determine their subjects' faith.

Ferdinand I found himself equally powerless to stop the spread of Lutheran doctrine among the townsmen of Bohemia, Austria and Hungary, where the traditional institutions of the Church failed to satisfy the spiritual needs of a small but growing bourgeoisie.[3] Ferdinand's agents at the Council of Trent sought to induce the assembly to concede the lay chalice to the Bohemian church, a move that seemed to him a very small doctrinal compromise which would reconcile that troubled kingdom with Rome. The Council remained adamant on the validity of tradition, however, and Ferdinand had to make the best of a bad situation. While he favoured the Roman Church wherever he could and encouraged the earliest efforts of the Jesuit fathers, he was forced in the end to allow Protestants to remain in his territories so long as they accepted his civil authority.

Ferdinand's heir, Maximilian II, proved to be notoriously indifferent to confessional disputes, and some of his contemporaries even suspected him of having converted to Lutheranism. Such ambiguity in doctrinal matters was not proof against family pressure, however. His own sons were sent to Spain to be educated under the stern eye of Philip II. When they returned to Austria they brought with them the intolerance they had been taught along with the stiff formalities of Spanish court ceremonial.

While there was no question that the Austrian Habsburgs intended to restore the religious authority of Rome in their domains, settlement of that issue remained a generation away. Rudolf II (1576–1612) had to rely on the Protestant nobility of Bohemia for assistance first against resurgent Turkish threats in the east and then against his rebellious brother Mathias. Rudolf's mental instability grew as the years passed, but still Bohemia remained loyal to him after Mathias split the hereditary states by engineering his own election as king of Hungary. Out of gratitude Rudolf conceded the Letter of Majesty in 1609, guaranteeing freedom of worship in Bohemia. When Mathias succeeded him in 1612 he had to accept the religious compromise in order to reunite Bohemia with Hungary.

In the absence of a direct male heir to Mathias's crowns the problem of the succession provided a focus for confessional as well as dynastic ambitions. The Catholic aristocracy in Bohemia supported Ferdinand of Styria, a capable, intelligent and genial prince, educated by the Jesuits at Ingolstadt and closely related by marriage and friendship to the duke of Bavaria, leader of the Catholic League in Germany. Ferdinand had already proved his zeal by expelling the Protestants from Styria, and looked forward to the triumphant restoration of Catholicism throughout the hereditary lands and in Germany once he held the Bohemian and Imperial crowns. With Mathias's help he was elected king of Bohemia in 1617 in spite of a Protestant majority in the Diet. When Mathias died two years later, however, the Protestant nobility refused to accept Ferdinand, withdrawing their previous assent to his election. In 1619 they chose a Calvinist German prince, elector Friedrich V of the Palatinate, to be their king. The rebellion spread through the Habsburg states, touching even Vienna where Ferdinand II narrowly escaped mob violence.

None of the centres of resistance was a match for Ferdinand's own efficient military forces once they were joined by troops sent from Bavaria. By 1620 he had totally defeated the Bohemian rebels at the White Mountain near Prague. Bohemia was sternly reduced to obedience. The noble leaders of the rebellion were executed, their Protestant supporters dispossessed. Ferdinand imposed on Bohemia a new aristocracy, all Catholics and supporters of the house of Austria, rewarded for their loyalty with the estates confiscated from the rebels.

The pacification of Bohemia proved only the beginning of a larger war.[4] Ferdinand's quick and decisive victory set up waves of apprehension among the Protestant states of Europe. The war expanded year by year as the United Provinces, Denmark, then Sweden and finally France joined the changing coalitions against Habsburg power. Twice in the course of the war Ferdinand II seemed to be within reach of his goal: a peace which would restore Imperial power in Germany and turn the balance in favour of the Catholic, Habsburg cause. Once in 1629 and again in 1635 Ferdinand threw away the advantages he had won by claiming more than his allies would let him keep. After his death in 1637 the war dragged on for another decade until it reached a stalemate.

Throughout the bloody struggle Spain had been the military and financial mainstay of the Habsburg cause. By 1640, however, it was clear that the Spanish colossus could no longer afford to waste its resources against so many enemies. A successful rebellion in Portugal, uprisings in Catalonia, the dismissal of Olivarez from the ministry, and finally the military disaster at Rocroi in 1643 all revealed the growing weakness of Spain. In 1648 Ferdinand III concluded peace in the name of the Empire, leaving Spain and France to go on fighting alone for yet another decade.

In the treaties of Westphalia Ferdinand III (1637–57) confirmed once again the religious settlement of 1555, adding Calvinism to the list of tolerated confessions. The Habsburg dream of a revived Catholic Empire in Germany faded, replaced once more by the principle of *cuius regio eius religio*. While this principle further weakened the Emperor's constitutional authority in Germany, it confirmed the restoration of Catholicism in his hereditary lands. A substantial increase of monarchical power in Austria and Hungary offset, and to some extent compensated for, the further erosion of Imperial power.

Ferdinand II and his two successors, Ferdinand III and Leopold I, have often been portrayed as the weak accomplices of Jesuit militancy. This is an exaggerated view. The traditional Catholic piety of the Habsburgs was not something imposed on the dynasty by the Jesuits; it was, rather, a major part of family tradition itself. The Jesuits received many favours at the hands of Habsburg monarchs, and rendered many important services in return, but the same could be said of most of the traditional religious orders. In areas where Jesuit leadership was outstanding, particularly in education, they were favoured over others. For the rest, the family did not need to be taught its divine mission in the world.

Habsburg tradition combined its belief in divine right with a strong sense of divine guidance.[5] Dynastic good fortune served to confirm a belief that Providence intervened directly, frequently and benevolently in its affairs. Such 'miracles of the house of Austria' were God's rewards for successful stewardship of the family's temporal responsibilities and in particular for the maintenance of the true faith and Christian behaviour among their subjects. Diversity of belief among the subjects entrusted to their rule seemed politically and ideologically indefensible. Uniformity of faith was dictated by prudence, not necessarily by fanaticism, and a generation of war seemed to confirm the inevitable association of heresy and rebellion.

Dedication to the Church of Rome did not imply political ultramontanism; indeed, as often as not the result was just the opposite. The

Emperor could not admit an intermediary between himself and God so far as his temporal rights were concerned;[6] dependence on the papacy carried with it special political dangers. The Church was an important, indeed an indispensable social institution, but it was expected to play its role in a partnership.

All the Habsburg rulers of the seventeenth century, most especially Leopold I, took seriously the idea of divine calling. They did not view the Church as an arm of the state, nor was it a master imposing, by virtue of its ideological supremacy, duties and burdens upon the monarch. The Church was the world under God; monarchs and popes served God and the Church, not dependently, but equally. Catholic tradition and ritual provided an ideological framework for the state, a set of concrete representations of those abstractions every society needs in order to believe in its own immortality. Holy days were the festivals of the court, while the saints of the calendar offered patronage to every circumstance, occupation and locality.[7] A dynastic enterprise that included so many divergent cultures and nationalities had need of such a universal and cosmopolitan doctrine.

There remained a strong element of the crusading spirit in both Spain and Austria which prevented this dynastic piety from becoming merely a passive, ritualistic formality. Both lines of the family could justifiably see themselves as the guardians of western Christianity against both militant Islam and Protestant heresy. The dangers were, or seemed to be, very real, and it is small wonder that they produced intolerance. This was intolerance from axiom, however, not the fanaticism of misdirected zeal. The Habsburgs had grown accustomed to taking their Catholicism for granted. They sincerely saw in the Roman faith the embodiment of a higher citizenship of Christendom which justified their own place in the world and gave purpose and meaning to the complex and diverse interlocking parts of the dynastic enterprise.

II

The Austrian Inheritance

Throughout the sixteenth century the senior Spanish line of the Habsburgs took the lead in the political and dynastic affairs of the family. During the following century the directing force gradually shifted from Madrid to Vienna, and upon the death of Philip IV of Spain in 1665, Leopold I became undisputed head of the family. This shift in authority from the senior to the cadet line reflected the shifting balance of European power as well as the genetic misfortunes of the house. The decline of Spanish power throughout the seventeenth century was obvious to contemporary observers, and while argument about the reasons for it continues after three centuries, the fact that it happened is clear enough.

The Spanish monarchy found itself impoverished in the midst of riches, stripped of great commercial wealth by the successful Dutch war for independence, with a domestic economy weakened by inflation, administrative neglect and poor fiscal management. Yet Spain still held its valuable possessions in Europe and overseas. The Thirty Years War may have brought to an end Spanish preponderance in Europe and the dream of a restored Catholic Empire in Germany, but it did not weaken the Habsburgs' proprietary claims to all the parts of their inheritance.

In eastern Europe Habsburg control over the various parts of the family enterprise had never grown so strong as regal power in Spain. Only in the Austrian provinces, and after 1627 in Bohemia, did sovereignty pass legally by inheritance. Hungary remained an elective monarchy.

When Leopold came to the throne the economic and demographic consequences of the Thirty Years War were still evident in central and eastern Europe. Unprecedented taxation, the expulsion of industrious Protestant townsmen, plagues and rural uprisings had left Styria and the Austrian duchies economically depressed. Hungary remained a frontier province periodically ravaged by Turks and Christians alike. In Bohemia and Silesia war, epidemics and migration produced a substantial decline of population with a corresponding net decrease of productivity in the richest of the Habsburgs' realms. Just what this demographic crisis amounted to in specific, quantitative terms is hard to judge, for regional differences were great; an over-all decline in production of about one-third would probably be a conservative estimate for Bohemia and Silesia,[1] with the market towns at intersecting lines of communication suffering most severely, and the incidence of rural depopulation varying from an insignificant proportion in some areas to as much as two-thirds in others.

In spite of these obvious disadvantages, the potential of the Danubian region was enormous. Upper and Lower Austria were rich areas for mixed farming, as were Styria, Bohemia and Moravia. Population decline produced serious economic consequences, but these were not permanent.[2] Especially in Bohemia, but elsewhere as well, the ruin of smaller landholders led to the enrichment of the more powerful and successful. The great landholders attracted new colonists to the land and developed a highly profitable system of production for the market, using the forced labour of peasants, the *Robot*, to rebuild agricultural capital and clear domainal lands that had returned to wood and waste.

Hungary, in spite of the violence that raged throughout the century, was a source of almost unlimited cattle driven in large herds up the Danube through Vienna on their way to Germany, where domestic livestock production no longer met the demands of the towns. Silesian linens were a major item in eastern European commerce, exported to the west along with the prized Bohemian glass. Silver mines in Upper Hungary (Slovakia) and the Tyrol provided substantial specie to help redress unfavourable trade balances. The iron of Styria, and the scythe blades and other agricultural tools forged from it, provided a large part of Austria's trade with the rest of Europe[3] as well as an important strategic resource for weaponry.

Agriculturally self-sufficient, blessed with considerable mineral resources and a tradition of good craftsmanship, the eastern Habsburg lands could stand alone economically in all but some luxury sectors.[4] Technological 'backwardness' may well have been a fact in conservative eastern Europe then as later, but in a pre-industrial society this relative, and debatable, disadvantage is not enough in itself to account for the repeated failure of eager and often very competent statesmen to create an effectively functioning political system in the midst of such plenty.

Many things distinguished the Austrian monarchy from the other European states of the seventeenth century: the cosmopolitan character of its ruling elite, the continuing wealth and influence of the landed nobility, a persistent localism in every branch of life, and a conservative respect for customary law which often seemed to frustrate even modest efforts to reform the political structure. In contrast to these apparently conservative influences were a number of forces leading to change and adjustment: the pressure of circumstances, threats to the security of far-flung frontiers, the economic possibilities of the central Danubian basin added to the dynasty's universalist, Catholic and Imperial aims.[5] In some ways the process which produced the great Habsburg empire of the succeeding two centuries resembled the growth of absolute monarchy elsewhere in Europe; but the peculiar character of the house of Austria sent it down a path distinctly its own.

Just as the Habsburgs assumed a Christian, in particular a Roman Catholic view of human destiny, so they took for granted a hierarchical society built upon ascending orders of social privilege. Rights were property, and as such were hereditary possessions for the nobility, corporate assets for the Church and the towns. All the privileged orders in society stood apart from the mass of the population, distinguished by noble rank, landlordship, ecclesiastical dignity or bourgeois franchise. This elite society made up the estates or orders who assembled in provincial diets (*Landtage*), an elite, or as it was usually called, *Obrigkeit*, who governed the larger population of subjects, *Untertanen*.

Unlike many European monarchs of the period, the Habsburgs made little effort to break down the traditional privileges of the aristocratic order. The monarchy existed to guarantee the physical survival of society, and social privilege was the accepted reward for military and political service to the crown in much the same way that salvation was assumed to be the natural consequence of service to God. Privilege combined with landed proprietary rights became an inheritance protected by the same law that upheld the principle of hereditary monarchy. The Habsburgs chose to regard privilege as a source of regal power rather than a challenge to it.

The crown could elevate any person it wanted to reward, but only through complex and difficult legal processes could it revoke privileges once granted or remove a magnate from the possession of his hereditary estates. The fact that it proved much easier to reward good service than to punish incompetence accounts for much of the awkwardness of Habsburg government in the seventeenth century, and for some of its strength and humaneness as well, particularly during the long reign of Leopold I, whose personality fitted such a system. Generous use of rewards and infrequent resort to severe punishment produced a rather wasteful system, but it could be effective and proved remarkably stable.

Persistent and widely diverse local institutions and customs remained the single greatest barrier to successful political centralization. Leopold I habitually referred to his monarchy in the plural, the 'Hereditary lands' (*Erblände*), and to the separate crowns individually. His view of the world, like that of his ancestors, did not reach to the vision of a single sovereignty administered uniformly under a single standard of law. Like all medieval European rulers he saw the world as a series of intricately interrelated clusters of privileges and rights, all sanctioned by usage and tradition or by his own binding oaths. A single body of ordinances, the *Hausordnung*, might regulate private, dynastic affairs; but many diffuse constitutions, customs and contracts governed his relations with each part of his inheritance, and each unit retained its special character within the total ensemble.

Localism was enshrined in a number of institutions which limited the sovereign power of the crown. The clergy and nobility remained separate and independent estates, generally immune from ordinary taxation except for certain customary contributions. These orders, holding the largest concentration of wealth, dominated the provincial assemblies and diets against the interests of the weaker estates of the lesser nobility, the towns or the peasantry. Since they could not be subjected to the direct will of the crown, they had perforce to be negotiated with, placated, and above all won by persuasion or the promise of further rewards.

Administration within such a vast confusion of local sovereignties had to take account of the special relation of the crown to each one. In general we can distinguish four separate though often overlapping governments united only in their varying degrees of obedience to a single man who possessed the royal title to them all. First in dignity if not in power was the Holy Roman Empire of the German Nation, of which the Austrian duchies and Bohemia were integral parts. Separate from the Empire but intertwined with it were the various administrations of the Austrian provinces as Habsburg dominions, as also of the kingdom of Bohemia and – outside the Empire – of Hungary.

Leopold's Imperial dignity, his claim to be the premier monarch of Christian Europe, derived from his election and coronation as Sacred August Emperor of the Holy Roman Empire of the German Nation. As such he was technically the sovereign ruler over all the many territories which had made up the fiefs of the great medieval German empire of Otto I, Friedrich Barbarossa and Friedrich II. In fact the office was more important for its ceremonial dignity than for any real power it offered him. From the civil wars of the thirteenth century onwards the noble 'vassals' of the Empire had transformed themselves into sovereign princes within a very loose confederation. By 1648, when the peace of Westphalia confirmed and placed under international guarantee the 'liberties' of the German nation, the territorial princes enjoyed virtually complete control over the management of their local affairs.

Only the loosest ties remained between the crowned Emperor and his independent German vassals. In spite of the many bitter conflicts among themselves, the fragments of Germany usually united to resist the centralizing of Imperial administration, and they tolerated only the minimum number of institutions necessary to take care of the complex legal relations among themselves. What little government there was for the whole of the Empire was represented by two institutions: the aulic council and the Imperial Diet.

Traditionally the main functions of monarchy were leadership in war and the dispensation of justice. All the Emperor's direct vassals had the right to appeal to the crown for judgment. The aulic council (*Reichshofrat*) served as the supreme appellate court, from which in theory decisions could be reversed only by the personal intervention of the Emperor. In fact it was but one more stage in a ponderous system of courts staffed by jurists learned in feudal law. Procedures were unbelievably complicated, made even more so by the division of the chancellery between the Emperor's own court, now permanently settled in Vienna, and the archiepiscopal see of Mainz whose prince-archbishop was *ex-officio* the Imperial chancellor.[6] From time to time a strong vice-chancellor in Vienna could provide the Emperor a means of influencing the process in his own behalf. From 1669 to 1694 count Leopold Wilhelm von Königsegg used the office to strengthen Imperial authority in Germany. Most of the time, however, the judicial system moved so slowly that there was little hope of using it effectively.

Without a large standing armed force to police judicial actions in Germany, there was little the Emperor could do but go to war against his own vassals when his judgments were challenged. Charles V and Ferdinand II had both tried to impose their will on Germany by force, and failed. Leopold I followed his father's policy of negotiating directly with his fellow princes. It is indicative of the state of German political development by that time that he found his strongest position not as head of the Empire, but as king of Bohemia and an elector. Diplomacy proved a more potent tool for achieving his purposes than the assertion of his sovereign prerogative.

The Imperial Diet (*Reichstag*) retained the traditional constitutional

right to declare wars and to tax itself to fight them, but these were
rarely exercised. The most select of the four bodies making up the Diet,
the college of electors, had the duty of choosing the Emperor. The full
Diet with its electoral college and houses of princes, knights and towns
seldom met except for great ceremonial occasions such as Imperial
coronations. Local affairs stayed in the hands of the individual states or
of the ten Imperial 'circles' (*Kreise*), regional groupings of political
units, most of them dominated by one or two of the larger territorial
principalities.

After 1663, when Leopold summoned the Diet to provide assistance
in meeting the Turkish invasion of Hungary, the Diet became what it
was to remain until its dissolution in 1806: a permanently settled diplomatic conference bringing together in Regensburg men representing
the powerful individual states and the regional circles along with foreign
envoys appointed from time to time by other European states with
business to conduct in Germany. This 'Perpetual Diet' (*Immerwährender
Reichstag*), as it came to be called, settled into a semi-dormant existence,
aroused by infrequent crises and visited by the princes themselves only
on great ceremonial occasions. It served as a diplomatic convenience for
all concerned, and a living monument to the fragmentation of Germany.

In the Austrian duchies Leopold ruled by hereditary right as absolute
sovereign. Each of the four Austrian territories, Upper and Lower
Austria, Inner Austria (Styria and Carinthia) and the Tyrol (which
Leopold did not rule until the last of the cadet line died in 1665),[7] had
its own diet and considerable autonomy in local administration. Upper
and Lower Austria were directly responsible to their sovereign prince
through the court chancellery (*Hofkanzlei*) for judicial and political
affairs, and through the court chamber (*Hofkammer*) for financial
matters. Styria and the Tyrol retained separate agencies (*Stellen*) in
Graz and Innsbruck, but as sovereign prince Leopold could exercise
direct control over both if he chose to do so.

All the officials within the system were directed from the court,
which was organized around the person of the monarch whose sovereign
will was the last court of appeal.[8] A variety of commissions and councils
developed over the years to organize business and advise the crown. A
judicial advisory commission, the privy council (*Geheimer Rat*), had
acted since the reign of Ferdinand I as a court of appeals for cases from
Upper and Lower Austria and as the central political advisory body, a
sort of primitive cabinet. The monarchs also consulted it for advice on
judicial appeals from the aulic council. By the mid-seventeenth century
the privy council had outgrown its original functions. From its original

membership of five or six in the sixteenth century it had grown into a body of several dozens, too unwieldy to perform its major function, which was to advise on legal and political matters. Leopold's father, Ferdinand III, had taken to consulting regularly with only a few key court officials, a sort of executive committee of the privy council. Leopold continued this practice. This inner circle of top advisers, a 'ministry' in all but name, remained an informal institution until Leopold gave it official status in 1669, but as the privy conference (*Geheime Konferenz*) it existed as the central agency of government from the beginning of the reign.[9] The members of this conference varied according to the questions to be discussed and of course at the pleasure of the sovereign, but they were invariably drawn from among the men who presided over the major agencies of the administration.

In 1657 the most important and visible official of the court was the grand chamberlain (*Obristhofmeister*). The office was reserved by court custom to a man of noble birth. Until 1676 Leopold gave this office to his favourite adviser. Although there was no formal designation of precedence among the ministers, the grand chamberlain usually stood foremost. He alone had unhindered access to the Emperor's person; he ordered the comings and goings of those who had business with the crown. As chief administrator of the royal household, he supervised court personnel and exercised enormous influence over appointments at every level, which made him a powerful patron. Few meetings of the privy conference took place in the grand chamberlain's absence and little business reached the Emperor without his knowing about it and approving it first.

The Austrian chancellor (*Hofkanzler*) headed the political administration. His office conducted diplomatic correspondence as well as overseeing domestic legal and judicial matters. Unlike the chamberlain, the chancellor did not have to be of noble birth, indeed most of Leopold's chancellors came from the ranks of the lawyers in the professional bureaucracy. A bourgeois chancellor's tenure and prosperity depended more on the good will of the Emperor than was the case with officials from the noble families. Usually he could be counted on to serve the dynasty loyally and impartially. In the course of Leopold's reign the chancellery gradually replaced the chamberlain's office as the political centre of government.

Traditionally the main business of a prince was to lead in war. In military affairs alone all Leopold's realms were treated as one. Recruiting, provisioning, strategic planning, all the complex matters relating to warfare were the direct responsibility of the crown. To advise him and to coordinate actual operations Ferdinand I had instituted a collegial body, the court war council (*Hofkriegsrat*), whose president held a critical position among the Emperor's advisers. The war council itself, a group of professional military men and bureaucrats, had both advisory and executive duties. Beyond dealing with routine military business, they also had charge of political and diplomatic relations with the Ottoman empire, a state of affairs that had a certain historical logic behind it, but which often led to conflict with the chancellery.

The financial administration, in contrast to the judicial, political and military institutions, seemed even to contemporaries a scene of utter chaos and disorder, throughout Leopold's reign a constant subject of court scandal, complaints and recrimination. Leopold himself, like his father and grandfather before him, understood little of finance, though it was here that the ambitions of the crown touched most closely the lives and fortunes of his subjects.

The crown's normal income derived from a variety of sources. There were large royal estates in all the realms; crown monopolies in mining and other enterprises; regalian rights over appointments, inheritance, feudal investitures and minting coins; special tolls and other excise duties, fees for licences, payments by chartered corporations and communities. As the system had grown piecemeal, each source of income generally required separate administration. General supervision of income was divided among several 'chambers' or treasuries (*Kammer, Camera*), one in Bohemia, one in Hungary, and the most important of all, the Viennese court chamber (*Hofkammer*).

In theory the court chamber operated as a central accounting office for the financial transactions of the whole monarchy, but it had little supervisory authority over Bohemia and Hungary. Like the war council, the court chamber was a collegial body whose composition varied from time to time, but usually included some members of the higher nobility alongside career bureaucrats. Their duties included budgetary planning, supervision of the diverse sources of income, verification of orders to disburse funds, negotiating loans and providing accurate accounts. The diffusion of subordinate agencies, the archaic system of accounting, and the inexperience of many of the councillors made it impossible to keep abreast of business.

Charges against the Emperor's public and private purses always vastly exceeded the money available, a situation never completely disguised by the multiplicity of financial offices. Military expenses were accounted for separately from the normal outlays of the court, while some sources of income were theoretically reserved for special purposes. There were some twenty offices (*Kassen*) for these disbursements. When one was empty, claimants were routinely sent from one to another until funds were found somewhere. Borrowing was a permanent feature of the system, but poor administration forced interest rates up and led the court chamber to secure loans against income at the source rather than through its own expectations. This merely increased the confusion, for when special contributions were voted by the diets their own debts and expenses were deducted before any money went forward to Vienna, with the result that only a small part of these levies, or of regular income for that matter, ever went through the hands of the court chamber.

The whole financial apparatus was overstaffed, cumbersome, inefficient, perennially subject to corruption. Periodically it lurched to the brink of total collapse, yet proved almost impervious to reform. The court chamber president regularly sat with the privy conference as chief financial officer of the crown, but his counsel seldom offered much encouragement.

These four officers, the grand chamberlain, the chancellor, and the presidents of the court chamber and war council, made up the nucleus of the conferences in which major political decisions were debated. Others were invited or not as the Emperor chose, and the conferences could meet in his presence or not, again as he chose. Normally the grand chamberlain called these meetings, presenting an agenda made up from inquiries directed to the conference by the Emperor. After examining the relevant documents the participants discussed the matter freely, sometimes acrimoniously. The chancellor, or more usually one of his secretaries, recorded the opinions (*vota*) and drafted a proposal. If opinions were strongly divided, each person present recorded his *votum* separately. If the Emperor was not present, the secretary sent him the draft and the *vota* for his decision. Once the Emperor reached a decision the chancellery formally recorded it along with whatever changes he may have made in the draft and then sent out the appropriate orders or instructions.

The central administrative system, though unwieldy and slow, was surprisingly informal. Everything depended on the Emperor himself and a few close advisers. Any one of them could delay business purposefully if he chose. As time went on and the problems confronting the monarchy grew more complicated, the privy conference, like most such bodies, shared the unfortunate tendency to increase in size as political questions seemed to demand the advice of an ever widening circle of officials.

Leopold's two most important sovereignties, Bohemia and Hungary, each had systems of administration separate from the Austrian court. Of the two, Hungary was by far the more independent. The Hungarian chancellery jealously guarded its independence; very seldom did appeals reach the crown from the regional Magyar courts. When Leopold was not actually within the boundaries of the kingdom, the palatine, a magnate chosen by the Hungarian diet, exercised viceregal powers. Within the framework of its venerable constitution, the medieval *tripartitum*, Hungary continued to govern itself largely without Imperial intervention except in those increasingly frequent instances when the Magyar nobility chose to exercise its traditional 'right' of rebellion and the crown was forced to use loyal troops to occupy its own kingdom. In the course of his reign Leopold and his advisers laid the groundwork for a system of royal absolutism in Hungary, but not until the reign of Charles VI (1711–40), after the Turks had been permanently expelled from the Danubian plain and the greatest of the Magyar rebellions put down, did the Habsburgs develop a system of their own for governing their most unruly kingdom.

Matters were quite different in Bohemia, where loyalty to the crown was no longer a problem after 1620. A Bohemian chancellery handled judicial business from Vienna under the direction of a Bohemian chancellor appointed from among the Czech nobility by the Emperor. So long as things ran smoothly, and so far as the Bohemian chancellery was concerned this was generally the case, there was little need for the crown to intervene. For one important aspect of its political life, then, Bohemia retained independent institutions and its nobility had little cause to complain about foreign (Austrian) interference in its domestic affairs. The same, unfortunately, could not be said for financial affairs. A separate Bohemian chamber in Prague dealt with the regular taxes and special contributions voted for the crown. This body, modelled after the court chamber, spent a good portion of its collegial energy squabbling with the Viennese chamber about its independent status within the financial bureaucracy.

Even at the very centre of the government Leopold's administrative apparatus was beset by the complex problems of localism. The system of government, if system it can be called, depended ultimately on the personalities and capacities of the monarch and the men he chose to act for him. Beyond the central agencies of the court were a multitude of national, provincial and local institutions each with its traditional rights and a self-conceived position in the whole. At this level central policy direction could have but limited results. Insubordination was a way of life, a comfortable habit.

A prince of different calibre from Leopold's might well have taken a course like that followed by the Great Elector Friedrich Wilhelm of Brandenburg, ruthlessly subordinating local institutions to the central authority of the crown. In fact Leopold took things as he found them; his reign produced no great bureaucratic revolutions except possibly in Hungary where he had the great advantage after 1683 of being able to start virtually afresh; and even here the results were modest. For the rest, development resulted from slow adjustment to circumstances, from well-meaning reforms halfheartedly pursued. What the Austrian empire eventually became has much to do with the gentle personality of Leopold I and with the fact that he had not been trained to rule, but was prepared instead for a more modest role in the dynastic enterprise.

III

The Troubled Succession

On 24 May 1654 the Imperial College of Electors adjourned their electoral session in Regensburg. Emperor Ferdinand III had capped his mediocre reign by securing the election of his eldest son, archduke Ferdinand Maria (Ferdinand IV as king of the Romans), to succeed him on the Imperial throne, without having to agree in advance to an electoral capitulation (*Wahlkapitulation*). He chose an auspicious moment for the house of Austria. France and Sweden, the foreign powers most interested in maintaining the power of the princes against the prerogatives of the Imperial crown, were both too preoccupied with internal troubles to stir up the electors against the Habsburgs. Satisfied with his political victory, Ferdinand III, a prematurely old man at forty-six and in failing health, led his entourage back to Vienna, 164 barges carrying the court and the trappings of majesty down the Danube.

Young Ferdinand IV survived his triumphal homecoming by only a few weeks. On 9 July he suddenly died from smallpox. He had been a promising youth, his father's favourite among his five children.[1] He had been given a princely education and political tutoring by some of the most experienced statesmen in central Europe. All his father's hopes were dashed in a moment. The Emperor fell into a state of shock; many at court doubted he would survive. He neglected urgent business just at the moment when the dynasty had to act with despatch if it was to secure the succession to Ferdinand Maria's younger brother, archduke Leopold Ignatius, Ferdinand's third child and second son, now a fourteen-year-old boy being prepared for a career in the Church. Yet the old Emperor absorbed himself totally in the tediously long obsequies for his first son, and with growing lethargy he let weeks and months pass; the precious time lost undid his victory at Regensburg.

By the beginning of 1655 the international situation had changed in a number of ways. In France Mazarin had freed himself from the internal disorders of the *Fronde* and turned rapidly to restore French security in

the east, rebuilding French alliances with the electors and princes of the
Empire. In Sweden Queen Christina abdicated the throne in favour of
Karl Gustav of Zweibrücken, no friend of the Habsburgs. For both
powers the sudden death of archuke Ferdinand Maria offered a welcome
opportunity either to exclude the Habsburgs from the Imperial succession entirely, or at the very least to weaken further their influence in
Germany by negotiating a stiff electoral capitulation in advance of a
new election. Sweden and France, working through the Wittelsbach
elector of Cologne, proposed the election of duke Ferdinand Maria of
Bavaria. When he refused to entertain the offer, they considered other
candidates including the young king of France, Louis XIV. Clearly the
cost of securing Habsburg succession to the Imperial throne was increasing rapidly.

While France and Sweden wooed the electors, Ferdinand III finally
bestirred himself to assure Leopold's succession in the hereditary lands.
The Austrian succession was automatic, but the crowns of Hungary and
Bohemia both required election by the diets and lengthy preparation
for the coronation ceremonies. On 27 June 1655, just over two weeks
after his fifteenth birthday, the shy young archduke was duly elected
and crowned king of Hungary. In the following year, on 14 September
1656, he became king of Bohemia. The Imperial chancellor, archbishop
Johann Philipp von Schönborn of Mainz, tried to induce the electors
to meet quickly to choose a new king of Rome to avoid the confusion
likely to follow an interregnum, but the German princes found delay
more profitable.[2] When Ferdinand III died on 2 April 1657 the Imperial
throne fell vacant.

With Ferdinand gone, his family divided among itself over the
question of the Imperial succession. While most supported Leopold's
right to succeed by primogeniture, some argued that the Imperial title
should go to Ferdinand's brother, archduke Leopold Wilhelm, an
attractive candidate for several reasons. He was both experienced and
capable, a conscientious servant of the family enterprise; being a churchman without progeny, he could hold the throne for the family until
Leopold was of age, at which time the electors could no longer object
to his succession on grounds of his youth. A second and different consideration arose out of the dynastic ties with Spain, where the misfortunes befalling the children of Philip IV had left the senior branch
of the family without a living male heir. Leopold's projected marriage
with Philip IV's first daughter would give him an almost indisputable
claim to the Spanish crown, an inheritance which all agreed was now
incompatible with the Imperial throne; but Leopold could not be

induced to hold back and give up his claim to the Empire. His uncle supported this decision with good grace. At seventeen Leopold emerged from the family dispute the unchallenged master in his own household.

The College of Electors finally assembled in Frankfurt on 4 August 1657. Unlike earlier conclaves, which had met largely to ratify choices already agreed upon, this gathering became a diplomatic conference of great importance. Much more was at stake than the protocol dignity of an empty title. In addition to the electors with their courts, Frankfurt played host to embassies from France, Spain, Sweden, Denmark, Poland, Savoy, Mantua, Modena and the Papal See. Prince Wenzel Lobkowitz led a delegation representing Leopold's electoral kingdom of Bohemia, acting as chief agent for the Habsburg interests.

The sides were clearly drawn. Against Habsburg claims stood the envoys of France and Sweden. In the middle were a group of uncommitted electors, still a majority of the eight. Cologne followed French leadership from the start, while Karl Ludwig, the elector palatine, had sold his vote to France for a large 'subsidy'. Bohemia was Leopold's own vote, though he could not cast it until June 1658 when he reached the age of eighteen. Ferdinand Maria of Bavaria secretly promised his vote to the Habsburgs in return for a solid defensive alliance, thus leaving France and Sweden without a really good alternative candidate. Lobkowitz then turned to bargaining with the uncommitted electors to find the necessary majority.

Initially Johann Philipp of Mainz had been a strong supporter of the Habsburg candidacy, but since 1655 he had changed his mind. A shrewd and experienced statesman, he realized that he, like other rulers of small and exposed states caught between great powers, must consistently seek stability and peace among his powerful neighbours or find himself the victim of their conflicts. The Westphalian peace, which he helped negotiate, represented to him the safest guarantee that both French and Habsburg ambitions could be contained. He had already taken the lead in building the League of the Rhine, a coalition of German states which he hoped would turn into a balancing force capable of frustrating both France and Austria. In such a situation Johann Philipp would have welcomed any candidate who was neither Habsburg nor Bourbon; the difficulty was to find one.

Ferdinand Maria of Bavaria stuck to his bargain with Leopold, refusing to be moved by either French bribes or pressure from his ambitious wife. In the circumstances, Johann Philipp agreed finally to cast his own influential vote for Leopold, but only on condition that the election be delayed until France had concluded peace with Spain, to which end he offered his services as mediator. This diplomatic pipe-dream pleased neither France nor Spain, so the elector retreated to a demand that the new capitulation bind Leopold to the strictest neutrality in the continuing war.

Yet another difficulty was removed when news reached Frankfurt that Philip IV had again sired a son. This temporarily allayed fears of a reunion of Spain and Austria under a single monarch. Negotiations then settled down to bargaining over the two remaining issues: the exact terms of the capitulation and the bribes Leopold would have to pay for the votes he needed. It was a profitable conclave for the electors who received substantial 'subsidies' from Austria and even larger temptations from France.

Leopold left the details of the bargaining at Frankfurt to Lobkowitz, remaining in Prague until the end of January 1658 when he began a slow progress to Frankfurt which he reached in March. By that time he was assured of the votes of four of the five secular electors: Bohemia, Bavaria, Saxony and Brandenburg. The last of these, Brandenburg, was the costliest vote of all, and in the end the decisive one. Elector Friedrich Wilhelm had announced his intention to cast his vote for the highest bidder, but only Leopold could offer him what he wanted most and what France could never give: an offensive alliance against Sweden. Having won all he could fighting against Poland with the Swedes, the elector was about to turn against his former allies.

Certain of the votes he needed, Leopold still had to wait in Frankfurt another four months while Lobkowitz negotiated the terms of his capitulation. France and Sweden, seeing that they could not prevent Leopold's election, tried vigorously to bind his hands to the extent that his election could be regarded as a matter of indifference to them. Though it went against his natural dynastic sentiments and strong attachment to Spain, Leopold finally signed an agreement with France in which both parties promised to refrain from aiding the enemies of the other. This satisfied Johann Philipp of Mainz, and the electoral capitulation was quickly completed. That document, similar to others of its kind, insisted somewhat more strongly than usual on the liberties of the German princes and unequivocally confirmed the sovereignty of their states.

Assured that they had rendered their sovereign helpless, the electors unanimously chose Leopold to reign over them 'by the Grace of God, Elected Roman Emperor of the German Nation, Eternal Augmentor of the Empire', on 18 July 1658. He had turned eighteen in June; now on 1 August, swathed in the symbolic robes and weighed down by

ancient regalia, he endured the ceremony of coronation and the subsequent festivities which included a ritual public feast on the *Römer* in
Frankfurt. The following week he left Frankfurt and made a slow and
stately progress to Vienna by way of Nuremberg, Augsburg and
Munich, making his ceremonial entry into his capital on 1 October.

For nearly five years the court at Vienna had directed its attention
largely to accomplishing the overriding dynastic aims of the ruling
family. Many of the central figures of the court, including the monarch
himself along with his highest functionaries, had been absent from the
city for much of the time. Local agencies carried on their usual functions
under instructions from above, but central policy direction was lacking.
The new Emperor was little known outside his most intimate circle of
friends and advisers. A new reign meant a new regime, new favourites,
new patterns of doing business at the top. Leopold's unexpected succession naturally led to uneasiness and obvious curiosity among place-
holders, courtiers and diplomats. The experienced advisers of Ferdinand
III had found it both natural and prudent to identify their future with
the vigorous Ferdinand Maria, even at the risk of offending his younger
brother, Leopold. Now much depended on the character of the new
monarch and the men he might choose to trust to advise him.

At eighteen the young Emperor Leopold appeared to the Venetian
ambassador to be an exceptionally calm and modest youth, 'favoured
by fortune, if not by nature.'[3] His features were undistinguished, though
he showed markedly the exaggerated, pouting lower lip and the elon-
gated chin that characterized his family. His eyes were large, dark, deep-
set and keen. Still unmarked by smallpox, his complexion was ruddy and
healthy. His great passions, music and the hunt, were the customary
diversions of the family, and he showed considerable talent for both.

Leopold's earliest years were spent largely in the company of his
Spanish mother, Maria Anna, sister of Philip IV. She bore three children
to Ferdinand III: Ferdinand Maria in 1633; Maria Anna, who later
married her uncle Philip IV, in 1635; and Leopold Ignatius on 9 June
1640. The Empress showed a deep affection for her last child which he
returned full measure. Leopold was not yet six when his mother died
on 13 May 1646. Two years later Ferdinand III married Maria Leopoldina
of the Tyrol, a sixteen-year-old cousin to whom Leopold transferred his
affection. At her death in 1649 Ferdinand again sought a new consort,
marrying in 1651 Eleanora of Gonzaga, a pert, vivacious Italian princess.
She was already Leopold's godmother, and now regarded him as her
own son. For his part, Leopold treated her with great affection and
forbearance, tolerantly allowing her to indulge her passion for royal

matchmaking and family politics to a degree normally permitted only to the head of the family.

When Maria Anna died in 1646, Leopold was given a 'court' of his own, governors and tutors appointed by his father to educate him to his station in life, a suitable entourage for a prince of his dignity. Unsurprisingly Ferdinand III surrounded Leopold with men who were more noted for their piety, scholarship, social grace and submissiveness than for their political acumen. These were precisely the qualities expected in a man who was to play a subordinate role in the affairs of the dynasty. Ferdinand's own brother, Leopold Wilhelm, provided the model for the future he envisaged for his second son: high ecclesiastical offices providing the means to support himself in grand style while he occupied himself usefully in the government of the Spanish Netherlands or possibly in Italy.

A Jesuit, Philip Miller, was perhaps the most influential of Leopold's early teachers, an accomplished scholar who had been professor of moral theology, philosophy and mathematics at Graz and Vienna. His teaching gave academic confirmation of the simple, rather superstitious piety of Leopold's infancy, and instilled in him a lifelong interest in natural philosophy.

The secular preceptors were men of gentility, loyalty, honesty and learning. Count Lamberg, who joined the archduke's court between 1651 and 1653, and count Portia, Leopold's favourite who appeared in 1652, were both men whose loyalty to the dynasty had been tested but whose political competence left something to be desired. Ferdinand III found placing them in his younger son's entourage a convenient way to reward their fidelity without having to put them in positions where their lack of understanding might endanger serious affairs of state. They could be counted on to be models of the submissive virtues appropriate to a younger son.

In an atmosphere that emphasized scholarly and spiritual development over ambition for martial glory and royal dignity Leopold developed the more gentle virtues desired for him. Yet at the same time, if some of the anecdotes about his early years are to be believed,[4] he often let slip evidence of a temperament ill-suited to the role he was being groomed for. Though his personality developed in many directions over the years, one curious characteristic never left him from his earlier years: a tendency to keep strictly accurate accounts of his own and others' behaviour, noting in his 'Cracow Calendar' great and small events with statistical dispassion and little sense of discrimination.

Since he had a sound understanding, a quick and almost unnaturally retentive memory, Leopold excelled at the scholastic exercises set for him by his tutors. He mastered Latin, Italian, Spanish and German, though later he was to speak and write informally an indiscriminate mixture of all these with a fine disregard for syntax. A certain bookishness stayed with him all his life; learned conversation with his confessors, librarians or physicians always gave him greater pleasure than did the political discussions of his ministers.

His informal pastimes were appropriate to a young prince whose destiny was to fill decoratively whatever position he might be assigned by the family. An excellent horseman, he loved the hunt with a passion that bordered on excess. He was clever with his hands, and could paint as well as carve expertly. Mechanical gadgets of all kinds fascinated him. He might in another time and place have become an excellent engineer or at least a gifted tinkerer. All these interests, however, took second place to his love for music.

Everywhere in Europe music played a large role in the ceremonial occasions of both court and church, but in Austria music became the favourite pastime and at times a consuming passion of the ruling house. Royal enthusiasm and the patronage it generated later made Vienna the musical crossroads of Europe, the source of an astonishing proportion of the greatest music of the western tradition. At least from the time of Ferdinand II onwards, music figured prominently in the education of young Habsburgs. Ferdinand III had composed some respectable works in the dramatic, rather pompous Italianate style of the period, and he encouraged Leopold in turn to indulge freely in his passion for both performance and composition.

Music, not the verbal arts, offered a perfect artistic medium for a court which ruled so many nations and had perforce to speak so many tongues. Completely cosmopolitan in its appeal and politically neutral in its artistic abstractions, music provided a common meeting ground of taste. It also served to universalize the appeal of the theatrical productions of a baroque court which, like the court of France, ritualized the grandeur of monarchy in sumptuous dramatic allegories.

Of all the Habsburgs who dabbled in musical composition Leopold was clearly the most talented. The impressive remaining corpus of his compositions includes oratorios, requiem masses, musical comedies performed by ladies of the court, and above all a seemingly endless list of arias and intermezzos inserted by invitation in operas performed at the court.[5] Leopold pampered his musicians, and this was sometimes held against him. When money was short, as it almost always was, the musicians were paid first, before any other officers of the court.

Habsburg family piety found in Leopold a nearly ideal representative. His early training for the Church emphasized spiritual exercises in place of the normal martial training of a prince. A strong faith in miracles took hold in his mind. To the end of his life his response to crises was to pray rather than to scheme, to wait patiently for the judgment or miraculous intervention of Providence rather than to throw himself into a flurry of activity. He sensed his association with God intimately. As Emperor he regarded every success wrested from a resisting and sinful world as a sign of special divine favour to him, as another 'miracle of the house of Austria', worked by God in response to the devoted intercession of its heavenly sponsors and protectors. In return for divine favour, Leopold considered it one of his main duties to be punctilious and attentive in observing all acts of faith, all ceremonies of petition, thanksgiving and commemoration calculated to maintain a true faith among his subjects and to preserve the quasi-sacramental character of his high earthly office. He also expected his advisers and the court to take part with him in these long and frequent devotions, a chore many of them found tediously burdensome, distracting them from the business of state or from their more worldly diversions.

Leopold had no sympathy for the less ritualistic approach to religion purveyed by both the mystical sects and sceptical rationalists. Any compromise with heresy was intensely distasteful to him, however necessary it might appear. With respect to the infidel Turks, the situation was tolerably clear to all; but in the case of Protestantism the relationship was always ambiguous, not only because Leopold ruled over many Protestant princes in Germany, but also because his most natural allies in his perpetual conflict with France were the Protestant sea powers, England and the Dutch Republic. *Raison d'état* usually overcame Catholic conscience in the end, but nowhere in Europe did it have a harder time of it than in Vienna.

Those who looked at the young Emperor in 1658 seeking portents of things to come would have found little to suggest any dramatic changes. They saw instead a young man, normally healthy, intelligent, courteous in a shy, formal sort of way, uneasy in the consciousness of the fact that he had not been prepared for the role he was now called upon to play. That he would be conscientious in applying himself to business seemed clear, though there were no signs of ambition or political imagination to disturb the ease of courtiers grown comfortable in the habits of the last reign. Here was no hotheaded young ruler anxious to make history, but a perfect prince for a tradition-bound dynasty and a deeply conservative aristocratic society: modest, prudent, pious, neither a libertine nor a spoilsport, a quiet young gentleman content to let things run as they had done in the past.

For the support and advice his youth and inexperience made indispensable, Leopold turned at first to the two men bound most closely to him by ties of affection and respect: first his uncle, the archduke Leopold Wilhelm, and then to his *Ajo* or governor since 1652, Johann Ferdinand count (later prince) Portia.

Leopold Wilhelm's career had been what Leopold's might have become had Ferdinand IV lived. Trained to be a churchman, he held the bishoprics of Passau, Strassburg, Olmütz and later Breslau. This ecclesiastical pluralism served the interests of his father, Ferdinand II, and then of his brother in the kaleidoscopic complexity of religious politics in Germany during the Thirty Years War. After a brief military apprenticeship under Piccolomini, he was considered qualified to become a *Generalissimus*, halfheartedly leading two unsuccessful campaigns against the Swedes in 1641 and again in 1645-46. In 1647 he represented the Spanish branch of the family as governor of the Netherlands, a position he enjoyed to the fullest as it allowed him to indulge his passion for collecting paintings. He shared the pious traditions of his family, though he was no ascetic, preferring to live quietly, favouring prudence above all virtues, using the immense riches his benefices provided him to live as a great gentleman. Such time as he could take from his ceremonial duties he spent surrounded by his cabinets of curiosities, perusing his books, reading poetry, and enjoying his paintings which made up the finest princely gallery in all Europe.[6]

Leopold gave his uncle all the trust and affection which he had probably never felt for his own father,[7] bonds that were strengthened by shared tastes and a common concern for the fate of their dynasty. The archduke offered a wide and perceptive experience of European affairs, an often shrewd appreciation of the personalities Leopold would have to deal with. Inclined himself to seek a peaceful way out of any entanglement, he encouraged his nephew's natural distaste for military adventures and the hazards of battle. Leopold Wilhelm, like his brother Ferdinand III, aged prematurely, and his failing health allowed him only a few brief years alongside Leopold. He died on 6 January 1662, aged forty-eight.

Leopold's *Ajo* Portia descended from an ancient feudal family of Friuli and from the patriarchs of Aquileia. He was born and raised in Venice, where his father represented Inner Austria at the Venetian senate. With his father he travelled widely on formal missions for one or another of his sovereign lords. His own political career began in Graz, where he served as a member of the governing council from 1634 to 1647, after which he returned to Venice as Imperial orator to the Signoria. His post as Leopold's governor was reward for his loyalty, if not his outstanding competence in that job. When Leopold was thrust unexpectedly into his brother's place as heir to the Habsburg crowns, Portia suddenly and equally unexpectedly became one of the most important political figures in Austria outside the Imperial family itself.

Upon Ferdinand's death in 1657 Leopold gave Portia the office of grand chamberlain. From 1657 until his death in 1665 he was recognized as the first minister. Proudly aristocratic and cosmopolitan, Portia hid his mediocre talents behind an aloof, cold, lonely demeanour. Secure only in the affection of his former ward now turned sovereign, he made an art of caution and procrastination. His careful avoidance of controversy led the Venetian ambassador to remark in exasperation that even Portia's enemies did not fear him. He was scrupulously honest but irresolute and unimaginative, discreet to a fault but equally inexpert. He presided over the privy conference, punctiliously performing his functions, but policy direction came from other and more experienced men.

Leopold was fortunate in his grand chamberlain for one reason at least: Portia had not been great enough for long enough to build up a large following of dependents and clients, hence he was free to seek talent wherever he could find it. A number of men who were to achieve high office later in the reign began in modest bureaucratic posts during Portia's years as grand chamberlain. One of his most interesting protégés was the Spanish Franciscan friar Cristóbal de Rojas y Spínola, an ardent reformer who saw in the assertion of Habsburg power a means to reconcile the divided religious confessions in the west, to defeat Islam in the east and create a true Christian empire in Europe.[8] An early spokesman for mercantilist ideas, he memorialized incessantly, presenting many schemes to promote manufactures, to develop colonial trading enterprises in conjunction with Spain, and to reunite the Protestants with Rome. As Rojas' diplomatic talents won him favour at court he in turn became a patron to men with similar reform ideas, bringing to Vienna both the greatest cameralist writers of the period, Johann Joachim Becher and Philipp Wilhelm von Hörnigk.

For the most part, however, Leopold filled the highest positions with men who had served his father, even those he never completely trusted like Johann Adolf count Schwarzenberg and prince Johann Weikhard von Auersperg. Schwarzenberg was unquestionably able, but had made the mistake in 1657 of supporting Leopold Wilhelm's candidacy for the Imperial crown. In 1659 Leopold appointed him president of the aulic council, a long-delayed reward for years of distinguished service.

Prince Auersperg had been the minister closest to Ferdinand III during the old Emperor's last years, and remained perhaps the most astute politician at the court.[9] His greatest failing, an overbearing self-importance combined with a sharp tongue, grated on the chilly aloofness of Portia whose deep dislike for Auersperg young Leopold came to share. Auersperg had failed to contemplate the possibility that Ferdinand Maria might not succeed his father, and had never treated young Leopold with anything but the contempt he had for all humanity save himself and his monarch. His experience and counsel were absolutely essential to the new privy conference, but he never received the dignities he expected for his years of service.

Prince Wenzel Lobkowitz had been president of the war council since 1650 and Leopold kept him in that office until Portia died in 1665, when Lobkowitz was given the grand chamberlain's post. Having been the chief engineer of Leopold's election as Emperor in 1658, he held Leopold's confidence for a number of years and his gratitude even after the confidence was gone. A hefty *bon-vivant* with a store of ready wit and good humour, he bustled about the court as though he were the busiest man in Europe. He visited every salon, acted the complete man of fashion, the arbiter of taste. He was a particular favourite of Leopold's stepmother, the lively dowager Empress Eleanora. As years passed it became increasingly obvious that this façade was nothing more than that. Lobkowitz did not, for all his superficial cleverness, understand very clearly the detailed operation of the agencies he directed, leaving most of his work to underlings. When it finally came to a real clash in the conference over important policy decisions, he proved inept and fundamentally stupid, and was cast from power without ever understanding completely how it had happened.

Neither the chancellor, Hans Joachim count Sinzendorf, nor the Bohemian chancellor, Johann Hartwig count Nostiz, played a great role in the conference. Nostiz' voice was heard frequently on Bohemian and Hungarian questions, but on the whole he stuck to his main concern which was the smooth functioning of the Bohemian chancellery. Sinzendorf was a political hack, the last Austrian nobleman to hold the chancellorship during Leopold's reign.

Another Sinzendorf, Georg Ludwig count Sinzendorf, remained as president of the court chamber, the chief financial officer of the crown. Even contemporaries agreed that it was an open question which was greater, his competent efficiency or his corruption. The complex network of financial agencies he presided over offered opportunities for peculation at every turn. After his fall from office in 1680 the commission investigating the court chamber, unable to untangle the accounts, could do more than guess how much he had siphoned illegally from the revenues of the crown. The sum was clearly enormous, perhaps as much as two million Gulden, possibly even more. Not the least of his accomplishments was to make Leopold believe him indispensable to the regime for over twenty years.

Leopold's long reign covered the last decades of the great European price revolution, an inflation stimulated in part by the introduction of American bullion to the continent and by increasingly rapid circulation in the arteries of commerce. Every European state faced the financial crises it spawned to a greater or lesser extent; the Austrian monarchy proved more backward than most of them in coping with the problem. The reign began and ended in a state of financial muddle.

In the hereditary lands the common coin of account was the Gulden of sixty Kreuzer. Its value fluctuated considerably over the years in relation to its silver content compared to the Reichsthaler, which had become an abstract unit of account rather than a coin of wide circulation. Since minting was very profitable in the seventeenth century, the temptation to enrich the treasury by manipulation of the coinage often proved irresistible. In 1659, for example, the Vienna mint made a profit of a million and a half Gulden by coining fractional silver currency in small denominations of 3, 6 and 15 Kreuzer to pay the troops.[10]

In August 1658, even before Leopold returned from his coronation, he set a commission to work in Vienna to inquire into and audit unpaid taxes from the province of Lower Austria. The results of the investigation illustrate the distance that separated the Imperial budget from financial reality.[11] The commissioners suggested that taxes still due for years *prior to 1600* be forgiven entirely, and that half the sums due for 1600–17 be collected, the remaining half to be compensated for by 'local works', presumably allowing landlords to use *Robot* labour to repair roads and bridges in the province. Taxes for 1617–23 should be forgiven, 1624–40 to be compensated for entirely by public works. Arrears for 1641–47 were to be collected in cash, but the interest due on these sums was to be collected by taking mortgages on the land. For the years 1648–59 the commission recommended cash payment.

Only a fraction of the taxes the estates imposed on themselves ever got collected, and of that portion a still smaller part ever reached the court chamber. In 1680, for example, the permanent commission of deputies from the Lower Austrian *Landtag* reported that though the estates had granted the crown 498,216 Gulden, and another 232,242 for provincial expenses, in total some 730,458 Gulden, only 409,400 had actually come in, leaving a deficit of 321,058 for a single year. This gap between expectations and actual returns occurred regularly. In the circumstances it is not surprising to find that the government was reduced to treating the various estates of the realm rather like a street peddler bargaining about the price of a pot. The crown always exaggerated its needs when submitting to the various diets requests for extraordinary contributions, knowing that it must bargain, and that the final sum, when settled, would never actually be paid.

In times of general prosperity the crown might get enough to manage with and possibly even pay some interest on its enormous debts. This did not happen often, and even in good times there was never enough forthcoming to begin to pay for the wars that continued to increase the indebtedness. In poor years even local administration, which had the first crack at taxes collected, went unpaid. Both the poverty and mismanagement of the public purse run like a *Leitmotiv* through the whole reign, reinforcing Leopold's natural inclination toward cautious, unadventurous policies that had the merit of being cheaper as well. As Leopold grew older he learned to choose more talented ministers than those with whom he began his reign, but it was circumstance rather than his or his ministers' ambition that forced Leopold to abandon prudence, to take great risks in order to preserve his patrimony.

IV

The First Battles

All the threats to the security of Leopold's conglomerate of states centred around the two greatest enemies of the Habsburgs: France and the Turks. Both were great powers, both found their ambitions frustrated by the house of Austria. When Leopold ascended the throne cardinal Mazarin had already reasserted royal authority in France and turned his attention to crushing Spanish power in the Netherlands and neutralizing Habsburg influence in Germany. The lifeline of Habsburg communications, 'the Spanish Road', ran from northern Italy across Savoy to the Franche-Comté, thence through Lorraine to the Netherlands. The great forts that commanded this vital link appeared to the French as so many doors through which invaders could enter France from the north.

If Mazarin and his apt pupil Louis XIV could not completely destroy the Habsburgs, and they were usually realistic enough to sense the impossibility of this, they could at least aim at breaking the encirclement around France and splitting the two parts of Habsburg hegemony on the northern frontier. At the end of the long war against Spain, Mazarin could even contemplate a higher goal: an eventual Bourbon succession in Spain itself.

Hemmed in by the house of Austria along the Rhine, the French sought allies beyond the Empire to divert and distract its enemy. In the seventeenth century Sweden and the Ottoman empire were the most useful to France. Turkish power had receded after the first siege of Vienna in 1529, even more after the Spanish victory at Lepanto in 1571. In parts of south-eastern Europe the Habsburg 'military border' provided a relatively stable barrier against invasion.[1] Yet the Turks still occupied most of Hungary, and Turkish and renegade Magyar warbands periodically raided the eastern provinces of Austria and Moravia seeking plunder, usually livestock and slaves.[2] Though the Emperor and the sultan were technically at peace, Turkish presence in

Hungary was a permanent and sporadically painful reality, a constant, often violent, danger to life and property all along the frontier.

France had consistently tried to stir up Ottoman aggression against Austria, to coordinate Turkish thrusts into Hungary with French moves towards the Rhine. French agents in Constantinople urged the Porte to give priority to its western front rather than to its other conflicts in the Mediterranean, Persia, southern Russia and Poland. Fortunately for Leopold mutual distrust between his two greatest enemies prevented their ever reaching complete accord on a joint operation against his empire.

As the court in Vienna brought together men from all parts of the hereditary lands, so there naturally developed among this cosmopolitan society factions that sought to put their interests first, to get the attention of the monarch and to influence the policy of the privy conference. Leopold seems to have accepted these divisions as an inescapable condition of his regime, and indeed even to have encouraged competition among his advisers.[3] Such factionalism may have weakened the regime, but at the same time it left him personally more freedom to manœuvre, to change his mind, or more often to delay decisions until a course of action was forced upon him by circumstances.

Prince Lobkowitz and prince Auersperg led the so-called 'easterners', a large party at court strongly supported by substantial elements of the Austrian, Bohemian and Hungarian nobility who put local interests first. In their view the Turk was the main enemy, the threat of France in the west merely peripheral to the vital interests of the monarchy. For them the military and political problems of the east always took priority, a view constantly running counter to the demands of Habsburg dynastic politics and to Leopold's own conception of his family's European destiny.

Over against these more local interests stood the 'Spanish' faction, or the 'westerners'. A succession of Spanish ambassadors to Vienna found a number of influential courtiers who shared their view that France, not the Turks, must be dealt with first. Overt French encouragement of Turkish aggression lent plausibility to their arguments. Depending on the direction of French aggression at any given time, the Spanish envoys could count on Italian or German nobles and on the Imperial family itself to give priority to the concerns of Spain and the Rhineland. In 1658 prince Portia leaned towards this party, as did the archduke Leopold Wilhelm who had governed the Spanish Netherlands and had a very clear perception of the potential danger to the Habsburg possessions bordering on France.

From time to time a specifically German, 'Imperial' faction emerged at court, urging Leopold to give more attention to the affairs of Germany and to the threat of Swedish interference. In moments of real danger these men even demanded a revival of Imperial authority and reform of the archaic institutions of the Empire. The cameralist writers of the reign and many of the best diplomats serving Leopold could be counted among this faction, which as often as not concentrated on internal reform rather than on foreign policy. This group grew or waned as the German princes lost or gained confidence in their own ability to hold on to their precious 'liberties'. Even at its zenith late in the reign it remained a movement of opinion and pamphleteering rather than a genuine political force.

The Church, through the papal nuncio primarily but also through Leopold's many intimate friends among the court clergy, exercised substantial influence over the monarch, but it can hardly be said to have made up a 'faction' of its own. There were quite divergent views among churchmen about papal politics to begin with. Jealousy among the different monastic orders, competition for influence at court, concern for revenues and endowment, all tended to scatter and diffuse clerical opinion. Prominent clerics could be found in all parties, though as French influence increased in Rome those who followed papal leadership most closely supported the 'easterners'.

The decade between the peace of Westphalia and Leopold's coronation had been a time of peace for Austria, years of restoration and recovery. Leopold I never enjoyed a comparable period of relative tranquillity however much he might have yearned for it. The first international challenge to the new regime resulted from Leopold's bargain with the elector of Brandenburg at the electoral conclave. Sweden and Brandenburg had been at work together expanding their states at the expense of Poland and Denmark. The war, which had gone badly for Poland, appeared to be spreading southward to the lands along the eastern borders of the hereditary lands when prince George II Rákóczy of Transylvania joined the coalition against Poland.

In September 1657 Friedrich Wilhelm of Brandenburg made peace with Poland, winning East Prussia's freedom from Polish sovereignty. Straight away he then joined with Austria and Poland to attack his former ally, Sweden, whose Pomeranian possessions, especially the seaport of Stettin, now excited his cupidity. This had allowed Lobkowitz to strike his bargain with the elector. Once Leopold's election was certain, he sent his armies north to discharge his debt. His best generals, Raimondo Montecuccoli and Louis de Souches, joined Friedrich

Wilhelm in a successful campaign in Pomerania which the Swedes stopped just short of Stettin. In 1658 and 1659 Sweden was isolated from France by the continuing war with Spain. Once Mazarin finally freed France from that conflict in the Peace of the Pyrenees in 1659, however, the balance of power in northern Europe again swung in Sweden's favour with the diplomatic intervention of France. On 3 May 1660, after some months of negotiation, peace was signed at Oliva, and all that Brandenburg obtained was a Swedish guarantee of East Prussia.

Austrian intervention in the northern war exposed the flaws in the administrative and military system Leopold had inherited. Both his diplomatic service and the field armies under Montecuccoli had functioned well, but to play a more daring international game took resources he could not command from his reluctant estates. The army was unpaid and, as a result, unruly. The swelling debt made it hard to find new credit. With youthful enthusiasm Leopold took up the cry for reform, ordered inquiries and set up commissions to study the administration and finances. He invited reform projects from every side, then, rather than staying in Vienna to see them through, set out on an extended tour of his realms.

Leopold knew Prague and Pressburg; he had never visited Styria, Carinthia or Trieste. For five months in 1660 he toured his southern realms receiving homage from the provincial diets, collecting curiosities and winning the loyalty of provinces that had not seen their sovereign prince for generations. Archduke Leopold Wilhelm had opposed the journey because the Turks were again threatening to march into Hungary, but Leopold insisted on going. The expedition turned into a major public relations success, especially in Carinthia where none of Leopold's ancestors had ever appeared.

Whatever remained of the young Emperor's reforming zeal moved into the background after his return to Vienna. The following years were dominated by two prolonged crises: a revival of Turkish power in the east and the near extinction of the dynasty itself. The dynastic crisis caused Leopold the deepest concern, for it involved nothing less than the future of the whole Habsburg enterprise, and most particularly the succession in Spain.

The problem of the Spanish succession, which in 1701 plunged all Europe into war, was already in 1661 a fixture of European politics. While the rivalry between the Habsburg and Bourbon dynasties lay at the heart of the matter, any decision on the disposition of Spain's widely scattered possessions concerned every European power. The Spanish empire was weakened and unwieldy, but joined directly either to Austria or France might well produce an exorbitant power which might dominate the continent, or at the very least overthrow the delicate balance among the existing powers within which the modern European system of nation states was even then developing.

So long as the two branches of the house of Austria remained separate and independent, Spanish affairs were governed largely by Spanish interests. But for some years the succession to the Spanish crown had been uncertain as disaster seemed to pursue the heirs to the throne with persistent regularity. Philip IV had sired two sons in 1629: the heir presumptive, Baltasar Carlos, and a bastard son, don Juan de Austria. Baltasar Carlos died in 1646 and for eleven years Philip remained without a legitimate male heir. Then in 1657 his second wife and niece Maria Anna, Leopold's sister, gave birth to a son, Philip Prosper, who in turn died after four hopeful years on 1 November 1661. Just five days later Maria Anna gave birth to another son, Charles, a sickly infant who seemed unlikely to survive childhood. There remained two daughters: Maria Teresa, born in 1638 to Philip's first wife, Isabel of Bourbon, and the younger daughter Margareta, born in 1651 to Leopold's sister Maria Anna.

From the beginning it had been assumed both in Madrid and in Vienna that the infanta Maria Teresa would marry the heir of Ferdinand III, first Ferdinand IV, then, after his death, Leopold I. These plans collapsed when Mazarin insisted on the hand of the elder daughter for Louis XIV as the price for a peace with France that would leave the Spanish empire more or less intact. Neither Philip IV nor Louis XIV liked the match, but both gave in to Mazarin. At the Peace of the Pyrenees Louis reluctantly engaged to marry Maria Teresa for reasons of state. The new queen of France formally renounced all her claims to inherit the throne of Spain, though Mazarin inserted a condition making the renunciation dependent upon payment of her proposed marriage portion. All this remained speculation so long as Philip Prosper still lived, but with his death a Bourbon succession in Spain became a possibility.

Philip IV hastened to reassure his Austrian nephew that the French marriage had been forced on him in order to preserve Naples and the Netherlands, and within a year of signing the treaty with France he made public his intention to marry his second daughter, Margareta, to Leopold. Since the young infanta was but nine years old, the formal engagement treaty had to be postponed until 1663; Leopold did not see his bride until December 1666.

Count Lamberg, Austrian ambassador to Spain, returned to Vienna in 1660, and unaccountably no successor was named for two crucial years. Finally in 1662 Leopold sent count Franz Eusebius von Pötting, a reliable friend but an unskilled diplomat, to represent him in Madrid. The situation he found hardly promised well for the dynasty. Philip IV, ageing and ill, could clearly do no more to assure his succession. The French in the meanwhile had won over many leading figures in the government. The council of state was fearfully reluctant to carry through the projected marriage between Margareta and the Emperor.[4] Von Pötting managed to conclude the marriage contract in 1663, obtaining an express guarantee of Margareta's rights to the succession over those of her elder sister. The infanta, however, remained in Madrid and nothing von Pötting could do served to speed her departure for Vienna.

Afraid now that the dynastic link could be broken before his own marriage was consummated, Leopold sent his most talented diplomat, Franz Paul von Lisola, to Madrid in 1664 to work alongside the un-energetic von Pötting. Lisola was typical of the cosmopolitan servants of the Habsburgs, born of Italian parents in Besançon under Spanish rule. Driven by a fierce hatred for the French, he quickly took charge in Madrid, encouraging queen Maria Anna to exert herself more strongly in state affairs. Through her he finally convinced Philip IV to make a will categorically reaffirming Margareta's right to the succession and securing for Maria Anna, and through her for the pro-Austrian party at the Spanish court, control of the regency for young Charles II. When Philip IV died in September 1665 Maria Anna took over the reins of government and Lisola left Madrid with Leopold's interests as secure as they could be, given the infant king's uncertain hold on life and the fact that Maria Teresa had presented Louis XIV with a son in 1661. In 1666 Margareta and her large entourage finally set forth from Spain, travelling slowly to Austria where a magnificently theatrical celebration saluted Leopold's wedding in December.

Leopold's almost frenzied impatience to marry must be seen against the background of dynastic disasters succeeding one another year after year. The same bad luck that pursued the Spanish line seemed also to stalk the Austrian Habsburgs. Archduke Leopold Wilhelm died in November 1662. Just a month later archduke Karl Ferdinand of the Tyrol followed him to the grave. In January 1664 Leopold's younger half-brother, archduke Karl Joseph, died at the age of fifteen. With the death of archduke Sigmund Franz on 25 June 1665 the cadet Tyrolean line was extinguished. When Philip IV of Spain died in September the survival of the dynasty itself now depended solely on the sickly

Charles II of Spain and on Leopold who was twenty-six years old and still unmarried. When Leopold married Margareta in December 1666 the lavish entertainments that livened the occasion referred frequently and bluntly to the malicious fickleness of fortune which the marriage now overcame.

In the midst of all these dynastic troubles Leopold had to face a new state of emergency in the east. Officially at least the Emperor and the sultan had been at peace since the treaty of Zsitva-Török of 1606, an armistice maintained more by Habsburg distraction in western Europe and by the stagnation of Ottoman government and society than by any satisfaction either party took in the terms of the treaty. Both sides still wanted what the other held; both intended to take it when circumstances allowed. The occasion for renewing the ancient conflict was provided, as was often the case, by Transylvania.

The princes of Transylvania had built themselves a state between three warring powers: Poland, Austria and Turkey. They had done this by making the best of their precarious situation and the constant wars among their powerful neighbours. Their autonomy was never complete, however, and they recognized the suzerainty of the sultan and paid tribute to the Porte. In return the Turks allowed Transylvania a large measure of political autonomy and religious liberty for its very mixed population. Prince George II Rákóczy's adventure against Poland in 1658 brought down on him the wrath of the sultan's energetic new vizier, Mehmet Köprülü, who induced the sultan to depose the prince. Rákóczy rashly decided to resist the Turkish mandate, counting on Leopold to forgive him for the Polish fiasco and to send him aid against the Turks. Leopold did indeed sympathize with any Christian prince who faced being engulfed by the Turkish armies, but he distrusted Rákóczy for many good reasons, and found his own forces quite inadequate to meet a full-scale invasion. Rákóczy fought on alone, winning a few engagements in 1659, until he died from battle wounds in May 1660. The Transylvanians elected Janos Kemény, who fled to Habsburg Hungary before a second Turkish invasion which replaced him with yet another Transylvanian noble, Michael Apafy (Abafi).

The furious effectiveness of the Turks' punitive expeditions against Transylvania and their vigorous pursuit of Rákóczy and Kemény came as something of a surprise to Vienna where the Emperor and his ministers had become accustomed to Turkish bluster unaccompanied by strong action. These ominous signs of Turkish revival were evidence enough of the ruthless efficiency of Mehmet Köprülü (vizier 1656–61) and his adroit son Ahmed (vizier 1661–76), a resurgence of Islamic power that reached its climax before the walls of Vienna under Ahmed's adopted successor, Kara Mustafa.[5]

Refugees from Transylvania, Hungarian nobles at the court and the 'easterners' in Leopold's privy conference pressed for firm action in the east. Freed from involvement in the north by the peace of Oliva, Leopold reluctantly agreed to send Montecuccoli to Hungary with such small forces as could be assembled and partially supplied from the nearly empty treasury. The means were meagre, the troops poorly paid and unreliable, the Hungarians inhospitable. Montecuccoli could do little but complain of his lot and leave Kemény to his fate, which overtook him in January 1662 when he fell in battle against the Turks.

Kemény's death forced Leopold to choose among unwelcome alternatives. He was unwilling to recognize Apafy as prince and thereby sanction Turkish suzerainty over a province which he himself claimed as an ancient dependency of the Hungarian crown. He was equally reluctant to appeal to France or its satellite German princes for the aid he would need in the event of war against the Turks. Yet it was clear that war was coming; the reports from his representatives in Constantinople were full of danger signals and quite accurate warnings about the aggressiveness of the new vizier Ahmed Köprülü. While Montecuccoli fretted helplessly in Hungary in 1661 Leopold began negotiating for assistance from the few well-disposed princes in Germany. Even the friendliest of them insisted that he convene the Imperial Diet.

Austrian assistance to Kemény had been ineffective, but it was enough to anger the Turks. With Kemény dead and his troops scattered, Leopold's own forces faced the Turks alone. Leopold bowed to circumstances and agreed to call the Diet. Almost a year elapsed before all the princes and cities sent their representatives to convene at Regensburg in January 1663. By that time the Turks had firmly occupied all of Transylvania and built up threatening new forces in Hungary. As Leopold and his ministers expected, the German princes still saw the external danger of a Turkish invasion up the Danube a less immediate threat than the prospect of a large army under the Emperor's command. The French agents at Regensburg encouraged their reluctance to help Austria, finding a strong ally in Johann Philipp of Mainz, who convinced the majority not to revive the traditional general tax for war. Instead, he offered a separate force, independently commanded, to be sent by the states joined with France in the League of the Rhine.

In April 1663 the Turks declared war. Ahmed Köprülü moved into the Danube basin gathering fresh corps from Moldavia, Wallachia,

Transylvania and the Crimean Tatars. Leopold had to accept whatever he could get quickly. In July the archbishop of Salzburg mediated a treaty between the Emperor and the Rhenish League providing a corps of over 6,000 men including unwelcome contingents of French troops. In return Leopold had to supply artillery as well as the ordinary provisions, guarantee Protestants among them freedom of worship, and recognize the absolute independence of their own commanders.

Fortunately for Leopold the Turkish armies moved slowly enough for him to use the threat of their presence to win further support before they were in a position to crush his own eastern defences. By September 1663 his negotiations with Brandenburg and Saxony brought contingents from both states marching through Austria to quarter for the winter in Moravia and Hungary. By January 1664 the two upper houses of the Imperial Diet had at last been brought to agree on raising an Imperial army of about 21,000, an impressive political victory for Leopold's agents in Regensburg even though it remained a paper army still to be recruited.

The Turkish offensive in Hungary began in the spring of 1664. Montecuccoli tried to coordinate his scattered forces in spite of the division of command, but the rendezvous planned for late April did not in fact come about until mid-July when Montecuccoli moved to intercept the main Turkish force along the river Raab, where a Turkish breakthrough would open the way to both Vienna and Graz. Here he was joined by a contingent of French auxiliaries commanded by count Coligny. Although he was grateful for the additional manpower for the coming contest, Montecuccoli found the division of command a serious problem, interfering with the mobility of his forces and the speed of operation. This confusion among the Imperial armies allowed the Turks to begin crossing the river unopposed near the monastery of Saint Gotthard on 1 August. The Imperial forces, ill-coordinated and unsure of the ground, were thrown back in confusion before Montecuccoli finally convinced both Coligny and margrave Leopold Wilhelm of Baden-Baden, who commanded the Imperial contingents, to attack simultaneously with massed forces in a wooded area where the Turks were reorganizing for a fresh assault. The move proved astonishingly successful. The Turks broke ranks and fled back towards the river, large numbers of them drowning in the confusion, which completely disrupted Köprülü's attempt to cross with the rest of his forces.

The victory at Saint Gotthard proved temporarily decisive even though the Turkish army remained numerically superior. Turkish losses were heaviest among the elite corps, and the vizier was left with an army of ill-trained irregulars and auxiliaries. For Montecuccoli the situation was just the reverse. His casualties had been heaviest among the inexperienced Imperial contingent, a majority of whose staff officers were dead or badly wounded. His best units had held up well and remained ready for action.[6] Although the numerical odds were against him by as much as three to one, he had the advantage in virtually every other sense: organization, firepower and the initiative to act. There was an even more hopeful sign: the Hungarian and Croatian nobility suddenly found themselves filled with enthusiasm for the Habsburg cause and ready to do their part in liberating the occupied portions of the realm.

To the surprise and disgust of his generals, Leopold concluded peace at once. His agents, who had been negotiating with Köprülü throughout the campaign, concluded peace preliminaries at Vasvár just ten days after the victory. The treaty took no account of what had been won, leaving the Turks in possession of Transylvania and the parts of Hungary they had held before hostilities began. In addition the treaty bound Leopold to payment of an annual 'gift' of 200,000 Gulden to the Sublime Porte.[7] Prince Portia and a majority of the ministers in the privy conference favoured ratifying the humiliating peace even though it appeared to be snatching defeat from the jaws of victory. Leopold accepted their advice and ratified the treaty on 7 September 1664. This outraged the Hungarian nobility and complicated Leopold's relations with his most independent subjects for decades. In general even Leopold's apologists have seen it as a blunder, a cowardly move that threw away important gains for an illusion of peace.

Leopold himself wrote to his cousin archduke Sigmund Franz of the Tyrol on 1 October 1664 that he had been forced to make 'a virtue of necessity' in view of the general danger to Europe and to the house of Austria represented by France, which could be expected to seize quickly any advantage offered by Austrian distraction in the east, and because of the pressing 'interests of our house in Spain'.[8] Portia wrote in much the same vein to von Pötting in Madrid to help him explain the situation to the Spaniards who had sent troops and money to assist Leopold against the Turks, and who could be expected to feel equally disappointed at the meagre results of so spectacular a victory.

Vasvár marked a victory for the 'Spanish' faction at court, and above all for Leopold's overriding concern for the future of his dynasty. His distrust of Louis XIV and of French policy in general had grown during the debates at the *Reichstag* in Regensburg. The contingent of French troops sent to Hungary posed another problem, since its officers fraternized with the Magyar nobles and encouraged Hungarian dissatisfaction with Vienna's policies. Leopold noted that the magnates, now so enthusiastic to pursue the war and so critical of his peace with the Turks, had taken little part in Montecuccoli's campaign and had been noticeably absent during the decisive action at Saint Gotthard.

Leopold's distrust and suspicion of his allies were powerful motives inducing him to conclude the war as fast as possible. He could not afford to continue the war without this foreign assistance, and however much he hated and distrusted the Turks, he feared and suspected Louis XIV and the Hungarian nobles as much or more. Once he had made his decision, Leopold calmly weathered the storm of criticism, patiently explaining his position to those few whose opinion mattered to him, and turning his attention to France and the problems of his own family.

V

Austria and France 1659–73

It is not easy to imagine two European rulers more different than Leopold I and his near contemporary and life-long rival Louis XIV of France, whom he never met. Their hostility was like that of a blood feud, inherited with their family traditions and the political imperatives of their realms. Leopold, the younger by two years, assumed personal rule first, when Louis was still learning the art of statecraft from the Italian cardinal Mazarin.[1] Married as an act of state to the Spanish princess originally intended for Leopold, Louis treated his consort as an unloved but necessary encumbrance so long as she lived. This union affronted Leopold's dynastic sense in the first instance, while Louis' notorious procession of mistresses offended his sense of propriety. Louis saw Leopold as a pompous young incompetent who stood in the way of his glory; Leopold regarded Louis as an insufferably arrogant hypocrite whose deceitfulness was matched only by his bumptious disregard for the conventions of good behaviour. Both men misjudged the other and often acted impetuously from a deep and shared mistrust.

Their part in the long struggle for supremacy began at the electoral conclave in Frankfurt where Leopold saw at first hand how effectively French diplomacy and bribery could frustrate Habsburg interests. Then in 1659 the Pyrenees peace raised the spectre of a Bourbon succession in Spain. After Mazarin's death in 1661 Louis XIV, determined henceforth to be his own first minister, fanned the flames of Leopold's distrust by attempting to induce Philip IV to nullify Maria Teresa's renunciation of her rights to the Spanish throne. France had much to offer Spain, including military assistance in regaining Portugal, which had established its independence in 1640.

Louis' move might well have succeeded. Leopold was temporarily unrepresented in Madrid; his sister the Spanish queen had wielded little influence so far over political decisions. Even leaving aside the question of the promised but unpaid dowry, there were serious doubts whether a princess could renounce her rights to the succession. Dynastic law was generally considered a part of fundamental rather than contract law. Not content with legal arguments alone, however, Louis mixed threat with his petition, demanding that Spain cede to France the Franche-Comté and parts of the Netherlands. This the Spanish council of state refused even to consider. These exchanges between Paris and Madrid in 1662 were no more than a preliminary skirmish in the great affair of the Spanish succession, but they served to make French objectives perfectly clear, raising danger signals that increased Leopold's fears for the future of his house.

Although the Habsburgs and Bourbons were the principals in this duel for empire, the outcome concerned all of Europe. Even before the death of Philip IV gave added urgency to the issue, a number of states-men considered the possibility of partition, a negotiated distribution of the various parts of the Spanish inheritance in such a fashion that no European state would gain a preponderance of power in Europe. As early as 1663 the Imperial chancellor, Johann Philipp of Mainz, discussed various plans for dividing the inheritance between Louis XIV and Leopold, hoping thereby to avoid a war that would be to the dis-advantage of the smaller states on the Rhine.[2]

Partition seemed the obvious, sensible and statesmanlike solution to the situation, but it completely failed to take into account the Spanish viewpoint. The Spanish ministers could not afford even to consider a division of the patrimony built up in Spain's glorious past. Leopold, who knew the Spaniards better than did the elector of Mainz, realized that any suggestion of partition could rally the council of state behind any candidate, including a French one, who promised to take and hold everything. For the time being Leopold refused to discuss a proposal which would, if known, bring down his own supporters in Madrid and delay even further his marriage with Margareta. Reports reaching Vienna from France made it clear that Louis would almost certainly attempt to seize the Spanish Netherlands and probably the Franche-Comté as well, as soon as Philip IV died. For Leopold it was a matter of great urgency to consummate his marriage before this happened, in the hope that there might be at least one heir from the match to secure Habsburg succession in Spain through Philip's testament. The Turkish war was an unwelcome distraction from which Leopold felt compelled to disengage himself as quickly as he could.

Events moved more quickly than anyone expected. Philip IV died in September 1665. France immediately published claims to the provinces of Flanders and Brabant, the heart of the Spanish Netherlands, on the grounds that they 'devolved' on Maria Teresa through a Flemish law under which children of the first marriage inherited before the children of the second. However dubious it may have been to try to apply private law to the succession of sovereignty, the argument was a convenient one for Louis XIV, for both Margareta and Charles II of Spain were children of the second marriage. Maria Teresa was the only surviving child of the first. French initiative caught the Viennese regime off balance.

Leopold had determined, upon the death of prince Portia (in February 1665), to give no one else the same degree of influence that Portia had exercised; in effect he resolved like Louis XIV to have no first minister.[3] He transferred prince Lobkowitz, a confirmed 'easterner', to the grand chamberlain's post and appointed don Hannibal Gonzaga, an importunate relative of his stepmother, to the presidency of the war council. Leopold began to attend privy conference meetings regularly, asserting his right to make all decisions, trying to imitate his French rival, the very model of a busy monarch. Unfortunately for the expedition of important matters, Leopold in his inexperience too often confused his own superficial activity with actual accomplishment and diverted much of the time and energy of his conference to the ceremonial details of his approaching nuptials.

The real job of meeting the French challenge fell on the diplomatic corps, and above all on Franz von Lisola, who proved as skilful a pamphleteer as he was a diplomat. In a series of vitriolic pamphlets Lisola pictured Louis as an avaricious megalomaniac disturbing the peace of Europe. Leopold he pictured as a defender of European liberty against ambitious French desire for 'universal monarchy'. Humbler Austrian agents also did their part, providing accurate information on French moves which permitted Vienna to pass on precise details about the French invasion plans to the Spanish governor in Brussels, the marqués de Castel Rodrigo. All this did little good, however, for Leopold did not send troops to assist the Spaniards, and Castel Rodrigo could not be induced to make energetic moves to defend his provinces.

As the French poised for an invasion of the Netherlands, Leopold finally received his bride from Spain. The Viennese court had rehearsed busily for months in preparation for the theatrical productions, processions and fireworks that were to greet the inauguration of her reign as Empress. Those among the high nobility who could still mount a horse worked daily on the complex manœuvres of the horse ballet. No one, however important his other duties, could avoid volunteering for this, so we find young duke Charles, heir of Lorraine, and general Montecuccoli cavorting among the 'Four Elements'. The wedding itself took place on 12 December 1666; the celebrations went on for six weeks.

The Hofburg provided the stage for the elaborate equestrian ballet, while to provide a suitable setting for the popular Italian operas and the Jesuit *Musikspielen* Leopold ordered the architect Burnacini to build a 'Comedy House' on the Kortina bastion. This large wooden structure reportedly cost over 100,000 Reichsthaler,[4] and accommodated probably as many as 1,500. This great theatre, destroyed in the Turkish siege of 1683, was completed in 1667 and sometime during that year the famous opera *Il pomo d'oro* was first performed there with ingenious baroque stage techniques.

Often cited as an example of court extravagance, *Il pomo d'oro* was also a refined vehicle for Habsburg propaganda. Around the classical legend of the apple of discord the Italian court poet Francesco Sbarra and the composer Marc Antonio Cesti wove a plot full enough of incidents to tax even Burnacini's clever stage machinery. For five and a half hours the goddesses intrigue to win the coveted prize for the fairest of them all, only to agree in the end with Jupiter's decision to dedicate the prize to Margareta, the new Empress. This pretty, if heavily overdone, compliment to the Imperial couple came as no surprise to Leopold who had a hand in the production from the beginning and had himself composed several arias inserted into it.[5]

The concluding scene was set against a monumental allegory representing the Court of Austrian Glory, with statues of Leopold and Margareta set in the centre of the stage surrounded by pictures of their illustrious ancestors. The scene alluded to the fact that Leopold was the last male in a dwindling dynasty: behind the Imperial couple were ranged images of a large and prosperous progeny, received with joy by allegorical figures representing not only the hereditary lands and states, but also friendly foreign powers, chief among them the Spanish Habsburg dominions.

While Vienna celebrated and made propaganda, Louis XIV prepared to make good his claims to the Netherlands by force. In May 1667 his troops crossed the frontier, marched past Castel Rodrigo's unprepared defence lines and occupied enough of the province to give France the initiative at the bargaining table. That Louis wanted the Netherlands and the Franche-Comté was clear to all; but it was also true, though not nearly so obvious, that he was unwilling at the time to risk a general war to get them.

Leopold felt the insult to his dynasty very keenly, since he was now the head of the family. His own ministers, however, did not share his

intense concern for his dynastic responsibilities to Spain. Prince Lobkowitz, still pushing the eastern policy, saw nothing to be gained
through involvement in the Spanish Netherlands; he wanted to bring
the French to accept a compromise that would not seriously weaken the
Spanish position there and still leave Leopold free to concentrate on
extending his power in the east.

Lobkowitz shrewdly avoided involving himself too deeply in the
negotiations which could only result in appeasement of France. Instead
he induced his rival in the conference, prince Auersperg, to undertake
the discussions with Grémonville, the French ambassador in Vienna.
In this contest of wits both Auersperg and Leopold were outmatched
by Grémonville, who knew that Leopold could not afford to make a
public agreement with France which would be interpreted in Madrid
as a partition of the Spanish inheritance. Auersperg foolishly let Grémonville play on his intense vanity, conceding point after point in return for
vague promises of French support for his ambition to win a cardinal's
hat for himself.

By January 1668 Auersperg and Grémonville had patched together a
treaty which, had it been ratified, would have amounted to a secret
agreement between Louis XIV and Leopold I to partition the Spanish
empire between themselves should Charles II die childless. Leopold
would have inherited the bulk of the empire and most of Spain, giving
France the Netherlands, Naples, the Franche-Comté, Navarre and the
Philippines.[6] Such an arrangement, abstractly sensible as it was, might
have pleased ardent pacifists like Johann Philipp of Mainz, but it could
not possibly have proved acceptable either to the Spanish themselves,
whose own kingdom would be dismembered, or to Leopold, who
could hardly hope to defend his portion against a France strengthened
by the accession of rich, compact territories.

In the end the treaty was never signed, but even the most stringent
security did not prevent the Spanish from learning about the general
nature of the discussions. The repercussions in Madrid nearly lost Maria
Anna the regency, undercut Austrian influence at the Spanish court for
several years and helped induce the council of state to make peace with
France. The war ended with only modest losses to France, but the treaty
left unsettled the question Louis XIV raised at the beginning concerning
his legitimate claims to substantial parts of the Spanish patrimony.

In Vienna Lobkowitz moved to use the Spanish fiasco to destroy his
rival Auersperg, whom he had duped into taking the initiative with
Grémonville. The charges against Auersperg amounted to treason, but
they could not be substantiated without embarrassing the Emperor

himself. Although Leopold had disliked Auersperg, he was reluctant to dismiss him from the conference. He would have preferred to keep entirely out of the affair by turning the accusations over to a judicial inquiry, but he could not do that without revealing the details of the partition treaty and his own knowledge of them. Finally, after much wrangling with his conscience, Leopold summarily dismissed the prince from his offices on 10 December 1669 and banished him from the court.[7] Auersperg withdrew to Laibach (Ljubljana) where he died within a year.

In 1669 Lobkowitz appeared to be at the very pinnacle of power. His greatest rival had been disgraced, there was now no one left among the inner circle of the privy conference who could offer a serious challenge to his leadership. Montecuccoli joined the conference in August 1668, replacing Gonzaga as president of the war council, but the ageing general regarded himself as a specialist and a technician holding himself above the intrigues of court politics. The one other strong character in the conference was the new chancellor, Dr Johann Paul Hocher, appointed in January 1667. Hocher's talents quickly won Leopold's approval, but his bourgeois background kept him remote from the aristocratic cliques at court.[8] For the time being the chancellor held back cautiously, unwilling to challenge Lobkowitz. Faced with a conference tamely submissive to Lobkowitz and the easterners, Leopold turned increasingly to the advice of a trusted friend, the Capuchin monk Emmerich Sinelli, whose spiritual guidance helped Leopold through a new series of personal tragedies.

The years from 1668 to 1673 were bitter ones for Leopold. Margareta bore him a son, Ferdinand Wenzel, in September 1667, but the child died within five months. A second child, Maria Antonia, was born in January 1669 and she alone survived of the children of Leopold's Spanish marriage. A third son Johann Leopold was born in 1670 but died almost immediately after birth. Early in 1670 Leopold himself suffered a severe illness that placed the dynasty in grave danger of extinction. Finally, Leopold's happy domestic life was shattered when Margareta died on 12 March 1673.

The apparent fragility of the house of Austria caused intense political dangers. France took the opportunity to increase its influence among the German princes to whom it could now hold out tempting prospects of dismembering Austria itself. In 1669 Louis XIV lured Brandenburg into an alliance in return for French support for the elector's claims to Silesia. Bavaria took the same path the following year in return for large subsidies and tempting, if vague, promises of parts of Austria. Without assurances of an heir to his own realms, there was little Leopold could do to counteract the French, who scored a diplomatic *coup* by neutralizing the two most powerful German states which had in the past often aided Austria against its enemies both in the east and in the west.

Protected diplomatically against any serious opposition to his plans Louis XIV occupied the duchy of Lorraine in April 1670, cutting direct communications between the Spanish Netherlands and the Franche-Comté. The blow was shrewdly struck, for while it was a disaster for the Habsburg dynastic interests on the French frontier, it did not threaten the German princes across the Rhine. Leopold gave asylum to his old ally the duke of Lorraine, now a landless exile, but he could not send an army to recover his duchy, for his own troops were tied down in the east by the threat of rebellion in Hungary. In the privy conference Montecuccoli alone wanted a more vigorous stand against France, but his influence was too weak to overcome the views of Lobkowitz and Hocher who both preferred appeasement. Leopold accepted the opinion of his grand chamberlain and chancellor, adding one more to the long list of sins he held against the king of France.

Franz von Lisola kept the western policy alive by trying to make an alliance with the English and Dutch against France, but the results were disappointing. Just as Louis moved to occupy Lorraine it became clear that Charles II of England had reached an understanding with France. Faced with a diplomatic impasse, without troops of his own and money to pay them, Leopold agreed to make a deal with France, signing a secret treaty of neutrality on 13 November 1671 which in effect left Louis XIV free to attack the Dutch from the west, outflanking the strong Spanish frontier fortresses. When the invasion began in April 1672, however, it created a situation which suddenly changed the diplomatic picture and showed the flaws in the apparent perfection of French preparations.

The first to break with France was the elector of Brandenburg, who had been friendly with Louis XIV during the war against Spain but who now decided to support the Dutch with whom he had strong family and religious ties. Friedrich Wilhelm tried but failed to stir up the Protestant princes of Germany, then turned to Austria. In Vienna the mood was changing rapidly. The Hungarian revolt was suppressed, the war in the west grew more dangerous. In June 1672 Leopold signed a treaty with Brandenburg binding each to have 12,000 men in arms within two months for the defence of the Empire.[9] It was a purely defensive league, mentioning neither the French nor the Dutch; but it was a move away from the eastern orientation of Austrian policy, a step that Leopold himself found heartening.

This new direction in Vienna was hailed by the Spanish faction, for in February 1672 Spain had unexpectedly joined its former rebellious Dutch provinces. This alliance strengthened Leopold's instinctive wish to help the Dutch against the French; Austria and Spain both seemed to be moving once more in the same direction to protect the family enterprise. There were stirrings in the Germanies as well, represented at the Viennese court by margrave Hermann of Baden, who had abandoned his own lands to seek at the Imperial court some military or civil position worthy of his high rank. He had dabbled in mercantilist reform proposals, offering advice and services to the crown that were often unsought; he had, in fact, made himself something of a nuisance. Hermann of Baden advised precisely the reverse of what Leopold heard from a privy conference dominated by Lobkowitz. It was better, the margrave said, to lose something to the Turks if one must, for it could be regained when Christian Europe united behind the crusade to destroy Islam; but what was lost to France was lost forever and weakened the Empire for a final onslaught against the Turk.[10] In the privy conference general Montecuccoli grew bolder and began to spice his analyses of the military situation with demands for vigorous action against France.

As Vienna learned of repeated French successes in the United Provinces, Leopold agreed to send Montecuccoli with a small force to the Rhine, hoping that his presence there would divert the French while Lisola negotiated an alliance with the Dutch. Montecuccoli's bluff failed to impress the French, who insolently demanded that Leopold hold to the treaty of 1671, disarm and recall his troops. Prince Lobkowitz was playing a dangerous double game: openly he appeared to move with the growing interventionist sentiment in the conference, but privately and on his own initiative he informed Grémonville that the expedition to the Rhine was merely for show. Meanwhile he used whatever excuses he could invent to delay formal ratification of the Dutch alliance until December 1672, though by that time the mood of the court was so strongly for war against France that Lobkowitz stood virtually alone in his wish to continue looking eastward while appeasing France.

Montecuccoli returned to Vienna from his fruitless demonstration on the Rhine in April 1673. Chancellor Hocher joined him in the conference opposing Lobkowitz, who was now blamed for the neutrality treaty of 1671. The grand chamberlain, putting as good a face on things as he could, pretended to support the war, though his heart was not in it. Lobkowitz's influence over his sovereign collapsed with his eastern policy. All along, the weakness of his position had been his failure to

understand the influence France could exert indirectly by encouraging
the Emperor's opponents in Turkey, Hungary and Poland. Montecuccoli, his new ally chancellor Hocher, and margrave Hermann saw
more clearly that the European territorial interests of the dynasty led an
expansionist France to seek every means it could find to distract Austria
from the west.

For Austria the crucial diplomatic move came in August 1673 when
a treaty between Leopold and his Spanish relations brought promise of
the cash subsidies he needed to bring his army up to a size large enough
to operate openly against France. Within four weeks the Imperial
forces marched to the Rhine while Leopold addressed an emotional call
to the Imperial Diet to bestir itself to defend the Empire against France.
The war thus begun was to last for the rest of Leopold's reign with but
two interludes of armed peace from 1679 to 1688 and again from 1697
to 1700.

Leopold's unwillingness to commit his meagre resources to a war
against France without substantial assistance from Spain and other
allies had held him back until the French struck at the Dutch. He still
remained suspicious of the Protestant sea powers, reluctant to combine
with them against Catholic France however much he hated Louis XIV.
Until he could overcome these qualms of conscience – and the Spanish
alliance with the Dutch helped move him in this direction – he remained
without strong allies in the west, trapped by constant threats arising on
his eastern frontiers. Once Leopold did master the fundamental political
necessity of uniting his human and material potential with the commercial wealth of England and the Dutch Republic, the house of
Austria's future as a great power was assured.

VI

The Zrinyi Rebellion and Repression in Hungary

Hungary was a nation divided, a nation that had learned the art of survival through using the antagonisms between the two alien empires, Habsburg and Turk, that occupied it. In theory the whole nobility of Hungary made up the Magyar nation, but in fact only a small number of them, the great magnates, concerned themselves seriously with national affairs. In Habsburg Hungary Emperor Leopold possessed neither the military nor the administrative apparatus to circumvent the magnates, but was forced to work through them and with them whenever he could. Their palatine, who was virtually a viceroy in the absence of the king, had greater freedom of action and more influence over local affairs than any member of the royal administration, the magnates collectively made up one of the 'tables' of the national diet.

In the absence of frequent national diets, the magnates exerted their leadership at the local level through the counties, or comitats, whose assemblies on both sides of the border helped keep alive the idea of a Magyar nation. The nature of warfare along the frontier also served to strengthen county organization, for except in moments of real crisis, when a massive invasion moved one way or the other, it was left to county authorities and their militia to deal with raiding parties and brigandage. For many years the magnates had allowed themselves the luxury of believing that all public affairs including the defence of the kingdom could be handled by the comitats without outside interference, objecting fiercely whenever the crown introduced 'foreign' troops, mostly Germans, into Hungary. The Imperial war council could neither supervise the militia nor dispense with it, but had to support the authorities which raised and controlled it. However unavoidable it was, this was in the long run a dangerous policy, for it put in the hands of the comitats weapons which rebellious magnate leaders could use against the royal authority.

The first of Leopold's many bitter contests with the Hungarians arose from the treaty of Vasvár.[1] The peace of 1664 appeared to many Magyar nobles a betrayal of victory and a frustration of their ambition to enlarge their possessions through new conquests in Turkish Hungary. Leopold's explanations of his ratification stung their national pride, for they saw quite correctly a sacrifice of Hungarian interests by their own king to what seemed to them less important concerns in western Europe.

The palatine, Nicholas Zrinyi, and his brother Peter, both scions of an ancient, powerful Catholic magnate family with vast estates in Croatia, spoke out openly and bitterly against Portia's peace. Nicholas angrily retired to his estates in November 1664 where he was killed on a boar hunt. Peter, his heir and successor, chose to ignore the truce with the Turks and began raiding the Turkish frontier. In a short time he added substantially to his already vast fortune through pillage and ransom. In the process he gathered around him a private cavalry of some three to four thousand mounted men living in the same fashion.

Zrinyi's private war openly defied the crown's appeasement policy while at the same time it endangered the economic and commercial concessions that Leopold had won at Vasvár. An Oriental Trading Company was formed in Vienna to open direct trade along the Lower Danube to Constantinople. This project, dear to the mercantilist publicists, got off to a modest but promising start in 1666. By 1668 small cargoes of luxury goods were moving up and down the Danube, while the Oriental Company set about organizing large cattle drives from southern Hungary into Austria. The success of Austria's economic thrust into the Balkans depended not only on the continuing acquiescence of the Sublime Porte, but also on the goodwill of the powerful local pashas at Buda and Belgrade, whose truculence increased as Zrinyi's bands grew more audacious.[2]

Vienna tried in vain to bring the magnates to heel by fiat, but nothing could be done without force. Threats alone accomplished nothing; Austrian bluster succeeded only in provoking a Croatian uprising against royal tax-collectors. In this setting a conspiratorial *junta* emerged as other Magyar magnates joined Zrinyi. The leaders of the group included the new palatine, Ferenc Wesselényi; prince Ferenc Rákóczy I, the son of George II of Transylvania, now married to Peter Zrinyi's daughter Helena, in many ways the most fiery conspirator of them all; Thomas Nádasdy, once a great personal favourite of Leopold I; and Ferenc Frangepáni, another immensely wealthy Croatian magnate. This band of fierce individualists came together with very mixed motives, but they all agreed in their desire to reassert their independence from Habsburg rule and revive the elective character of the crown, in the process dividing royal estates in Hungary and Croatia among themselves. To insure against Austrian revenge they first offered to hold their little kingdoms as fiefs of the Turkish sultan in his technical role as prince of Transylvania, but the Turks sensibly refused to get involved. The plotters then tried to interest Louis XIV with very modest success.

Leadership proved the most serious problem the disaffected nobles faced. While most of them shared a dislike for the Habsburgs, they had little else in common. Popular discontent centred around the Hungarian Lutherans and Calvinists who distrusted the Zrinyis and the other magnates who were nearly all Catholics. The palatine Wesselényi hated his colleague Nádasdy, who headed the Magyar judiciary. The French envoy Grémonville, to whom the junta had made various appeals, found them all to be men who were easily led astray by unrealistic visions of the future and by their total incomprehension of European affairs on a larger scale. The personal animosities and controversies within the conspiracy did not strike Grémonville as the stuff of which successful rebellions are made.

From the first the Vienna regime knew the general outlines and scope of the plot. Indeed, from time to time various conspirators betrayed each other to the government in hope of reward.[3] Leopold was well informed, but he held his hand. It seemed to him and to most of the privy conference a childish and relatively harmless enterprise on the part of a few nobles whose dislike of Habsburg authority, indeed of authority of any kind, was too well known to deserve comment. Since it was equally clear by 1668 that the French would not underwrite a general uprising in Hungary, giving no support beyond a few kind words and some small pensions, the danger seemed modest.

Early in the spring of 1670, however, the situation changed ominously. Insurrectionist pamphlets swept through Hungary in alarming numbers. Reports reached Vienna that Protestant preachers in Upper Hungary had given thanks from the pulpit that the Turks, having finally driven the Venetians from the island of Crete after a twenty-three year siege of Candia, were now free to come 'rescue Hungary from its oppression and papist slavery'. When at the same moment Rákóczy called the Protestant comitats to assemble in Kaschau (Košice) in February, the possibility of a violent insurrection in a confessional cause suddenly appeared alarmingly real.

Leopold summoned the estates of all Upper Hungary to meet at Neusohl (Banská-Bystrika) on 16 March, but they refused to assemble at royal command. Convinced now that the Hungarians anticipated a call for a general uprising, the privy conference took rapid action to meet the rebellion in urgent sessions on 20 and 27 March. With unusual speed troops were sent from Styria to Croatia, cavalry from Silesia moved into Upper Hungary, and units of troops from Austria, Bohemia and Moravia marched to the Waag (Váh) river. Prince Lobkowitz, whose eastern policy was now clearly 'on the line', seconded Leopold in trying to win over Zrinyi and the other leaders of the insurrection. Both sent messages promising 'imperial clemency', not realizing that matters had gone beyond their power to forgive. In the midst of all this confusion news reached Vienna that the magnates had in fact issued the call to revolt. Leopold quickly signed decrees outlawing both Zrinyi and Frangepáni and setting a price on their heads. Their estates were declared forfeited and Frangepáni's office as *ban* of Croatia given to count Nicholas Erdödy, a thoroughly reliable magnate.

While the conference awaited the outcome of events in Hungary, it learned that a Styrian nobleman, a lover of Zrinyi's wife, count Hans von Tattenbach, was involved in the conspiracy. In a swift move the authorities in Graz captured him and with him all the correspondence between him and the Hungarian rebels. Tattenbach was arrested on 22 March, the same day that general Herberstein began operations in Hungary. The rebellion in Croatia collapsed quickly before the Austrian troops. The pasha of Pest refused to bestir himself to save it. Zrinyi and Frangepáni, remembering Leopold's earlier offer of clemency, threw themselves on his mercy. They arrived in Vienna on 18 April 1670 only to find the Emperor's clemency as exhausted as his patience.

The rebellion in north-eastern Hungary could not be dealt with so easily. On 9 April Rákóczy and Stevan Bockskay called out the comitat militias, managing at one point to kidnap count Ernst Rüdiger von Starhemberg, governor of the royal fortress at Tokay. These militia-turned-rebels ranged through the region taking a number of small fortresses and annihilating a few isolated units of Austrian troops. Rákóczy, like Zrinyi, failed through miscalculation, for he also had counted on the Turks to aid him once he openly defied the crown. Lacking that support he found himself with a purposeless, virtually leaderless insurrection which failed to win the prudent Protestant towns, and which could not dislodge the substantial and well-armed garrisons in Tokay and Szatmár. When they learned of Zrinyi's collapse in the south, the northern rebels also decided to submit to Leopold on 1 May, though they couched their surrender in the form of a defiant list of grievances.

Leopold I, Holy Roman
Emperor at eighteen years of age,
surrounded by the coronation
regalia: crown, orb and sceptre.

2   The portrait by Velasquez of the Spanish
infanta Margareta Teresa, sent to Leopold at the
time of the negotiations for their marriage.

3   A scene from the opera *Il pomo d'oro*, performed in 1667 at the wedding celebrations
of Leopold and Margareta.

4 Painting of the Turkish siege of Vienna, 1683. The victory gained when the Ottomans were put to flight is an important landmark in European history.

5 Left, Ernst Rüdiger, Graf von Starhemberg, commander of the military forces in Vienna during the siege.

6 Above, John Sobieski, king of Poland, who played an important part in the raising of the siege.

7 Fireworks at Vienna to celebrate the victory of 1683. Note the Austrian Habsburg coat of arms in the firework display at left, and the Hofburg on the right.

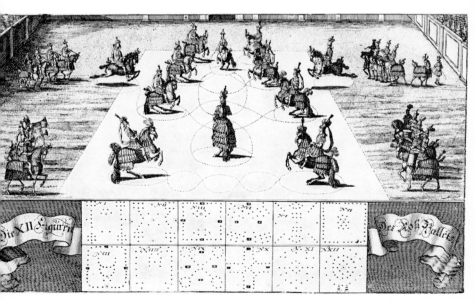

8 The Turkish attack postponed the building of a riding school. Equestrian ballets, like this one of 1667, therefore continued to be staged in the open air. The school was eventually built between 1729 and 1735 to the design of J. B. Fischer von Erlach.

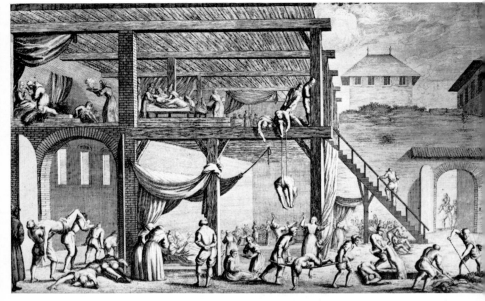

9   A scene from the great plague: a hospital in Vienna, 1679.

Dein lob SERIN gieng durch die welt,
Man hat dich hoch Erhoben:
Nun aber wird verachtung gmelt,
Auß ist das vorig leben.
O buntes thon, wie hast du dein,
So gantz, und gar vergessen,
Vnd teschest auß den edlen schein,
Durch untyreü hoch vermessen:
Bildnüß Peter Serini welcher Zur Reustadt im Zeighauß Haupt m̄ ....
Anno 1671.

10   Peter Zrinyi, *ban* of Croatia, who
rebelled against Leopold and was
executed in 1671.

11   Prince Ferenc II Rákóczy who raised
the standard of the Magyar fight for
independence in 1703.

12   The battle of Zenta, 1697, in which prince Eugene, as Imperial commander
in Hungary, won the decisive battle in the long war against the Turks.

13 Eugene, prince of Savoy-Carignan, Leopold's most important general and war office administrator.

14 Charles V, duke of Lorraine, brother-in-law of Leopold, as an Imperial cavalry commander.

15 An English print of Ludwig Wilhelm, margrave of Baden, known as 'Türkenlouis' because of his victories over the Turks.

16 The conference pavilion at Carlowitz with ground plan showing how the delegates from the Holy League, the Turks and the mediators, to avoid problems of precedence, were enabled to enter simultaneously and separately.

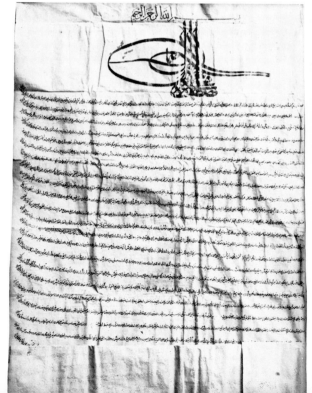

17 The Turkish copy of the treaty of Carlowitz.

18 Leopold's favourite sport was hunting. This engraving shows a stag hunt organized in the Prater as a spectacle before the Emperor.

19 The old moated castle at Laxenburg, one of Leopold's favourite refuges from the ceremonial of the court, and the scene of many hunting parties.

LAXENBVRG

20   The opening bars of Leopold's Requiem Mass (top) written in 1673, probably in memory of his 'beloved Margareta' who died in March of that year.

21, 22   Title page and excerpt (left) from a musical comedy composed by Leopold for the ladies of the court in 1686.

23   The Emperor in theatrical costume (above).

25 Maria Antonia, daughter of Leopold by his first marriage, was forced by her father to sign away the claims to the Spanish succession of herself and her descendants on her marriage to Max Emmanuel, elector of Bavaria. Her renunciation, in Leopold's eyes, strengthened the claim of his sons by his third, 'German', marriage.

24 Charles II, king of Spain, 1665. From birth a semi-invalid, the assumption (which proved correct) that he would never have 'an heir of his own body' presented Europe with 'the problem of the Spanish succession'. The painting shows him, the last of his line, surrounded by portraits of his ancestors, whose incestuous unions were largely responsible for his physical and mental weakness.

26 Max Emmanuel of Bavaria during the war of the Spanish succession in which he took the part of Louis XIV.

27 Leopold's third wife,
Eleanora of Pfalz-Neuburg.

28 Archduke Joseph, Leopold's
eldest son and eventual successor.

29 Archduke Charles, Leopold's
second surviving son, proclaimed
Charles III of Spain in 1703, later
succeeded his brother Joseph as
Emperor Charles VI in 1711.

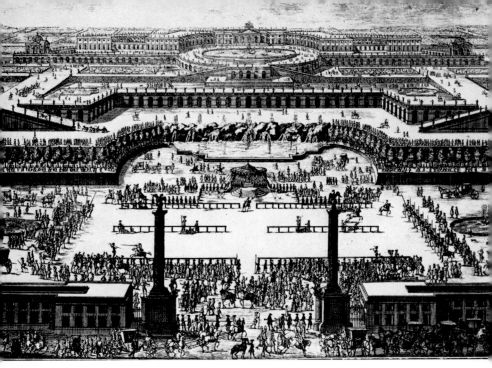

30　First project by J. B. Fischer von Erlach for the Imperial Palace of Schönbrunn.

31　Leopold I in the 'Spanish dress' customary at court.

32 The Capuchin, Emmerich Sinelli, Leopold's closest personal friend during the middle years of his reign.

33 Title page of Philipp Wilhelm von Hörnigk's *Österreich über Alles . . .*, one of the most important cameralist tracts of the century.

34 The 'Court Jew', Samuel Oppenheimer, who financed Leopold's wars.

35 War with France: the burning of Heidelberg, capital of the Rhine Palatinate, in 1693 during the Nine Years War (1688–97).

36 Georg Ludwig, elector of Hanover from 1698, like his father a prominent ally in the Hungarian campaigns and in the wars against Louis XIV.

37 Medal celebrating the momentous victory of Marlborough and Eugene at Blenheim (Blindheim-Höchstädt) in 1704.

8-42 Some of
Leopold's admini-
trators. Prince Wenzel
Lobkowitz (1609-77),
president of the war
council 1650-65, grand
chamberlain 1665-74
(above left); count
Georg Ludwig von
Sinzendorf (1616-81),
president of the court
chamber 1656-80
(above right); count
Franz Ulrich Kinsky
(1633-99), Bohemian

chancellor 1683-99
(centre); count Johann
Wenzel Wratislaw von
Mitrowitz (1669-
1712), ambassador to
England 1700-04,
Bohemian chancellor
1711-12 (below left);
count Leopold
Kolonitsch (d. 1707),
bishop, later cardinal,
a ruthless opponent of
Protestantism in
Hungary (below
right).

JOSEPH I. REX HVNGARIÆ DAL SCLAVONIÆ

APOSTOLICVS MATIÆ CROATIÆ BOSNIÆ &C.

Archidux Austriæ. Dux Burgundiæ Princeps Sueviæ. Marchia Styriæ Carinthiæ Carniolæ. Luxemburgiæ Wertembergæ Sileciæ &c. Princeps Sueviæ: Marchio S.R.I. Burgaviæ Moraviæ utriusque Lusatiæ. &c. vena Habsburgi Tyrolis, Kyburgi, Goritiæ, et Landtgravis Alsatiæ. in nativ.Vienna fu a 6 July Ab 1678 coronatus Posonij die 9. Decembris 1687. VIVAT FELICITER.

43 The succession secured in Leopold's lifetime: his son Joseph who was elected king of the Romans in 1685 and king of Hungary in 1687.

44 The lying-in-state of Leopold I. He died in his sixty-fifth year on 5 May 1705. Note, at the foot of the bed, the crown of the Holy Roman Empire of the German Nation; the other two crowns are those of Bohemia and Hungary.

Between May and August 1670 general Spork and Charles of Lorraine won back all the fortresses the rebel magnates had taken, capturing in the process most of the conspirators' secret correspondence. Having won his battle with few casualties, Leopold intended to follow a relatively mild course of action, hoping to win back the loyalty of the rebels. The new primate of Hungary, archbishop Szelepcsényi of Esztergom, and even prince Lobkowitz seemed to agree with him, though both advised Leopold that changes would have to be made in the Hungarian system of government. The captured evidence was so damning, however, that there was no way to avoid legal proceedings against the leaders of the movement. Once these began, the sensational revelations that came out led to a reign of terror in Hungary.

Chancellor Hocher and the secretary of the privy conference, Christof Abele, undertook the preliminary investigation against Zrinyi and Frangepáni. They worked slowly and carefully. Neither of the rebel magnates appeared to good advantage. First they tried lying, then when confronted with their own correspondence, each placed the blame on the other. The evidence presented, which included a plot to murder Leopold, led to accusations which were then sent to a larger special court (*judicium delegatum*) of twelve high court functionaries, none of them Hungarian.[4]

Thomas Pálffy, the Hungarian chancellor, insisted that only the Hungarian diet had the right to try Magyar nobles. Archbishop Szelepcsényi, however, agreed with Hocher that rebels against the crown could be tried in special courts. The trial lasted for months, though the evidence was so clear that the defence had little to challenge but the constitutionality of the proceedings. In April 1671 Zrinyi, Nádasdy and Frangepáni were sentenced to death and confiscation of all their estates, having been pronounced guilty of *lèse majesté*, rebellion and high treason. Still hoping to avoid the capital sentence, Leopold presented the verdict to a still larger commission of his privy councillors and high court officials, a majority of whom recommended that the sentences be carried out. The privy conference, meeting in Leopold's presence on 25 April, argued vigorously against clemency; Leopold then signed the warrants. On 30 April 1671 Nádasdy went to the block in Vienna, Zrinyi and Frangepáni in Wiener Neustadt. The same sentence fell on count Tattenbach, who was tried and convicted by the Inner Austrian government in Graz. Again the privy conference persuaded Leopold to confirm the sentence; Tattenbach was beheaded on 1 December. Leopold wrote to von Pötting that he favoured clemency, but would not have it said that he distinguished between his German and Hungarian subjects.[5]

Evidence brought to light during the investigations and trials revealed widespread, if vague, circles of involvement throughout Hungary; the conspirators had corresponded with everyone who might be inclined to support their cause. To pursue these inquiries Leopold agreed to the establishment of a special commission in Pressburg, chaired by the Austrian count Rottal. The Hungarian chancellor Pálffy, already disturbed about the Vienna trials, now feared for the independence of the Hungarian judiciary. He responded to what he saw as a new challenge to his authority by undertaking an investigation of his own, ordering the imprisonment of hundreds of suspected rebels and confiscating their estates into the Hungarian treasury.

Both moves were reasonable given the nervous mood of the court on one hand and the desire of loyal Hungarian officials to preserve their independence on the other. Both started out trying to preserve the forms of legality, but very soon the competition between the inquiries resulted in wholesale arrests and every suspicion quickly led to proceedings in one or both agencies. Most of the accusations were directed against the Protestant nobles, who were suspected of supporting Rákóczy, and against the Protestant preachers and teachers they protected. By the end of 1671 there may have been as many as 2,000 people imprisoned in Hungary on suspicion of rebellion. Many nobles and Protestant commoners fled to Transylvania or to Turkish Hungary to escape the net.

Count Rottal saw clearly that these proceedings could only lead to more violence. He urged the court in Vienna to restrain Pálffy and to moderate the zeal of its own investigators. Archbishop Szelepcsényi, however, argued for even harsher measures, particularly against the Protestant towns of Upper Hungary, and his views prevailed in Vienna. While Zrinyi and his associates were being tried, an extraordinary prerogative court set to work in Pressburg. Count Rottal presided over the tribunal, but all the other members were Hungarians and the proceedings were conducted, at least in theory, according to Magyar law.

Between 26 February and 18 July 1671 over two hundred cases were heard by the special tribunal. Many of the suspects imprisoned in the early days of suppression were freed unconditionally or on payment of a fine. Several death sentences were imposed, but only one was carried out – that in the case of one Ferenc Bonis, who had raised armed forces against the crown until the very last. In every case, however, those found guilty of rebellion or treason forfeited their estates to the crown, the court refusing to permit inheritance by brothers or children, a direct contradiction of Hungarian custom. To get at the estates of all the rebels, several great nobles who had died in the meantime were tried posthumously, notably Stevan Thököly, Vitnyedy, and Ferenc Csáky.

By the time the work of the extraordinary court was finished in July 1671 Hungary seemed on the surface at least to have been pacified with a minimum of bloodshed and great profit to the crown. Hocher, Lobkowitz and Montecuccoli, men who strongly favoured the growing absolutism of the monarchy, now saw a chance to impose on Hungary the sort of regime established in Bohemia fifty years before.[6] Even some Magyars, notably archbishop Szelepcsényi and chancellor Pálffy, argued that the time had come to root out Protestantism in the kingdom. Margrave Hermann of Baden and the new Imperial vice-chancellor count Königsegg urged Leopold to establish a large, permanent occupying force of German soldiery in Hungary, hoping that in time the Magyars would learn German, accept German customs; in effect lose their national identity and 'germanize' themselves. Virtually every faction at the court, except possibly the Emperor himself, favoured a radical reordering of government and society in Hungary. Each group had its own goals in mind, but all of them saw in the extension of absolute royal power a means to their particular ends.

Building royal authority in Hungary clearly required a continuous occupation of the kingdom by Imperial troops. To the Viennese authorities this was a simple question of maintaining public order, and therefore it seemed logical to them that the Hungarians should pay for their own military occupation. Count Rottal, in his capacity as Leopold's special agent for Hungary, called an assembly of magnates to meet in Pressburg in January 1671, at which he revealed to them the Emperor's plan for their future. The magnates responded angrily to this rape of their old liberties, raising again their major grievance, the stationing of foreign troops within Hungary. From their point of view it was bad enough to have to tolerate German troops in Hungarian garrisons; to have to pay for their support was outrageous. Leopold responded on 21 March with a decree issued 'in his full sovereign power' (*aus kaiserlicher Machtvolkommenheit*) which made every town and every comitat in Hungary responsible for the upkeep of each soldier on its territory.

Even the most loyal nobles greeted this decree with sullen resentment. In June the decree was modified to reduce the total sums demanded by one-half, but the principle established in the original decree remained in full force. The June decree also struck a blow at the magnates as a class by forbidding them to pass on more than half the occupation costs to their peasantry and the comitats, making them responsible for collecting the remainder from the nobility itself. To enforce these hated regulations, Leopold named count Leopold Kolonitsch, the stern bishop of Wiener Neustadt, to the presidency of the Hungarian chamber in February 1672.

To confirm the hold they thought they had on Hungary, the privy conference ministers led by Hocher and Lobkowitz produced a series of proposals which amounted to a thoroughgoing reform of the Hungarian constitution. Carried to their logical conclusion, these measures would have abolished the elective nature of the monarchy, substituting dynastic inheritance according to the Habsburg *Hausordnung*. They would have completed the work of the counter reformation by eliminating Protestantism throughout the kingdom. Ultimately they looked towards abolishing the office of palatine, with its viceregal powers, and replacing the independent Hungarian financial and judicial administrations with a bureaucratic organization directly dependent on Vienna. They even contemplated doing away with the diet and comitat assemblies.

Leopold, however, remembered his coronation oath to respect the Hungarian constitution, objecting to his ministers that these proposals violated his solemn promise. The privy conference met the Emperor's objections by arguing that the rebellion of some of the Magyar magnates had in effect cancelled Leopold's oath to respect the liberties of the whole Magyar nation. This argument unsettled Leopold, who turned to his spiritual advisers, particularly Emmerich Sinelli. Still in a quandary about his conscientious duty, Leopold then set up a special commission of theologians and lawyers to advise on the matter. This panel all agreed that the Magyar liberties had indeed been forfeited by an act of rebellion, yet Leopold still could not be persuaded that they were right. The Emperor fell back into his habitual indecisiveness, his usual reaction when confronted by a question of conscience, and withheld his consent to decrees and appointments. The initiative seized in 1671 might have brought Hungary to heel since the effective sources of resistance in the kingdom were scattered and impotent in the face of repression. As the weeks and months passed, however, and Leopold wrestled with his conscience, the Hungarian opposition had time to prepare itself to meet the new threats to the constitution.

The central agency envisioned in the reform proposals was to be a governing council in Pressburg, the *gubernium*, a body like the Inner Austrian *Stelle* in Graz which depended directly on royal appointment and direction from Vienna. It would represent the sovereign's will in all political and judicial affairs of the kingdom. The Hungarian treasury was to be placed directly under the court chamber and made responsible to it for all transactions, a move which would theoretically centralize financial policy in Vienna and for the first time make Hungarian resources serve the larger needs of the Imperial government.

Archbishop Szelepcsényi, who encouraged the religious repression, had grave doubts about the political reforms, urging Leopold to make no such sweeping changes without consulting the diet. Leopold continued to withhold his assent to the prepared reform decrees from month to month. During the summer and autumn of 1672 raiding parties, largely made up of émigrés from the previous year's arrests, stormed from Turkish into Royal Hungary. Leopold finally assented to the appointment of a royal governor in February 1673, sanctioning the new *gubernium*. The new governor, Johann Kaspar von Ampringen, was the Grand Master of the Teutonic Knights, a well-known soldier born in Hungary, with a reputation for scrupulous honesty, a man thought to be on the whole sympathetic to the Magyars.

Effective royal absolutism required more than a central office, however; it needed also the means for extending authority downwards to provincial and local levels. Accomplishing this in Hungary would have required restructuring the whole lower and intermediate administration. Vienna simply did not have the means to do this. Both the Hungarian chancellery under Pálffy and the treasury under Kolonitsch continued to deal directly with the comitats as they had done in the past without consulting the *gubernium* in Pressburg. Even in Vienna the central court agencies with jurisdiction over Hungarian affairs worked at cross purposes. This was particularly true of the war council, which was responsible for the military occupation. Jealous of its control over the military establishment, the war council ignored both the new authorities in Pressburg and the court chamber itself, dealing directly with the existing local Magyar administration to arrange for provisioning and quartering the troops.

The *gubernium* was quickly reduced to ineffectiveness, and Ampringen to pathetic frustration. Yet the mere existence of the new government, however impotent it proved to be, provided a focus for Magyar discontent against which all opponents of the monarchy could unite. Ampringen himself became a symbol of Habsburg efforts to destroy the Hungarian constitution and the ancient liberties of the kingdom. The hapless governor saw what was happening and sensed the growing alienation of the population. He warned the privy conference repeatedly against further rash measures of suppression, speaking out particularly against the anti-Protestant campaign. Still he sat helplessly in Pressburg, unable to enforce the Emperor's will in Hungary, and equally powerless to stop the politically dangerous work of the fanatical Catholics.

The confessional issue rapidly became the focal point of all the problems and contradictions in Hungary. There is no question that the regime in Vienna intended to restore the Roman confession throughout the kingdom. Leopold is supposed to have said in 1670 that he intended, if God allowed him to defeat the rebellion, to make that kingdom truly 'Apostolic' as its traditional title claimed it to be.[7] Even though the 1670 conspiracy was led largely by Catholic nobles, Leopold and his ministers assumed that heresy and rebellion were allied. Their experience had also shown that tolerating large communities of Protestants in Hungary offered many opportunities for foreign intervention in what they regarded as purely internal matters.

The pattern of confessional differences in Hungary was complex. In the towns, most of which had mixed populations, the Germans were usually Lutherans, the Magyars Catholic or Calvinist, depending largely on the religion of the local magnates.[8] Urban disputes over possession of churches or schools, municipal offices or market privileges, had important social and ethnic implications. The Magyar nobility was divided, part Catholic and part Calvinist. As a separate 'table' in the diet, the magnates often united as a class against both the crown and the lower 'table' made up of representatives of the small landholders in the comitats and from the towns. Yet the confessional division within the higher nobility divided the magnates among themselves on many issues. While the Catholic magnates had no more enthusiasm for the monarchy than their Calvinist colleagues, many of them were willing to join heartily in persecuting the Protestants in hopes of enriching themselves with confiscated estates.

Opposition to the reforms initiated in Vienna developed in several centres independent of one another. First it appeared among the Calvinist nobles of Upper Hungary who had good reason to fear for their estates and their safety. Alongside this, discontent grew rapidly in the largely German-speaking Protestant towns, where the Germans, lording it over the Magyars of the surrounding villages, might have been a support for Vienna's efforts to 'germanize' Hungary had they not been driven into the party of the extreme Magyar nationalists by the fanatical anti-Protestant campaign undertaken by the primate and the Catholic magnates.

Harassment of the Protestants grew far out of proportion to any support they had given Zrinyi's uprising. The few firebrands who had preached rebellion or expressed a preference for the Turks over the Habsburgs now became an excuse for a systematic attack on the whole Protestant community. Persecution began unofficially at the local level as Catholic prelates moved into Protestant communities with armed followers, taking possession of Lutheran schools and churches, driving out the pastors and teachers. By 1672 archbishop Szelepcsényi took the lead in a coordinated campaign to eliminate all Protestant chapels in Hungary. In Pressburg the Lutherans armed themselves against the local bishop's men; bloody riots followed. Vienna responded by occupying the city with Imperial troops, handing over all the Lutheran churches to the Catholic bishop. Elsewhere resistance to the Catholic onslaught resulted in the arrest of Lutheran pastors, many of whom were sentenced to death. Leopold commuted all such sentences to fines, but in the summer of 1672 he sanctioned a decree ordering all Protestant preachers to quit Hungary and threatening to quarter troops on any Protestants who did not convert.

Leopold and the privy conference followed the lead of the Hungarian prelates and the Catholic magnates in spite of Ampringen's warnings that the persecution was raising issues that went far beyond confessional differences. In the towns, for example, the replacement of Protestant magistrates by Catholics usually also meant the replacement of Germans, who were often the ethnic majority, by Magyars.

Szelepcsényi and Kolonitsch, his ardent collaborator, climaxed their purges by assembling a special court (*judicium delegatum*) in Pressburg in January 1674. Here some 330 Protestant preachers were tried for treason, found guilty, and given the choice between conversion or death. Some ninety-three of them stood firm and were sentenced to death. Leopold quickly commuted the sentences to imprisonment. In 1675 Kolonitsch on his own initiative sent some forty of these recalcitrants as galley slaves to Naples, a senselessly cruel gesture which produced serious international complications.

As the persecutions grew more vigorous, the whole policy came under increasing criticism at the Imperial court. Some of the Magyar courtiers who had at first gone along with the repressive policy, among them the Hungarian chancellor Pálffy, began to realize that the primate's actions were creating a situation which could easily slip out of control. Even Sinelli, now perhaps Leopold's most intimate friend, suggested that the results of Szelepcsényi's ruthlessness would ultimately serve neither the Emperor nor the faith he was supposed to be defending.[9] International pressures increased as well, particularly after the plight of the Lutheran preachers in the galleys became generally known. Protestant refugees carried tales of persecution, often embroidered, to all parts of Europe. These stories created a wave of indignation among the Protestant German states just as Vienna was seeking to build up its alliance system with the

Dutch Republic, Brandenburg and Saxony for the war against France. While Leopold officially pretended that he took no notice of foreign protests, insisting that the matter was strictly an internal one, it is clear that these protests had an important effect. The Dutch, now allied with Spain, induced the viceroy of Naples to liberate the galley slaves in February 1676, by which time Leopold himself had decided to terminate the functions of the special courts.

The anti-Protestant campaign lasted as long as it did because it represented the will of the Catholic magnates supported by an Imperial army of occupation. Without the continuing support of the Emperor and the war council, the campaign gradually abated. In May 1676 all the preachers remaining in prison were released. With Vienna's attention diverted now to the war in the west most of the occupation army was withdrawn and the whole effort to reduce Hungary to a status similar to Bohemia's collapsed, leaving the kingdom once again the battleground for a vicious civil war growing out of accumulated animosities.

Throughout these years of rebellion and halfhearted attempts to establish royal authority in Hungary Leopold was still facing the problem of succession. Had he died during the troubles in Hungary the whole dynastic structure in eastern Europe would have collapsed for want of an heir. After Margareta's death in March 1673 Leopold was inconsolable.[10]

At first he refused even to contemplate remarriage, though the conference and Sinelli began tactfully urging him to take a new wife at once, pointing out the political necessity of having an heir to succeed him and preserve the hereditary lands. Hocher and Sinelli had already made their choice for a new consort for Leopold: Claudia Felicitas of the Tyrol, daughter of archduke Ferdinand Karl, the last male but one in that cadet line. Their combined pressure and Leopold's own sense of dynastic duty brought the reluctant and bereaved Emperor to the altar again on 5 October 1673.

Writing about his decision to von Pötting, Leopold rehearsed the arguments for the marriage and gave some clues to the tactics of his advisers. First of all, both his sister the queen of Spain and the pope himself had made him see God's hand in the matter. Claudia had originally been the subject of some serious marriage bargaining with James, duke of York, but the negotiations had come to nothing.[11] Claudia Felicitas was only twenty, strong and healthy. She had a good figure ('but oh, not like my only Margareta!'), a pleasant disposition and 'all virtues and great piety'. She was a Habsburg by descent and could be expected to make his daughter the best possible stepmother. Finally, since she was already his own ward, there would be fewer gifts and other expenses, and the wedding could be held with little ceremony.

From the dynastic viewpoint, this second marriage turned out to be even more disappointing than the first. Claudia Felicitas lived but two and a half years, producing two daughters who both died shortly after birth. When the Empress died in April 1676, Leopold still remained after nearly ten years of marriage the last male Habsburg of the Austrian line.

VII

A New Regime at War with France

In the summer of 1673, beset by personal tragedy, frustrated politically by French aggression and by Hungarian rebelliousness, the Emperor Leopold began the fifteenth year of his reign with little positive accomplishment to show for his stewardship of the family fortunes. He had recovered his physical vigour after the nearly fatal illness of two years before;[1] but he had as yet no heir. He already looked middle-aged, his features showing the marks of illness and strain. Although he continued to enjoy the theatre, when he was not in mourning as he now seemed to be most of the time, and though he still followed the hunt with his youthful ardour, disappointments had reinforced his pessimism and his superstitious dread of divine displeasure.[2] His accustomed phlegmatic calm, which had seemed charming dignity in a youth of eighteen, now became an almost permanent mask that hid his feelings from the busy world that surrounded him, making him seem ever more aloof, more wooden in his demeanour, conservative, slow to respond, tolerant, even indulgent, towards men around him who would long since have felt the wrath of a more attentive prince.

The only important men who had remained in the privy conference since his coronation, prince Lobkowitz and court chamber president count Sinzendorf, had both become embarrassing hindrances. Lobkowitz's single-minded concern with eastern affairs and his pro-French stance at the beginning of the Dutch War went directly against Leopold's dynastic interests in western Europe. Sinzendorf's incorrigible corruption had produced an administrative morass impervious to reform yet incapable of producing the resources necessary for a war with France. The failings of his ministers were not kept secret from Leopold, yet as his natural conservatism grew stronger he became increasingly reluctant to part with familiar advisers. He found it easier to forgive the sins of those he knew well than to punish them and have as a consequence to take new and untried men into his confidence.

The prospect of war against France raised financial demands much greater than those faced during the pacification of Hungary, where troops could be quartered on unwilling but helpless towns. While enough money generally filtered up through the system to provide for the normal expenses of the court, the needs of the military could never be met by ordinary revenues. Direct foreign subsidies from Spain, the papacy or the Dutch Republic were a possible solution, though all Austria's allies shared an understandable mistrust of the court chamber. The Imperial treasury was like a leaky grain sack gnawed at by contractors, creditors and courtiers alike. In spite of Sinzendorf's sticky fingers, however, the system limped along for several more years; there were always unexpected windfalls to help cover urgent needs, extraordinary revenues increased in this period by the wholesale confiscations in Hungary and Croatia following the Zrinyi uprising. Nevertheless Leopold found it necessary from time to time to alienate crown lands, selling estates or villages to wealthy nobles in return for hard cash.

One incident in 1670 which is usually ascribed to Leopold's religious intolerance and fanaticism probably had as much to do with the need for money as with the Emperor's bigotry. This was the expulsion of the Jews from Vienna. Although the court and the city lived within the same walls, they were different worlds which seldom came together. The merchants of Vienna, jealous of their various commercial rights and yet dependent on the court for much of their business, had long resented the presence among them of a prosperous Jewish community which had, in their eyes, no reason to share the city's wealth. Here, as in the Imperial cities of Germany, the Jews and their quarter of the city were technically the property of the Emperor, a legal device dating back to the Middle Ages, intended originally to protect the financially useful Jewish communities from periodic outbreaks of violence against them by their Christian neighbours.

There had been many petitions by the 'Good Christian' merchants of Vienna against the Jews, but the Emperor's law protected them until July 1670 when Leopold signed an agreement with the city council. The city of Vienna bought the Jewish quarter from the Emperor for 100,000 Gulden, and in return for the right to expel its inhabitants promised to cover all their debts up to 10,000 Gulden and to build a church on the site of the old synagogue. If Leopold himself thought very seriously about this move, and his correspondence does not suggest that he did, he might well have been concerned at the existence in his capital city of a non-Christian population whose loyalty might be doubtful in a contest with Islam.³ It seems more likely, however, that this was as much a financial transaction as an act of religious fervour. Later on many exceptions were made. Towards the end of his reign Leopold found himself relying on his 'Court Jew' Samuel Oppenheimer as much as he did upon the court chamber to handle the finances of the realm. Meanwhile, at considerable cost to the Jews of Vienna, Leopold transformed a periodic income from the special taxes the Jews paid into an immediate payment from the city of Vienna.

By such hand-to-mouth measures the regime managed to survive total financial disaster. Sinzendorf kept his place until 1680. Lobkowitz was less fortunate, though he had served so long and so well that he found it difficult to conceive of a regime he did not direct.

It is not clear what finally induced Leopold to dismiss the Bohemian prince. His policy of appeasing France ran counter to Leopold's own inclinations. Lobkowitz had also opposed the Emperor's marriage with Claudia Felicitas, preferring instead Eleanora of Pfalz-Neuburg, whom Leopold did in fact marry in 1676. His views about Leopold's second wife were well known at court, and Lobkowitz had antagonized the Empress's clique by making some witty but highly tactless and insulting remarks about Claudia's mother, a Medici princess.

Like all men who hold great power for many years, Lobkowitz had made a number of enemies and had become the object of many intrigues.⁴ Still it seems unlikely that this alone would have brought him down, for Leopold was quite used to hearing the worst about his advisers from their colleagues, and he generally paid little attention to accusations that seemed to arise from jealousy. Though Lobkowitz's influence was clearly declining, Leopold showed no ill will or animosity towards him, even though it was increasingly the chancellor Dr Hocher, once Lobkowitz's protégé, whom Leopold summoned to his presence and through whose hands the major decisions were now channelled.

Lobkowitz would not yield to the changing mood of the court after 1673, and in September of that year had asked Leopold to let him resign his office. Leopold refused; Lobkowitz remained in spite of his failing health. Early in 1674 Franz Paul von Lisola, Leopold's roving ambassador among the coalition powers against France, returned to Vienna. Around the same time Hocher discovered among intercepted French dispatches proof that Lobkowitz had betrayed Montecuccoli's plans to distract the French in 1673. Lisola convinced Hocher that it was now necessary to remove Lobkowitz from office; several other members of the privy conference agreed with him, including prince Adolf Schwarzenberg, president of the aulic council, and count Lamberg. The group began meeting secretly with the conference secretary, Christof Abele, to draw up a detailed accusation against the grand chamberlain. This they presented to Leopold without Lobkowitz's knowledge. On 16 October 1674 Leopold signed an order stripping Lobkowitz of all his offices, banishing him from the court, and ordering him to retire incommunicado to his estates in Bohemia.

Three days later Lobkowitz left Vienna. His papers were seized, and his ready cash, some 190,000 Gulden, was turned over to the court chamber. Father Emmerich Sinelli, whom Leopold seems strangely not to have consulted, tried to effect a reconciliation. Leopold refused to reconsider his decision, offering the rather odd explanation that Lobkowitz's innocence could have been proved only by an open trial, and for the prince's own good he had chosen not to permit one.[5] Some of Lobkowitz's friends hoped that he would return to power in 1676 when Claudia Felicitas died and Leopold quickly married the former chamberlain's original candidate, Eleanora of Pfalz-Neuburg; but the once great minister was too sick to respond to a call even had there been one. He died in April 1677.

When Leopold determined to be his own first minister, he hoped to avoid having an over-mighty subject about him, someone who could use the power of the crown to his own purposes by virtue of the monarch's reliance on him. In fact Lobkowitz had become such a one simply because Leopold had confided in him for so long. After 1674 Leopold appointed weaker men to the chamberlain's office: first the ageing count Lamberg, then later in his reign a succession of old cronies of his youth whom he trusted as friends and who could be counted on not to exert themselves to wield great political influence, prince Ferdinand Dietrichstein and count Ferdinand von Harrach.

In the absence of a powerful or ambitious chamberlain, the character of the regime gradually changed. The new focus of leadership was the Austrian chancellery (*Hofkanzlei*) with its large cadre of professional administrators, most of them lawyers. Chancellor Johann Paul Hocher built up this bureaucratic apparatus, and grew powerful not so much by virtue of his own talents, which were considerable within the limits of the administrative mentality, but rather because of the importance of the bureau he directed. From Lobkowitz's fall until his own death in 1683 Hocher acted as virtual first minister.

The Austrian chancellery had grown to overshadow the Imperial chancellery as Austrian and dynastic affairs began to occupy more of the attention of the crown than did the affairs of the Empire. By the time of Leopold's accession the Austrian chancellery had already become the centre for diplomatic correspondence as well as the secretarial organ for Austrian judicial and legal decisions or decrees. The chancellor, if he was energetic enough, was thus in a position to oversee virtually all the most important business of the crown. If he was intelligent as well as energetic, as Hocher was, he could use his detailed knowledge of the monarch's business as a lever to direct policy. Through his control over the paperwork, Hocher gradually got control over the agenda of the privy conference as well.

Unlike Lobkowitz, who loved playing the role of *grand seigneur*, and who lived for the game of intrigue and high politics, Hocher did not try to hide his bourgeois origins. Though Leopold later made him a baron, Hocher never attained that sense of effortless superiority which marked the born aristocrat. His qualities were rather those of the good bureaucrat, a stubborn loyalty to the crown, industrious energy, a precise and careful appreciation of detail, a conservative, cautious, unimaginative approach to decisions which suited Leopold's own view of the art of government well.[6] Hocher had a fine memory and could keep his counsel behind a dour, unapproachable demeanour. He was reputed to be absolutely incorruptible. With the provinciality of many Germans at the Imperial court he disliked and distrusted the other nationalities that swarmed there from all over Europe, particularly the Hungarians whom he thought he had come to understand during the long investigation preceding the trial of Zrinyi and Nádasdy.

Hocher never had a personal following of his own at court, aside perhaps from the army of clerks and subordinate officials in the chancellery. In fact he did not need one, for in any event his influence and prosperity depended entirely on Leopold's favour. Hocher could afford to be heartily disliked so long as his business was done to the Emperor's satisfaction. His political outlook could be summed up as thoroughgoing absolutism. He used his influence consistently to further the interests of the crown against the diverse privileged elements in the realm. His sense of the overwhelming authority of the crown left him no sympathy for the aristocratic tradition. Hocher alone, of all Leopold's many ministers in the course of a long reign, seemed able to strike a good balance between the local concerns of the Austrian hereditary lands and the wider European interests of the dynasty.

With Lobkowitz gone, the privy conference unanimously agreed on vigorous action against France and support of the Dutch. The problem was to turn a vigorous policy into vigorous action. Subsidies and loans from Spain and the Dutch Republic helped solve for the moment the pressing need for money, but no amount of money could solve the perennial problem of divided leadership in the army. Aside from a core of units recruited in the Habsburg hereditary lands, commanded directly by the Emperor's delegated generals, the Imperial armed forces were made up of whatever units the German princes chose to donate, usually under conditions that upheld the independence of their own commanders in the field. Division of command plagued the Imperial armies for as long as the Holy Roman Empire lasted, becoming particularly difficult when various princes themselves decided to play general. Since Leopold wisely chose not to go on campaign himself, he always had the task of finding for his commander a man who could bring some unity of action out of a force split into many parts, each one of which jealously guarded its own independence of action.

In 1673 Montecuccoli conducted a brilliant campaign of manœuvre on the Rhine, forcing the French to fall back from their advanced outposts in the Empire and capturing the city of Bonn, the residence of the troublesome Fürstenberg, archbishop of Cologne. The personal controversies among the Imperial commanders grew so intense, however, that Montecuccoli left the army in the hands of his mediocre subordinate, the duc de Bournonville, and returned to Vienna to demand from Leopold both the resources and the authority he needed to do his job. Leopold sympathized with his redoubtable old commander, but there was little he could do beyond that without losing essential auxiliary forces. Montecuccoli remained in Vienna 'for his health' while de Souches was sent to take command next season.

In 1674 the divisions within the Imperial command allowed the French to regain the initiative. Turenne briskly scattered the Imperial forces along the Rhine, then turned to devastating the Palatinate north and south of the Neckar in order to prevent an attack on the great fortress of Philippsburg. In May the Imperial Diet at Regensburg finally bestirred itself to declare war against France; in June Brandenburg broke its lingering ties with France and directly joined the alliance. Not until August, however, did the Imperial forces muster enough manpower to challenge Turenne's invasion of the Palatinate. By that time the French had done their work and held unassailable positions far inside Imperial territory.

Faced by the virtual collapse of Imperial defences, Leopold again induced Montecuccoli to assume command in 1675. The old fieldmarshal decided to concentrate on Strassburg, an Imperial city coveted by France, which had tried to remain neutral to preserve its independence. Striking directly into Alsace, Montecuccoli lured Turenne's main force after him. The resulting series of manœuvres in an ever smaller space became a duel of masters. After two months of campaigning, Turenne gained a momentary advantage of position and forced Montecuccoli to attack. The battle at Sassbach on 27 July was a draw, but Turenne was killed by a cannon ball during the engagement. The French retired unbeaten having lost their greatest general. Five days later, on 1 August, Montecuccoli again attacked the French at Altenheim and defeated them soundly. The remains of the French army retired from the Rhine, and the Imperialists entered Strassburg, which abandoned its neutrality and joined the coalition.

A second Imperial contingent operating with Spanish and Dutch forces on the lower Rhine helped tip the balance there as well, defeating Créqui and retaking the city of Trier. On 18 September 1675 the old duke Charles IV of Lorraine died just as it seemed his way was open to regain the land of his ancestors. His nephew and successor, duke Charles V, at the time a cavalry general fighting under Montecuccoli, left the main army to join his own Lorraine troops. In spite of the many allied successes during the summer, however, he could not break into Lorraine which remained firmly under French occupation.

Montecuccoli returned to Vienna too weak and ill to take field command again.[7] Leopold chose duke Charles, the marshal's apt pupil, to succeed him as Imperial commander in chief. It proved to be a happy choice. The personable young duke was a man of considerable talent, a warrior diplomat whose high rank among the princes of Europe gave him a measure of authority over the prickly and independent commanders of Imperial contingents that no professional soldier of lesser status could hope to exercise.

As the armies manœuvred for advantage Leopold sought vainly to induce the German princes to join forces against France, but to no avail. With the French safely beyond the Rhine the Germans again sat back to cherish their liberties. Furthermore, the new military balance created in 1675 opened the way for peace negotiations, a possibility Louis XIV quickly utilized to break the coalition against him. In January 1676 Spanish, Dutch and French representatives gathered at Nijmegen under English mediation to argue about protocol, the usual preliminary to a peace conference. Leopold at first refused to participate, but when the campaign of 1676 produced no positive results except the capture of Philippsburg from the French after a two-and-a-half-month siege, he agreed to send a representative.

The French found it relatively easy to divide the coalition by dealing gently with the Dutch and directing their territorial demands against the Habsburgs. The Dutch yielded to persuasion, signing a separate peace with France on 10 August 1678. Left alone to face the French on the lower Rhine, Spain in turn gave way and ceded to France the Franche-Comté and a string of fortresses in the Spanish Netherlands in return for peace. When Spain signed its treaty with France on 17 September, the Empire stood alone. Without subsidies from his erstwhile allies, Leopold could do little to build up his forces in the west. Renewed guerrilla warfare in Hungary forced him to draw heavily on what was already there. Charles of Lorraine made a desperate effort to recapture the city of Freiburg im Breisgau, a Habsburg possession since the Middle Ages, but failed in this even though he did prevent the French from retaking Strassburg or any other towns of importance. Leopold recognized that he could not continue the war alone, even though the opinion of his own court favoured fighting on.

When the 'western' or Spanish faction in Vienna defeated Lob-kowitz in 1674 they had done so in the name of those German-Imperial ideas earlier preached by margrave Hermann of Baden, and now aggressively and enthusiastically taken up by Montecuccoli and the Imperial vice-chancellor, count Königsegg. The man Leopold chose as his delegate to the Nijmegen conference, Heinrich Stratmann, wrote a pamphlet urging the Empire to unite behind its sovereign and punish recalcitrant princes who would not march to the defence of their German fatherland. This enthusiasm for war pervaded Leopold's family as well as the privy conference, but the Emperor himself had little faith in its power to move the German princes. That his appreciation of the situation was indeed the correct one became clear when Bavaria, which had remained neutral during the whole conflict with France, began to recruit other German states into a peace bloc. Saxony and the Palatinate had already joined Bavaria when the coalition broke apart in 1678. With only chancellor Hocher supporting him in the privy conference, Leopold decided late in 1678 that he would have to make the best bargain he could with France before his armies melted entirely away.

Stratmann and his colleagues at Nijmegen negotiated a peace with France which they signed on 5 February 1679. It was a better bargain than Leopold might have expected, surely a better one than Louis gave either the Spanish or the Dutch. The French gave up Philippsburg, but kept Freiburg. Charles of Lorraine was to be recognized as duke of Lorraine, a face-saving provision for Leopold, but the French kept Longwy and Nancy along with military access roads across the territory and the right to maintain garrisons along them. Since this amounted to a partition of the duchy, Charles refused to accept the compromise. Lorraine remained in fact under French occupation, though Leopold himself managed for the time being to avoid recognizing French sovereignty.

Leopold was profoundly disappointed by the outcome of his first war with Louis XIV, a war which ended in the loss of important dynastic strongholds to France and the disruption of the strategically vital 'Spanish road'. It was no consolation to realize that he had been forced to make peace in order to meet new threats to the hereditary lands in the east. He showed his annoyance by refusing to accept the congratulatory messages that customarily came to him at the conclusion of peace.[8] There were festive celebrations at the Imperial Diet in Regensburg, and Munich was illuminated by the Bavarian elector to solemnize the peace. Leopold grumbled that he supposed he must thank God even for calamities.

VIII

Civil War in Hungary 1676–81

The peace of Nijmegen, like the treaty of Vasvár, disappointed many of Leopold's ambitions for his house, though in this instance at least he gave up nothing he could claim to have won. The most distressing outcome of the peace negotiations was the betrothal of Marie Louise d'Orléans to Charles II of Spain, a move that brought the French one step closer to breaking the Habsburg hold on Spain. On the other hand the prospect of dynastic extinction now seemed more remote. Charles II still lived, to the surprise of all, and Leopold could take deep satisfaction in his own marriage to Eleanora Magdalena of Pfalz-Neuburg in 1676.

The new Empress was not a particularly talented or accomplished person, but she quickly won Leopold's affection and tender concern by proving herself a capable mother to Leopold's daughter and a strong bearer of healthy children. Devoting herself to her children and to her exaggerated, often eccentric acts of devotion and piety, she left politics to the men. Her first child, the archduke Joseph, was born in July 1678 and showed every sign of surviving in robust good health. During the following twelve years she bore Leopold nine more children; five of the ten outlived their parents, a good record for any family in the seventeenth century.

Though the dynastic future seemed brighter, the troubles in Hungary grew more serious each year. Diplomatic pressure from Austria's Protestant allies in the war against France forced Leopold to call a halt to the persecution of Protestants in Hungary, while the battle to drive the French out of the Empire induced him to strip the Hungarian occupation forces to provide troops on the Rhine. Most of the forces sent west had soon to be recalled, however, to meet the violent *Kuruczók* raiding bands that streamed across the frontier from Turkish Hungary in greater numbers every summer.

Magyars fleeing from the persecutions that followed the collapse of Zrinyi's rebellion generally had no great distance to go in order to find safety in Turkish Hungary. Whatever the reasons that drove them into exile, these refugees (*bujdosók*) took with them a deep hatred for the Austrians and for their Catholic Magyar collaborators. Having little to live from, the émigrés turned to raiding across the frontier into their former homelands to take what they needed. At first they came in small bands, badly organized and without any purpose but plunder. Gradually they merged into larger units for their own protection.[1] By the summer of 1672 these bands, now calling themselves the *Kuruc* (crusaders) had already grown bold enough to challenge and defeat a small detachment of regular troops under general Spankau, whom they then besieged briefly in the fortress town of Kaschau (Košice). Several smaller towns in the border area left unprotected opened their doors to the *Kuruc* and paid the tribute the raiders demanded. One band got as far as the River Waag (Váh), raiding as far north as Arva. Most of the bands sooner or later ran into regular units of the Imperial army and were defeated by them, but the survivors withdrew again to Turkish territory, in no way discouraged.

The Turks, though still formally abiding by their treaty with Leopold, tolerated the refugees since their violence was directed exclusively across the frontier towards the west. As long as the Austrians did not violate the treaty by pursuing the bands into Turkish Hungary, the local pashas could find no fault with border raiding, a long-established tradition on both sides, which gave the refugees a modest livelihood without compromising the sultan's officials.

The *Kuruc* were a constant embarrassment to the Austrian *gubernium* and the military occupation. Their very existence proved that while Leopold had defeated rebellion, he had still not won the nation to his allegiance. Since they were unequal to the trained and disciplined regular troops, the *Kuruc* clearly could not destroy the regime's political hold over the area it occupied. At the same time they constantly perplexed the thinly stretched garrisons of the Imperial army which could not hope to protect all the scattered villages from unpredictable and swift attacks by raiders on fast horses, who used deliberate brutality and terror to demoralize their opponents. The *Kuruc* quickly gained a fearsome reputation from their habit of treating their victims with spectacular cruelty, torturing and mutilating, taking no prisoners. In response the Imperial field commanders replied with equal or worse brutality, the response of frightened, beleaguered men. Inevitably, this led to even more violence as the threshold of restraint retreated before deliberate terror.

The raids continued each summer, intermittently, with little pattern until 1678 when the guerrilla bands were forged together into a powerful machine for national insurrection. The cumulative effect of these raids produced a wasted no-man's land along the frontier, desolating large sections of the Máramaros and the northern and north-eastern comitats of Hungary.

Compounding the misery of that unhappy land beset by the systematic persecution of its Protestant population and the *Kuruc* raiders, a plague epidemic broke out in 1676. The disease grew in intensity as it spread westwards, reaching a climax in 1679 when the virulence reached Bohemia and Austria. First the border villages, then the city of Vienna itself suffered the agony of contagion. Military operations had to be virtually suspended.

Hungary's miseries offered the French many opportunities to weaken Leopold's position in the west. French agents were active in Poland and Transylvania, encouraging the *Kuruc* at small cost to themselves.[2] By 1677 French diplomats had arranged a treaty between king John III Sobieski of Poland and the Transylvanian prince Michael Apafy, both agreeing to provide refuge and support for the *Kuruc*. Fortunately for Leopold nothing of importance resulted from this potentially disturbing alliance among his eastern neighbours. Sobieski was already cooling in his attitude towards France, turning his attention to the Turkish menace to his own kingdom, while the spread of the plague made any organized operations risky.

Leopold still had to concede that the repressive campaign to impose royal authority in Hungary had failed. In spite of the stubborn position of Hocher and of a few Magyar extremists like archbishop Szelepcsényi, Leopold turned to new avenues of pacification. Even the papal nuncio in Vienna, cardinal Buonvisi, spoke out in favour of compromise with the Magyar malcontents, warning, as did others, that the Turkish forces were falling back into their old habit of raiding independently across the frontier. Islam, not Protestantism, was the real enemy; the pope himself had begun to give his support to moves which he hoped would lead to a reconciliation between Protestants and Catholics in Europe so that all Christendom could be mobilized for a war to rid Europe of the Turkish menace once and for all. Leopold now began seriously to support the irenical negotiations of his old friend bishop Cristóbal de Rojas y Spínola, accepting at least on the surface his programme for reuniting the Protestants with Rome.[3]

The Vienna regime made other gestures indicating a change in its approach to the troubles of Hungary. At the beginning of 1678 Leopold replaced general Cob, who had indulged in the most brutal reprisals against the *Kuruc*. At the same time he called all the magnates and prelates to an assembly in Pressburg, and even considered with his privy conference the possibility of restoring the Hungarian constitution by decree, rescinding in effect the decree which set up the *gubernium* and nullifying the legal pretext that a rebellion by some of the magnates had forfeited the rights and liberties of all.

At Pressburg the Magyar nobles, encouraged by what they took to be clear evidence that Leopold was ready to retreat entirely from his Hungarian reform programme, demanded withdrawal of all Austrian troops from Hungary. When the Hungarian chancellor, Thomas Pálffy, delivered this 'request' to Hocher the two men engaged in an angry argument. Hocher was convinced by the diet's truculence that the Hungarians would never compromise, and induced Leopold to withdraw his concessions. The *Kuruc* war resumed in the summer of 1678, its character now vastly changed.

The *Kuruc* found a talented leader in the person of count Imre Thököly, the twenty-two-year-old son of a Calvinist nobleman whose estates had been confiscated after Zrinyi's rebellion. Count Imre had been brought up in Transylvania, carefully educated as suited his station, imbued with the stern opposition view of his fellow refugees. His native intelligence and good education made him stand out among the *bujdosók*, as did his talents for persuasive speaking and commanding obedience. When one of the war bands chose him as their leader its successes quickly drew other *Kuruc* to his side. In October 1678 he led a large-scale attack on the mining towns in the northern Hungarian hills (modern Slovakia), retreating when threatened by general Wrbna's Imperial regulars, but taking with him an enormous booty of coin and unminted silver to sustain the insurgents' cause.

For the first time in the long years of informal warfare the Austrians now had someone to negotiate with. Leopold took advantage of the situation to open negotiations with Thököly, who agreed to a temporary armistice. By negotiating with Thököly, however, Vienna recognized him as the real leader of Magyar opposition and strengthened his hand by treating him virtually as a sovereign prince, a position Thököly hoped to consolidate by marrying Rákóczy's widow, Helena Zrinyi, who was now a ward of the Emperor. The peace talks began at Sopron in the winter, but Leopold broke them off as soon as the conclusion of peace with France suddenly left him free to use his whole military force to restore order in Hungary. Troops from the Rhineland hurried eastwards as the *Kuruc* war erupted but soon found themselves in the midst of one of the worst disease epidemics of a plague-ridden century.

In these circumstances military might alone could not restore order. Kaspar von Ampringen, using the plague as an excuse, resigned his office as governor and withdrew from Pressburg. Leopold named no successor; the *gubernium* simply ceased to function.

Even in Vienna the spreading plague brought public business virtually to a halt.[4] Leopold and the Imperial family hastily removed from Vienna to Prague to escape the pestilence, while many courtiers and high officials retired to their country estates far removed from the capital. With the government thus scattered about the hereditary lands, affairs of state were put aside as men coped as best they could with the epidemic.

In Bohemia Leopold faced violence of another kind: peasant uprisings against harsh exploitation of *Robot* labour by some of the greatest landholders. The peasants sent Leopold a long statement of grievances in November 1679, then took arms against the troops despatched to put them down. As usual the regular troops outmatched the peasants and restored order quickly. Some of the leaders of the revolt were executed 'as an example and a caution'. On 28 June 1680 Leopold issued his famous *Robotpatent* for Bohemia setting forth clearly the limits on forced labour.[5] He decreed that no landlord (*Obrigkeit*) could demand more labour from his peasants (*Untertanen*) than was set down for them by regulations of the general diet of Bohemia; any additional service had to be paid for in cash. *Robot* labour was prohibited on Sundays and holidays, and limited in every case to a maximum of three days in the week. Given the general unhappy lot of the peasantry throughout the hereditary lands, the *Robotpatent* was a generous response to the grievances of a class still ruthlesly exploited throughout the European continent. It also indicated the extent to which the royal authority could be exercised in Bohemia.

During the court's sojourn in Prague disturbing news reached Leopold from both Paris and Constantinople. In the west Louis XIV had begun his campaign of 'reunions', quasi-judicial proceedings to incorporate into his kingdom territories not specifically ceded by the treaty of Nijmegen, but held by him to be dependencies of such cessions. From the east came word of growing Turkish enthusiasm for another war against the Empire, an aggressive mood openly encouraged by the French envoy to the Sublime Porte. Since his own regime had been seriously weakened by the plague and peasant unrest, Leopold concluded that he would have to come to terms with the opposition in Hungary before he could hope to deal with even more serious threats. At Linz, on his way from Prague to Vienna Leopold (in February 1681) issued a formal summons to the Hungarian diet to meet in Sopron on 28 April. He included in the summons a promise that he would appear personally and conduct the diet according to traditional procedures. However reluctantly, he was now determined to restore constitutional government as the only alternative to continued violence.

The diet assembled with agents appearing to represent Thököly and other Protestant nobles who still thought it prudent to keep their distance. Leopold formally opened the proceedings on 25 May; the diet elected as their palatine count Paul Esterházy, a candidate acceptable to Vienna. In fairly quick order Leopold accepted a proposal formally abolishing the *gubernium* and another restoring the Hungarian treasury to its original independent status. This last move cost the court chamber its authority over the fiscal affairs of Hungary, but since it had in fact failed to make good its claim to supervision, the concession changed little.[6] Leopold and the diet arranged compromises dealing with most of the rebel grievances: foreign troops, unconstitutional taxation, and a variety of minor issues. But the confessional problems could not be settled so easily.

Leopold clung to his position that religious matters were private, not public concerns, and hence not a subject for debate in the diet. The Catholic majority supported the crown in this, not wanting to give up the commanding position the Roman Church had won during the past ten years of suppression. Thököly's friends, however, demanded a restoration of all 'liberties', including the right of Protestants to own property and to worship freely and publicly throughout the kingdom. To accept this would have made necessary the wholesale restoration of confiscated property to its original owners. Worse yet, it would probably have set Protestant and Catholic Magyars to fighting among themselves again. Esterházy and the Protestants negotiated for weeks without either side giving an inch. Finally in July Leopold ordered the diet to set aside all discussions of 'private affairs'. The Protestants angrily refused to accept this decree and declared the diet to be illegal, withdrawing their assent to any agreements and compromises already reached.

Leopold had conceded as much as he thought his conscience would allow. In his mind political concessions were one thing, religious compromise something quite different. Still, he had to recognize the fact that the Catholic majority at the diet did not represent the whole Magyar nobility. The agents sent by Thököly and the Protestant dissidents, though few in number, represented a large part of the aristocracy which had not come to the diet, but waited upon its outcome in the security of Turkish territory.

As the diet approached an impasse, Leopold found himself once more caught between the easterners and westerners at his court. The Spanish ambassador, the marqués de Borgomanero, harangued him about the growing danger from France and the threat posed to both Spain and the Empire by the French courts of reunion. The easterners on the other hand demanded that Leopold take account of the disturbing reports from Christoph von Kunitz, his resident in Constantinople, who sent repeated and increasingly urgent warnings that the peaceful demeanour of the Sublime Porte was a deliberate deceit, that war preparations were moving ahead and were clearly directed against the Emperor. On one point only were both factions now agreed: Leopold must come to terms with the Magyar rebels whatever the cost in order to meet greater perils.

Pressed by his courtiers and by the Hungarian dissidents, Leopold remained calmly indecisive until the beginning of October 1681 when news reached Vienna that the French had seized the Imperial city of Strassburg. This would seem to have convinced Leopold that he would have to fight France again very soon. By decree he restored the peace of 1606 in Hungary, thus affording complete confessional freedom to the towns. This represented a retreat to an earlier position which his conscience could accept. It did not satisfy the Protestant nobles, however, for their position remained the same in spite of the decree; their confiscated estates remained in the hands of the Catholics. The Catholic clerical faction in Hungary was equally disappointed, for the decree effectively nullified their commanding position in the market towns. Neither side was satisfied, but neither side could defeat the other without support from either the Turks or the Emperor. A temporary and uneasy restoration of constitutional government thus went forward during the winter of 1681–82. For the moment Leopold felt free to turn towards the new menace from France.

The misfortunes of the years between Nijmegen and the diet of Sopron brought into sharp focus all the inadequacies that plagued Austrian financial management. Complaints against count Georg Ludwig von Sinzendorf, the court chamber president, persisted throughout the twenty-four years he held the office. Leopold ignored or dismissed them until 1680, when they were accompanied by a universal refusal by Leopold's creditors to advance the state further loans until the court chamber had been reformed. Faced with what amounted to an ultimatum from the moneylenders, Leopold finally agreed to investigate the accusations, an inquiry whose revelations probably surprised no one but the Emperor himself.

So far as could be determined, Sinzendorf had appropriated for himself some two million Gulden beyond the normal, legal and acceptable income and perquisites of the office. On 2 April 1680 Leopold dismissed Sinzendorf, at the same time setting up a commission to investigate the court chamber operations and recommend reforms. In time a part of Sinzendorf's embezzled millions was recovered, but the more immediate problem was to restore the state's credit by administrative reform. The commission of inquiry included chancellor Hocher, the Bohemian chancellor count Nostitz, and count Albrecht Sinzendorf, a privy councillor with some reputation for fiscal competence. They met under the chairmanship of the privy conference secretary Christof Abele, who on 15 April was formally appointed president of the court chamber. No member of the court chamber sat with the commission. This may have helped the commissioners to avoid the charge that their investigation would not be independent, but still it was unfortunate that they did not include count Quintin Jörger, the vice-president who had brought most of the original charges against Sinzendorf and who had long demanded reform, making many excellent proposals which the commissioners appear not to have taken into account.[7] There was, in fact, no lack of new ideas from which to work. Both count Jörger and abbot Anton of Kremsmünster had submitted detailed plans for a unified financial administration based on a centralized accounting system which would make it possible to survey the total financial picture at any given moment.

The commissioners, however, held to the old system of separate agencies and disbursing offices to handle the expenses of the court and the military, contending that it was enough for all to be responsible to the court chamber. The results of the investigation were published in the *Hofkammerordnung* on 2 January 1681, which took its departure from the original *Ordnung* of 1568, to which it added little that was new, nothing that was original. The commission seemed convinced that the monarchy's current financial problems were the product of bad administration, and that they could be overcome by more precise instructions for the administration of royal estates and greater probity in the handling of public monies. Consolidation of the military budget, by then a commonplace in most European states, was not even considered. Individual regiments were left to collect the 'contributions' budgeted for their upkeep, a procedure that made accurate accounting and control impossible.

The *Hofkammerordnung* did, it is true, oblige the court chamber to keep accurate records and to prepare quarterly and annual consolidated accounts. The president was instructed henceforth to report to the Emperor annually on 'the total sums taken in and spent for the whole year, payments on capital, interest and other loans, and the amount of each still unpaid; *Item* what still remains unpaid from grants voted by the Landtag and others'.[8] Even the tone of the document suggests a certain pessimism about any fundamental changes in the way money could be handled in the future. The accounts which the provincial treasuries were expected to send to Vienna came in irregularly and late; the court chamber paid little attention to them when they did appear.

The actual operation of the court chamber changed very little. Business could be conducted only at meetings of the whole body, a board of ten men: five from the nobility, three from the knightly estate, and two from the learned professions. Certain routine items were entrusted to the president's discretion, but even this sensible provision had its disadvantages, for the councillors lost touch with the day-to-day operations of the treasury, though they were still expected to deliberate sensibly on policy matters.

The Bohemian treasury in Prague and the Silesian one in Breslau as well as the two Hungarian chambers of Pressburg and Kaschau were all expressly subordinated to the court chamber, and from now on ordered to send promptly all their reports and accounts to Vienna for review. This represented the one substantial move to assert the supremacy of the central monarchy over the separate states it ruled. Yet it immediately produced even more confusion, particularly while the court was absent from Vienna. In such cases some of the court chamber officials remained in the capital, others followed the monarch. Those who travelled with the court had control of all expenditure, while the reports from the provinces had first to go to Vienna where the collected income was accounted for before it was reported to the Emperor. A separate instruction permitted the registrar of the chamber in Vienna to keep the Imperial seal for verifying documents, with the casual injunction that he 'should not misuse it, and not entrust it to anyone else, but keep it safe'.

This amateurish attempt to centralize fiscal affairs under the court chamber never worked to anyone's satisfaction. Within months of accepting the new *Hofkammerordnung*, Leopold bargained away one of its most important provisions at the diet at Sopron, restoring the independence of the two separate Hungarian treasuries. Still, for all its faults, the *Ordnung* remained in effect with only modest changes until 1714.

Leopold, who understood nothing of finance, was dangerously misled by his commissioners who saw in their programme a strong and positive reform, a view which was reinforced by the renewed confidence of the Emperor's creditors. A gradual, and probably rather small, increase in revenues resulted from improvements in estate management and the elimination of corrupt officials, but these adjustments had little impact on the underlying problems. In fact it was probably Leopold's shrewd choice of reputable men to handle his finances that to a certain extent restored his credit. As in the past the funds actually transmitted to the court chamber still did not cover normal expenses plus interest on the debts for which it was responsible. To produce revenue for the military the monarchy still had to rely upon expedients, windfalls or foreign subsidies.

On the eve of the greatest crisis of his reign, Leopold still conducted his business affairs like an old-fashioned debt-ridden landlord, convinced now that because he had honest stewards all would go well. When the test came in 1683, his triumph over the Turks served only to confirm his belief that faith and loyalty, not bureaucratic reform, was the true path to victory.

IX

The Turkish Invasion

When Leopold restored the constitutional *status quo ante* in Hungary on 8 October 1681, both he and the Magyars knew he was acting from desperation. The move was made with little grace and with many reservations. The Magyars knew that the privy conference had to look to its safety in the west after the French seizure of Strassburg (now renamed Strasbourg) and that it was this that had forced the Emperor to give in, not any genuine respect for the traditional liberties of Hungary. Still, the east could not be entirely forgotten, even though the troubles on the Rhine led the conference to discount Kunitz's repeated warnings from Constantinople as exaggerations. The twenty-year armistice of Vasvár was due to run out in 1684. Worse yet, Thököly and his *Kuruczók* remained unsubdued.

Thököly saw in Leopold's predicament the opportunity to reach for power for himself in Hungary. Claiming that Leopold's decree did not meet his followers' legitimate grievances, he sent Vienna an insolent petition demanding pardon for himself and all his followers, restitution of his estates, a principality of his own in Upper Hungary, religious freedom throughout the kingdom, and the hand of Helena Zrinyi.[1]

Leopold could hardly welcome making so troublesome a subject so mighty, yet Thököly now had some twenty to thirty thousand men in the field, with additional support from the Transylvanian prince Michael Apafy and from some of the more adventurous Turkish pashas as well. If Leopold were to concentrate his forces in Hungary, it would mean ignoring French depredations in the Empire. It might even lead to a serious breach with Spain, still smarting from the humiliation of its last encounter with France.

Hocher, Hermann of Baden, Königsegg and the other Imperialists at the court inclined to support the westerners led by the Spanish ambassador Borgomanero. The privy conference came up with a plan which they hoped offered a third way out of the unhappy situation. The first step was to negotiate directly with the Sublime Porte for an extension of the armistice. If that succeeded, they could then deal at leisure with the Hungarian malcontents, while they braced for another war on the Rhine. Appeasing the Turks involved an ambitious diplomatic under-taking, but it seemed worth the attempt.

French diplomats were by now well-versed in the manipulation of Leopold's eastern difficulties to the advantage of Louis XIV.[2] Their small subsidies to the Magyar rebels were well invested; they could hope for even more from the Turks and from Poland. In Constantinople they had to be subtle, however, for it would not do for His Most Christ-ian Majesty to be caught publicly encouraging the sultan to storm the Christian Empire in the east while he pillaged it in the west. French envoys in Constantinople did not seek a formal alliance, but contented themselves with cautious encouragement of the war party in the *divan*, judicious bribes and careful management of rumour.

In Poland the French could be more open and straightforward. King John III Sobieski and his French wife Marysiénka (born the marquise d'Arquien) had for years found France a natural ally against the Habs-burgs as well as a source of money. At the same time Sobieski hated the Turks even more than he loved French *livres*.[3] To satisfy the French Sobieski had only to remain neutral if the Turks attacked Austria, but neutrality was not an easy course to follow.

The Polish nobility on the whole favoured war against the Turks. Louis XIV, on the other hand, wanted to keep the Turks and Poles apart, for a Turkish war in Poland would gain him nothing, while it would free Leopold for action in the west. If possible he wanted to turn both against Austria. In this he miscalculated badly, overestimating his influence over Sobieski and underestimating the general fear the Turkish armies could still awaken in central and eastern Europe. He also reckoned without the stubborn singlemindedness of pope Innocent XI and the skill of papal diplomacy.

Ever since his elevation to the papal throne in 1676, Benedetto Odescalchi had pursued his dream of uniting all Christian Europe for a crusade against the Turks. Though in other matters he was inclined to favour the French, on this question he was unmovable. Against his capable and eloquent nuncios, Palavicini in Warsaw and Buonvisi in Vienna, the French made little progress.

While Palavicini took advantage of anti-Turkish sentiment in Poland, Buonvisi, nuncio to Vienna since 1675, did what he could in the midst of a war against France to encourage what remained of the 'eastern' party at court, urging Leopold to make up his differences with France and collect his resources for the coming great battle with Islam. This reiterated advice, more often given than sought, met with little response from the Emperor and his close advisers. Even after Nijmegen, when it became clear that the Turks were offering more than passive assistance to Thököly, the privy conference clung to the conviction that France, not the Turk, was the real enemy of the house of Austria and the Empire.

Buonvisi's offer of papal mediation with Poland was welcome, though here again Leopold and the privy conference saw an improvement of relations more as a blow to French influence than as preparation for war in the east. Warsaw received Leopold's initial overtures cordially, especially as they were strongly seconded by Palavicini and by personal notes from Innocent XI in 1681 and 1682. The nuncios carefully tempered the mutual suspicions Leopold and Sobieski held towards each other, and so laid the groundwork for their momentous last-minute alliance when the storm finally broke in Hungary.

What Buonvisi could not do was overcome the Emperor's fear and hatred of France. Long experience as a neighbour of the Turks had in a fashion inured the Viennese government to having a permanent crisis in the east, where the often repeated prayer '. . . and protect us God from the Turk' had become a habit. Experience also suggested that the Ottoman state of the degenerate Mehmet IV was not the awesome power of Suleiman I. After the war of 1664 many Austrians even doubted that the Turks could ever again hope to achieve more than small frontier gains in Hungary, losses which could easily be won back once the Empire was safe from the rapacity of Louis XIV.

This optimistic view found no encouragement in the reports that reached Vienna from Constantinople. During 1678 and 1679 no less than four diplomatic missions had been sent to the Porte from Vienna, but all the envoys had died before serious talks could begin. When Christof von Kunitz arrived in 1680 he discovered that some Turks superstitiously interpreted his predecessors' fates as a sign that God did not want peace between the Emperor and the sultan; hardly a comforting beginning to a peacemaking mission. From the moment of his arrival Kunitz saw that the *divan* was more concerned with the affairs of the Hungarian rebels and with preparations for war than it was about renewing the Vasvár armistice.

In 1676, the same year that the crusading Innocent XI came to the papal throne, Ahmed Köprülü the grand vizier died, leaving his office in the hands of his carefully groomed successor, the Anatolian upstart Kara Mustafa. In strong contrast to his mentor, the new vizier was unwilling to trust his ambitions and his fortunes to the intrigues of the indolent Ottoman court. He understood the fundamentally military character of the Ottoman state, and knew that its strength and his own authority in it rested on military success.[4]

Kara Mustafa's main assets were a reputation for bravery on the battlefield and a proven ability to work tirelessly at whatever business was put in his hands; beyond that he lacked any of the refined characteristics. His aggressive avarice, his corruption and extreme jealousy of power made him capable of sacrificing anything and anyone to his own ambition, as he was to do ruthlessly and repeatedly in order to protect himself from his sovereign's wrath after the 1683 debacle. From the beginning he had in mind many projects to bring glory to Turkish arms and win him favour with the military. These probably included an expedition against the Imperial capital. Kunitz, at least, suspected as much and shared his fears with the privy conference even before it was clear in which direction the vizier's ambition would lead him.

In February 1681 the Turks made peace with the Russians at Radzin, freeing themselves from war on their northeastern border. By the summer of that year Turkish forces supporting Thököly were clearly operating with official sanction in violation of the treaty of Vasvár. Prince Michael Apafy openly collaborated with Thököly, accepting the sultan's appointment as commander of the Turkish–Transylvanian forces supporting the *Kuruc*.

All these moves confirmed Kunitz's reports and lent weight to Buonvisi's view that a clash with the Turks could not be postponed. Emmerich Sinelli, now bishop of Vienna, went over to the nuncio's side during the summer of 1681, though Hermann of Baden and the Imperialists in the conference remained firmly behind the western group. As late as June 1682 the chancellery still directed its main diplomatic efforts toward creating an alliance with key German states to provide an Imperial army to hold off the French. To win over the francophile elector of Bavaria, Leopold offered the hand of his daughter Maria Antonia to young Max Emmanuel. Given the complicated problems of the Spanish succession, this clearly was the dynastic catch of the century. Max Emmanuel found the offer irresistible, and joined the Imperial side. As things turned out he won his spurs fighting the Turks, not France.

Only the certainty of war with France can explain Leopold's response to the eastern crisis in 1682. In spite of all indications to the contrary, he and his privy conference clung to the view that the Hungarian rebels could be won over, and with that source of discord out of the way the Turks could then be induced to keep the peace. In this optimistic frame of mind Leopold dispatched yet another emissary, count Albert Caprara, to Constantinople to work alongside Kunitz, while the discussions with Thököly continued. Leopold could not afford to meet all the rebel's demands, but to keep the negotiations open he offered to consent to Thököly's marriage with Helena Zrinyi. It was a substantial concession, for as long as Helena remained an unmarried widow and the Emperor's ward, the income of the large Rákóczy estates went to the crown. By consenting to the marriage Leopold also gave up the last advantage he held in his bargaining, for the Turks could promise Thököly everything else, but they could not offer him the fascinating rich widow.

Imre Thököly and Helena Zrinyi Rákóczy were married on 15 June 1682. Nine days later Thököly renounced his armistice with Leopold. In July and August, with the help of forces sent by Ibrahim Pasha of Pest and Michael Apafy, Thököly seized three important towns in Upper Hungary including Kaschau. In September he received a patent from the sultan designating him 'Prince of Middle Hungary' under the suzerainty of the Sublime Porte. By October the rebels held all of Upper Hungary and were sending *Kuruc* raiding parties west and north into Moravia and Silesia.

On 1 August 1682 Leopold summoned his privy conference to an urgent session where he posed the question of accepting French peace proposals in order to free himself to meet the crisis in Hungary. In spite of Caprara's warnings and a note of almost hysterical urgency in Kunitz's reports, the privy conference decided firmly against making an agreement with France that would sanction the reunions. Afraid to fight on two fronts simultaneously, and still more afraid of France than the Turks, the conference determined to concentrate on the Rhine rather than the Danube. Instructions were drafted for Caprara and Kunitz, urging them to redouble their efforts to appease the sultan, while Austrian diplomats in the west were instructed to continue breathing defiance at France.

By this time events were moving more rapidly than news of them could travel. The instructions agreed upon in August did not reach Constantinople in time to be of any use. France explicitly promised that it would not aid the Emperor under any circumstances, though Louis XIV indicated he might support Poland if that kingdom were attacked. With this assurance, the sultan and Kara Mustafa decided to strike at Hungary, and left Constantinople to join the army at the beginning of October 1682. When Caprara and Kunitz received their instructions and the money they needed for bribes, the court had moved to Adrianople. Diplomacy could accomplish nothing further.

The combined threat of France and new troubles in Hungary lent urgency to Austrian negotiations in Warsaw. In the spring of 1682 Sobieski agreed to expel the Hungarian rebels from his realm, and to prevent the French from using Poland as a base for transmitting subsidies to them. By this time there was little the French could do but try to delay an alliance between Austria and Poland. The treaty was concluded on 31 March 1683. Leopold pledged himself to field 60,000 men, Sobieski to bring 40,000 to war against the Turks. If the Turkish attack were directed against either Cracow or Vienna, the two armies would operate jointly. Pope Innocent XI cheerfully joined the coalition as guarantor, opening his purse generously to subsidize both Austria and Poland. From his point of view it was an offensive alliance, a crusade against Islam. For Leopold and Sobieski it was a more urgent matter of self-defence. In addition to sending direct cash grants of about half a million Gulden to each monarch, Innocent gave Austria and Bavaria, now partners in what was coming to be called the Holy League, permission to tax church property, an unusual concession.

Innocent XI tried to help Leopold in one more way: by using his influence to restrain Louis XIV from taking advantage of the eastern crisis to fall upon the Empire again. In this he was less successful, though he accepted Louis' protest of his innocence with unseemly gullibility. For his part, Louis XIV declared himself satisfied with the reunions of 1681 plus Strasbourg, and invited Leopold to accept them in return for French restraint in the future. When Leopold refused, Louis demanded additional reunions in return for which he promised Leopold thirty years of peace. At the same time he began mobilizing his troops in Alsace. Friedrich Wilhelm of Brandenburg, once again at odds with the Habsburgs and allied with the French, added bribery to blackmail by offering Leopold 16,000 men for the Turkish war if he accepted the French terms. Even Innocent XI, fearing the collapse of his crusade, encouraged Leopold to come to terms, but the Emperor remained firm. So deep now was his distrust of France that he refused to conduct any further negotiations on the subject of the reunions. What happened in the west would have to be dealt with later, for the moment Vienna had to see to its own defences.

Even with the sudden and unexpected sums of money the pope's generosity made available, the mustering of an Imperial army was a slow process. After Nijmegen the army had been reduced; by 1682 Leopold still had some 36,000 men under arms, but it was a widely scattered force. Most of it was tied down to garrison duty in the hereditary lands, especially in Hungary, the bulk of the field units was concentrated on the Rhine. Any additions to the force would have to come from the German princes, and this meant months of bargaining over the terms, then even more weeks until they could reach Hungary.

The Turks moved more rapidly than the Imperial war council had expected. Kara Mustafa used the winter months to assemble scattered Turkish units and to order the auxiliaries to meet the main army along the line of march. The main force left Adrianople on 31 March 1683 and camped around Belgrade on 3 May. Here it was joined by rein-forcements from Asia along with the auxiliary corps from the vassal states on the Danube. The core of the Turkish force was the regular army of some 40,000 well-trained men. The allied and vassal forces assembled around it brought the whole up to nearly 100,000 men not counting the inevitable train of servants, slaves and camp-followers. In mid-June the Ottoman troops marched through Hungary, where they were joined by the cavalry of the Tatar Khan. By the end of June they joined the local forces of Ibrahim Pasha of Pest opposite the Imperial fortress of Györ on the frontier of royal Hungary.

Once the war council knew the direction the Turkish army was taking, it developed a plan for an offensive strike into Hungary, presum-ing that this would contain the war there. They set 20 April for the rendezvous of Imperial forces south of Pressburg. The plan was a good one, but the time was too short for the scattered Imperial units to reach their destination. Another problem arose over the appointment of a supreme commander. Leopold wanted to give the command to his brother-in-law, Charles of Lorraine, but first he had to override the opposition of his war council president, Hermann of Baden, who coveted the appointment for his own nephew, Ludwig Wilhelm, also an accomplished soldier. Not until 21 April, the day after the armies were to have assembled, did Leopold confirm duke Charles as commander of all his armies.

On 6 May 1683 Leopold and his prospective son-in-law, Max Emman-uel of Bavaria, reviewed a force of about 30,000 men near Pressburg. The Imperial army was still only half the promised strength, and much less than Leopold needed to face the Turks in battle; but the force grew steadily as new units joined the encampment. Paul Esterházy, the Hungarian palatine, brought 6,000 men from the 'insurrection forces';[5] another 12,000 of that force remained scattered among the garrisons in Hungary and along the military frontier in Croatia.

The speed of Turkish movements and the growing conviction that the Turkish thrust at Vienna could not easily be distracted by movements on its flank led the war council and the privy conference to give up all

thought of an offensive in Turkish Hungary which might leave the
capital defenceless and cut off the main Imperial army from the slowly
assembling allied forces in the west and Sobieski's army in the north.
Instead, Charles of Lorraine was ordered to put the main barrier forts
of Györ and Komárno in order and remain on the defensive, avoiding
battle and keeping himself always between the main Turkish force and
Vienna.

This conventional strategy was endangered almost at once by the
outbreak of Tatar raids in western Hungary and *Kuruc* attacks in the
north. Lorraine dared not split his defence force into many small units
to protect the whole frontier region against guerrilla attacks. Keeping
his forces concentrated, he began to retreat up the Danube, just as Kara
Mustafa appeared before Györ on 2 July. Seeing the Austrians pulling
back before him, Kara Mustafa left a small detachment to besiege that
small but well-armed garrison and concentrated his own forces for a
thrust across the Raab (Rába). Lorraine quickly sent the main body of his
artillery and infantry back towards Vienna, spreading his cavalry as a
screen to protect the withdrawal of his slower units.

About two o'clock in the afternoon of 7 July, general Aeneas Caprara
reached the Hofburg bringing news that the Turks had pushed past
Charles of Lorraine's defensive screen on the Raab and were on the
march to Vienna. Shock gave way to confusion. Leopold hastily met
with the privy conference and decided to remove the Imperial family and
the court from Vienna, leaving the city in the hands of its own defenders.

The precipitate flight of the court understandably produced consterna-
tion in the city.[6] Leopold has ever since been judged quite harshly for
what may well have been the one truly hasty decision of his reign.
Whatever the damage done to his reputation, there is little doubt that
Leopold took not only the prudent, but the only intelligent, course
open to him. Shut up within a besieged capital, Leopold might have
become a symbol of resistance, but there would have been little else for
him to do, while his court would be a useless burden on supplies. When
the Emperor's carriage left the Hofburg a crowd of frightened, grumb-
ling citizens barred the way briefly. His guards began to force their way
through the mob, shoving aside the crowd who begged the Emperor
not to desert them. Leopold calmly ordered his guards to go gently, and
the entourage slowly moved through the crowded streets beyond the
Hofburg.

In the countryside around the city, an area that was to suffer more than
any other from the siege operations, there was general panic. Angry
bands of peasants harassed parties of refugees fleeing the city, providing

an impromptu *jacquerie* with many ugly incidents and possibly some danger to the Imperial family itself. Wherever his carriage was recognized, Leopold was roundly cursed for bringing war on the country, or for supporting the Jesuits whose policies had so angered the Protestants that they had called in the Turks to free them. Not until late at night did the Imperial party push through the villages west of Vienna and reach the great monastery at Klosterneuburg, whence it set out again the next day, moving with few pauses up the Danube to Krems and Linz, until it reached the episcopal city of Passau on 17 July.

Passau proved an excellent choice for a command post. Though the small town was soon uncomfortably crowded, it provided good communications in all directions. The scattered remnants of the central administration quickly gathered, set up an emergency government for the crowded city, and arranged temporary offices to carry on the work of forming an army of liberation. Once the administration was again functioning sufficiently to carry on the normal routine, Leopold felt free to get closer to the battle. On 25 August he and the pregnant Empress Eleanora went to Linz by boat. Installing Eleanora comfortably in Linz (where she was delivered of a daughter on 7 September) Leopold went further downstream with a small following, awaiting the decisive moment on his barge anchored in the Danube below the ruins of Dürnstein castle, where once a Babenburg Leopold held an earlier crusader, Richard of England, for ransom.

Through the night of 7–8 July, while the court fled up the Danube, the city of Vienna had been a scene of noisy uproar as the great nobles and the foreign embassies hastily packed their carriages. As thousands left the city, other thousands crowded into it in their place to save themselves from Turkish raids on their unprotected villages.[7] The following day order gradually replaced chaos. When count Ernst Rüdiger von Starhemberg arrived during the evening of 8 July, the emergency government planned for the city quickly took hold.

Leopold had chosen carefully and well the men he left to defend Vienna. Starhemberg, military commander of the defending garrison, was a simple, straightforward, soldierly type, crude and outspoken, energetic and highly skilled in the complex techniques of siegecraft. His personal bravery was a living legend in the Imperial army, his brusque and unaffected manners brought out the best in the men he commanded. He was no diplomat, not the sort of man to handle the complex intrigues of aristocratic war councils, but for this assignment he was probably the best man in the Imperial service.

To direct the civil government Leopold had designated the Czech

count Kaspar Zdenko Kapliřs, the vice-president of the war council.
Kapliřs was seventy-two, a sensible, competent old soldier-courtier,
understandably reluctant to undertake the arduous assignment on
grounds of his age. At first he fled the city with the court, but in Krems
Leopold kindly but firmly ordered him back to his post. Kapliřs returned
to the city and performed his job with remarkable energy and good
sense. Leopold Kolonitsch, now a cardinal and bishop of Wiener
Neustadt, came to Vienna on his own initiative to organize the hospital
and medical services of the city. He had long experience as a soldier of
the Knights of Malta, and was a veteran of the long Turkish war on
Crete. He knew his business and did it well. He also provided dubious
ecclesiastical sanction for the confiscation of the wealth stored up in
Vienna by various Hungarian prelates.

Vienna enjoyed over a week's respite between the court's flight and
the arrival of Kara Mustafa's army. First the Turks halted near Deutsch-
Altenburg on the Danube near Pressburg while supplies were hauled
upstream from Buda. This gave Vienna extra precious days to prepare.
The city had been provisioned to withstand a long siege by foresighted
work on the part of the war council staff. Now still more food and
military supplies were brought in at the last minute. With the whole-
hearted cooperation of the city officials and the Bürgermeister Johann
Andreas von Liebenberg, civilians were drafted to help improve the
earthworks around the main walls of the city. On 13 July the suburbs
close to Vienna were burned down so the Turks could not use the
buildings to cover their own siege operations. In the course of this a
tragic disaster was narrowly averted when fire threatened to spread to
the main armoury with its vast deposits of gunpowder. Quick action
by a young officer, the future fieldmarshal Guido von Starhemberg,
saved the situation.

Charles of Lorraine, whose forces had remained camped near Vienna
since their retreat from the Raab, reinforced the city garrison with as
many units as Starhemberg could support. Then the Imperial army
withdrew north of the Danube as the Turkish army approached and
surrounded the city on 16 July.

X

The Siege of Vienna

Amid preparations to meet the Turkish invasion Leopold lost several of his most important advisers, a majority of the men he relied upon for all the normal business of government. The old grand chamberlain, Leopold's scholarly friend count Lamberg, died in December 1682. Then the 'spring sickness' claimed the life of chancellor Hocher on 1 March 1683; within the month it also killed the court chamber president, Christof Abele, and the Bohemian chancellor, count Nostitz. Only two central figures on the privy conference survived: the Imperial vice-chancellor count Königsegg and the war council president margrave Hermann of Baden. The sudden disappearance of so many men from the privy conference was in itself a crisis for the regime.

Leopold turned over to Königsegg the diplomatic business Hocher had been conducting. The Imperial vice-chancellor had sat in the privy conference for many years, overshadowed first by Lobkowitz, then by Hocher. He was a convinced 'Imperialist', competent if not brilliant, a man whose experience and steadiness Leopold could count on to carry through the work others had begun. His age and chronic gout made it impossible for him to undertake much greater burdens, however, and future leadership in the conference depended on stronger men.

To replace Hocher as court chancellor Leopold chose a career diplomat, Theodor Stratmann. Stratmann's personality was as different as possible from that of his dour, earnest and somewhat ponderous predecessor. Stratmann was a Rhinelander, open, hearty, vivacious, a man who handled both men and business with intelligence, light wit and tact. He had come to Vienna in the entourage of Empress Eleanora, who remained his unswerving patroness.[1] For three years before he became chancellor he had been Leopold's chief representative at the Imperial Diet in Regensburg, where he acquired an encyclopædic knowledge of German affairs. During the crisis year 1683 Stratmann was overshadowed by Königsegg, but as the vice-chancellor's health failed, Stratmann took over political leadership in the conference. His instinctive tact and a talent for keeping Leopold in good humour even in the most serious situations won him increasing favour.

The only real rival to Stratmann's domination of the privy conference was the new Bohemian chancellor, count Franz Ulrich Kinsky. A scion of one of the few old Bohemian noble families who had prospered because of their loyalty to the house of Austria, Kinsky assumed high office as a matter of course. For generations his family had served as diplomats, administrators and soldiers. He had been educated to be a statesman, and had developed a good understanding of European and German, as well as local Bohemian, affairs. Scholarly, almost pedantic, he still had a fund of good sense and native intelligence alongside a phenomenal stubbornness that made him a valuable if often contrary voice in the privy conference.

The grand chamberlain's office had lost so much of its political importance since the dismissal of Lobkowitz that at Lamberg's death Leopold could afford to leave it vacant for four months. In April 1683 he appointed count Albrecht Sinzendorf, who died in October of the same year. Leopold then named an old friend, the pleasant but politically insignificant count Ferdinand Dietrichstein, who performed his duties with dignity and loyalty, but whose role in the conference was largely ceremonial.

To preside over the court chamber Leopold named count Wolfgang Aeneas Orsini von Rosenberg, a man whose name is almost a compendium of the cosmopolitan aristocracy of the Viennese court. Little was heard of him in the years that followed except persistent complaints that he was not up to meeting the demands of his office. Yet Leopold kept him in office long after he had proved his mediocrity possibly convinced still that the aborted *Hofkammerordnung* and the vigorous work of Abele had in fact accomplished the necessary reforms in financial administration.

The new privy conference included both able and incompetent men, prickly personalities and bitter rivals. There is little doubt that they were all deliberately chosen by Leopold for the qualities he saw in them, not because they represented one or another of the cliques at court. It was, however, a hastily patched-together regime that Leopold left in Passau to conduct his affairs through the agonizing summer weeks of 1683, while the Turks fought to capture Vienna. As usual he had chosen men who, whatever their faults and shortcomings, served him well enough in a crisis and to whom he remained grateful even when their service was no longer to his own advantage.

During July and August 1683 time was the greatest enemy; everything depended on Starhemberg's ability to hold the capital for as long as it took to assemble the relief force. Through the first weeks of the siege the Turks had concentrated on building lines and approaches to the city's defences, using captives swept up in their march through Hungary to dig trenches and build earthworks. Starhemberg organized sorties to interrupt that work whenever possible, and continued with the help of the townsmen to work on his own defences.² Unlike the stately siege warfare common in western Europe, with its textbook precision and geometrical calculations, its rules of etiquette, this was a savage war without quarter. Assaults against the city's defences increased in frequency and the Turks came ever nearer success; normal restraints broke down and both sides resorted to deliberate terror. Kara Mustafa ordered the wholesale slaughter of recalcitrant Christian captives outside the walls from which the defenders could see the butchery. The Imperial soldiers in turn took first to impaling the heads of captured Turks on the walls, and then to flaying their prisoners alive. By mid-August the stench of decomposing human flesh was a permanent accompaniment to the constant din of artillery and mines, the clamour of assaults and sorties.

The Turks directed their main assaults at the corner of the city dominated by the Hofburg, which was defended by a series of outerworks called the *Burgbastei*. By early August Turkish mines and artillery had knocked away important parts of the bastions there and elsewhere around the city. On 12 August a Turkish mine blasted away part of the earthworks near the *Burgbastei*, piling up a mound of earth in the moat. This made a rough sort of causeway that permitted a direct assault on the main walls. The assault was driven off, but at great cost to the garrison, which had by then already lost 1,200 men. Dysentery spread through both armies, but proved nearly disastrous for the defenders. Starhemberg himself, along with most of his men and the rest of the city, suffered from its debilitating effects, made all the more intolerable by the August heat and a general breakdown of sanitary arrangements.

Conditions were little better outside the walls, where the disease became a great problem for the Turks, who had not bothered with setting up adequate sanitation. Kara Mustafa faced serious morale problems, particularly among the auxiliary forces who were unenthusiastic about the whole operation. Assaults on the city drew him ever closer to the inner defences, but they were increasingly costly. The casualties among his elite forces grew alarmingly. The vizier called for reinforcements from the east, but with little success. Imre Thököly, who had played so large a role in the beginning of the war, had already tasted the sharpness of Imperial arms in Hungary, and refused now to heed the vizier's command to bring his army to Vienna.

At the end of August the Turks took heart from clear signs that the defenders were growing desperate. One after another the outer defences around the *Burgbastei* fell before Turkish assaults. The Turks prepared to mine the curtain wall and the inner bastions. On 4 September an assault against the outer wall near the Hofburg, now broken by a thirty-foot breach, nearly succeeded in penetrating the city. Starhemberg and some of his officers rallied the weakening defence, leading a charge that threw the Turks back from the wall. That night Starhemberg fired the first distress rockets from the tower of St Stephen's Cathedral to signal the relief army to hasten. The Turks understood the signal and began celebrating, carousing immoderately with the abundant wine they found in suburban Viennese cellars.

The following day Starhemberg found he had little more than a third of his original garrison still fit for duty, a small force of regular troops that he now had to stretch thinly along sixty-four defence posts around the walls. Behind them stood only an ill-trained and unreliable municipal militia. On the night of 7 September, after three more days of desperate fighting near the breaches in the walls that brought the Turks still nearer to the streets inside, Starhemberg's distress signals were answered by fires from the hills west of the city.

When Charles of Lorraine had withdrawn his diminished force from Vienna on 16 July, he did not at first move far from the city, trusting the Turks to concentrate all their attention on the siege.[3] His immediate plans had to be made in the field without direction from the court, which was still hurrying towards Passau. For the moment at least, he was perhaps as independent as any field commander has ever been. His most urgent task was to protect as much of the hereditary lands as he could from Turkish and Tatar raiding parties, and if possible to hold the northern bank of the Danube. This also involved protecting Pressburg from Thököly, who was trying to build a kingdom for himself in Hungary while the Turks screened him from the Imperial army. Thököly did manage at one point to reach Pressburg, but his irregulars got completely out of hand looting the town. When Lorraine approached the city with regular forces Thököly withdrew into Upper Hungary and did not again offer a serious challenge to Lorraine's control of the lands north of the river.

As early as 20 July duke Charles had developed a plan for the relief of Vienna, setting the Tulln basin as the rendezvous point for the allied armies. The attack on the Turks would come through the Vienna woods. Corresponding directly with John Sobieski, Lorraine won the Pole's approval for his plan. The exiled regime in Passau, particularly the war council president, margrave Hermann, had many other suggestions to offer, but Lorraine's plan changed only in detail as the campaign progressed. Leopold reviewed the plan, offering no more than counsels of caution, and insisting that no attack be made on the Turks until all the allied forces had assembled. While Lorraine waited for the relief force to assemble, he camped around Marchegg, north-east of Vienna, where he could be ready to move quickly when the time came while remaining in a good position to harass the Turks and keep an eye on Thököly.

While Lorraine fidgeted in impatience at Marchegg and Vienna's defenders grew weaker, the work of the diplomats began to bear fruit. On 6 August Max Emmanuel of Bavaria finally signed an agreement implementing his new alliance with Leopold and then marched off to join his new and well-trained army of over 11,000 men which he had sent ahead into Austria. Another 8,000 Germans under prince Waldeck came from Franconia and Swabia, passing through Passau on 21 August. Slowly and reluctantly the Empire sent its regiments eastwards from their stations facing the Rhine. Duke Ernst August of Hanover, protesting that he could not send his army so far from home, contributed a force of some 600 cavalry, largely, it appeared, as a bodyguard for his two sons (including the future George I of England) who wanted to see a real war. Leopold's pleas for aid fell on deaf ears in Berlin, where it was hoped the elector might still send as many as 12,000 of his tough Brandenburgers. In spite of the obvious danger in the east, the elector held to his bargain with France and refused to send a single unit until Leopold accepted the reunions. Leopold had better luck in Saxony, whose elector Johann Georg III personally led off his 9,000 men in spite of strong anti-Habsburg sentiment among his own subjects arising from the persecution of Magyar Protestants. This band of Saxons performed some of the most gallant of all the action before Vienna. All these men were needed. Their total when they finally assembled probably gave Lorraine an Imperial army of nearly 50,000, which he judged large enough to allow him to take the risk of attacking the Turks before the city fell.

A confident, decisive move to break the siege depended on Sobieski and his large force of Poles. Poland had begun mobilizing in the spring, but Sobieski held back until he was certain that Kara Mustafa's offensive was not directed north towards Poland. Even when it was clear that Vienna was the Turks' objective, Sobieski delayed his departure from

Warsaw until 18 July. He arrived in Cracow where his troops were assembling at the end of the month. There he stayed yet another two weeks and more exchanging letters with Charles of Lorraine. When he did finally move from Cracow, he left behind substantial units of infantry. Of the 40,000 men he had promised to the alliance, only about 18,000 actually joined the Imperial army in time to take part in the battle.[4] Leopold had come closer to providing his promised force of 60,000, and may even have exceeded his commitment if one includes the garrisons holding out in Hungary and within Vienna itself.

The allied armies gathered along the Danube between Tulln and Krems during the last days of August. Charles of Lorraine left his encampment in Marchegg and marched west to join them. On 31 August he dashed off with a modest guard for a bibulous meeting with Sobieski. Charles used all his charm to win the touchy Pole's friendship and to prevent the usual pre-battle squabbles over command that were the plague of combined military operations. After a series of war councils Charles worked out, and got the others to accept, an order of precedence that put Sobieski in chief command so long as the Emperor Leopold did not appear in person to lead his armies. Final rendezvous for the attack was set for 7 September at Tulln.

The question of supreme command forced Leopold to make a critical decision about his own conduct. He was quite aware that the flight from Vienna had been a blow to his personal prestige not only in his capital but throughout Europe. His friends and advisers were sharply divided, some urging him to join the army, others counselling him to stay away. Both bishop Emmerich Sinelli and the Spanish ambassador Borgomanero thought that he should take command himself and not give the world the impression that other princes had to come to save his empire for him. In the middle of August Leopold apparently agreed with this view. He left Passau for Linz intending to join the army. Once in Linz, however, he learned more about Sobieski's strong reaction against submitting to even nominal command by a superior. Leopold moved down the Danube still debating the matter, deciding finally on the very eve of battle that his presence would only cause confusion and disrupt the delicate system of command that Charles of Lorraine had so painstakingly built at the sacrifice of his own ambition. Leopold awaited the decision at Dürnstein.

By 6 September the allied armies began to move into the Tulln basin just west of the hills that ring Vienna. The next day Lorraine sent a small cavalry detachment ahead to the Kahlenberg to signal their approach to the defenders. On 9 September, when the rendezvous was complete, the army broke camp and began the hard two-day march through the Vienna woods. Marching in four widely separated columns, through thick woods and up stony ravines, the army pushed its way to the summits looking down on Vienna, dislodging some small Turkish outposts there on 11 September.

Kara Mustafa was not caught by surprise, but he had done little to protect his own encampment from an attack by the relieving army. His arrogant conduct during the siege had damaged morale, while the long duration of the siege, staggering casualties, disease and poor provisioning had left his men and horses weak. Only at the northern end of the siege camp, near the gap through which the Danube flows out onto the plain, did he have any proper trenches and lines to protect himself. Others had been ordered but none was complete when the relief army appeared.

The battle for Vienna began early on the morning of 12 September after the Capuchin monk Marco d'Aviano celebrated mass in a burnt-out chapel on the Kahlenberg, preaching a short, stirring sermon. The many columns began moving down the broken hills between the summit and the plain, looking to the Turks like 'a stream of black pitch',[5] flowing towards the main Turkish camp along the whole line from the Danube to the river Wien. The Imperial forces had the left wing along the Danube, Sobieski's Poles the right, the position of honour according to the military protocol of the period.

Austrian and German troops coming around the hills nearest the Danube had an easier march than the others. They also had the longest fight, as they struck the upper end of the Turkish camp early in the day and began slowly hewing their way southwards as additional columns emerged from the foothills and struck the Ottoman flank. For the first three or four hours the battle was a series of sharp skirmishes that coalesced gradually into a long battle line across the whole north-western perimeter of the Turkish camp.

Shortly after midday the Poles, who had the longest and most difficult march, began moving down from the hills to the south near the major siege works, fighting their way towards the centre of the now shrinking Turkish lines. By around five in the afternoon the separate assaulting forces working independently struck sharply at the Turkish line in several places at nearly the same moment. The whole Ottoman battle front quickly collapsed. In the confusion Kara Mustafa tried to rally his forces, but in less than an hour his position was hopeless. He fled from his tent with a few sacks of treasure and the flag of the Prophet, leading the general retreat towards Győr.[6] By sunset the battle was over, the Turks gone and Vienna freed.

Leopold had news of the victory late that same night. As soon as it was light enough to travel he hurriedly left Dürnstein and arrived before Vienna near noon the next day. There he was met by the electors Max Emmanuel of Bavaria and Johann Georg III of Saxony, the latter's bandaged wounds giving proof of his valour. With them he joined the duke of Lorraine and count Starhemberg in reviewing the siegeworks. Leopold then entered his capital to the sound of bells that had been silent for seven weeks, proceeding to St Stephen's for the *Te Deum*. Leopold and his small escort took up temporary quarters in the Stallburg, then surveyed the damage to the city. Palaces, churches, townhouses, all had suffered severe damage in the parts nearest the walls. At the sight of the ruined Leopoldine old quarters (*Trakt*) of the Hofburg, Leopold wept. Rubble filled the streets, along with corpses awaiting burial, heaps of undisposed sewage, the wreckage of siege engines and all the unavoidable trash of war. Obviously the government could not function in the city for some time to come. Leopold sent to summon his ministers from Passau to Linz to take temporary quarters there while Vienna was cleansed and repairs started on the Hofburg.

In his official entry into the capital, Leopold had been outdone by Sobieski, who on the very night after the battle conducted an impromptu triumph, dramatically emphasizing his role in the victory. This had been a source of deep embarrassment to the Austrian officers, who knew of Leopold's desire to be the first to enter Vienna. The affront to the Emperor's already tarnished dignity, added to the fact that the Polish army had seized for itself the cream of the rich booty left behind in the Turkish camp, intensified the touchiness of men exhausted by days of hard marching and fighting.

Furious at being upstaged by Sobieski, Leopold seemed distracted and unable to handle the problems put before him by the Imperial commanders who presented themselves at the Stallburg. Even Charles of Lorraine, faced with the urgent problem of provisioning and quartering the large relief forces, got little satisfaction from his conversation. Johann Georg III of Saxony, tactlessly giving Leopold a lecture on the mistreatment of the Hungarian Protestants, felt so aggrieved by Leopold's unreassuring response that he indignantly marched his troops back towards Saxony the next day.[7]

Leopold finally overcame his resentment of Sobieski's conduct. On 15 September he rode out to Schwechat, where the Poles were camped, for a personal interview with the self-proclaimed 'Saviour of Vienna'. In spite of a long argument about protocol, the meeting began well, both monarchs remaining mounted, exchanging their cordial compliments in Latin. Then Sobieski presented his son Jákob to the Emperor. Leopold seemed to ignore the lad in a cold manner, deeply offending Sobieski and his officers. Leopold's motives for this apparent breach of courtesy have been endlessly debated. Sobieski, encouraged by Francophile nobles in his entourage, chose to magnify the incident. Leopold's actions may well have been prompted by serious dynastic and political motives. There had been talk of a marriage between Jákob and one of the Habsburg archduchesses, a scheme pushed by Sobieski and Marysieńka, but not at all pleasing to Leopold. Young Jákob himself put the slight down to the fact that Leopold was having trouble managing his floppy hat, flowing court peruke and a nervous horse.[8] King John Sobieski, however, reacted to the incident as symbolic of all the real and imagined difficulties he was having in Austria. Nothing Leopold did later could make amends or restore cordiality between them.

The battle before Vienna produced a sudden, startling, apparently total victory. Like the battle of Lepanto in 1571, this was widely seen as a Christian, European triumph over an alien, infidel civilization. A mood of jubilant self-confidence spread throughout Europe, even in countries that had little reason to rejoice at the political consequences of a Habsburg triumph. The euphoria that comes with success after a long period of agony does not last long, but for the moment there was glory enough for all the victors which their own unseemly bickering could not tarnish.

While Christian Europe celebrated, Kara Mustafa retreated from the scene of his debacle. To save himself from the sultan's vengeance he blamed his subordinate commanders, executing a number of pashas and generals who might give witness to his own mismanagement, but none of these ruthless sacrifices could hide the magnitude of the defeat. On 25 December 1683, while he was at prayer in the palace in Belgrade, Kara Mustafa was interrupted by emissaries from Constantinople bearing the sultan's order of dismissal and the silken scarf of execution. Kara Mustafa lifted his long beard, the sultan's agents quickly strangled him, recited the office for the dead, and then sent his head to Constantinople.[9]

Leopold left Vienna on 19 September, his duties to the allied armies and his brave city completed. In Linz, a more suitable temporary capital than crowded Passau, he met his court and resumed the routine of government.

XI

Austria turns Eastwards

When the privy conference took up its work in Linz in the early autumn of 1683 it faced, as its first order of business, the exploitation of the victory won at Vienna. The military stores taken after the Turks had fled left little doubt that it would be some time before the grand vizier could replace his valuable artillery. The powder alone was valued at a million Gulden, a windfall for the allies, however prosaic it might seem to plundering soldiers, a treasure which the Turks could not replace quickly. The news that filtered back from the retreating Ottoman army suggested, moreover, that the Turkish leadership was in total disarray, the army itself rendered helpless by the confusion and lack of supplies.

The opportunities opening in the east drew Leopold's attention in that direction in a way that the constant threat of invasion had not done before. He even began to think of pushing Islam out of Europe entirely, a spark of ambition the papal nuncio was careful to cherish. As always, the problem was to find and organize the resources to continue the crusade. As the war had caused widespread desolation in Lower Austria and Royal Hungary, little could be expected from those regions. Victory left Leopold still as dependent upon foreign assistance as he had been before the Turks invaded. To mobilize that support he had to maintain the alliances of 1682 and 1683, and if possible lure new powers to join him. This could not be an easy task, for the coalition of 1683 was already showing signs of strain, of jealousy and competition for precedence and mutual suspicion that had immobilized so many such enterprises in the past.

Success overcame the timidity of the privy conference, which now seized the initiative from Rome; it proposed first an alliance with Venice, a state usually neutral in European conflicts, but now smarting from the loss of Crete to the Turks and anxious to restore its valuable shipping empire in the eastern Mediterranean. Innocent XI seconded the move and enthusiastically offered still further subsidies. At the same time he kept up his pressure on Sobieski to hold Poland in the coalition. These negotiations led to the Holy League, confirmed by a treaty signed in Linz in March 1684 by representatives of Venice, Poland, the papacy and the Empire. All bound themselves to continue the war against the Turks and renounced any war against a Christian state while they were engaged in that enterprise.

The Holy League represented Leopold's intention to take the offensive in the east. It suggested a relaxation of his uneasiness about France, perhaps a pious hope that the pope would be able to restrain Louis XIV long enough to let the League get on with its work in Hungary. The question of the reunions remained unresolved, but the French did not take up arms against the Empire during the relief of Vienna. This sense of security was very rudely shaken in December 1683 when news reached Linz that Spain had again declared war on France.

Spain had done what little it could to assist in the relief of Vienna, but it was little indeed. From the beginning Spanish fears centred around French moves against its fortresses in the Netherlands. In response to Innocent XI's vigorous appeal for peace among Christian states in the spring of 1683 Madrid had responded courteously, but with a damning catalogue of French violations of the peace of Nijmegen and other 'invasions and insults'.[1] Borgomanero's reports from Vienna and Passau led the Spanish council of state to the optimistic view that, once Vienna was saved, Leopold could be persuaded to turn his attention back to the west. By late November 1683, however, it was clear that the Holy League would be renewed and that the Poles would hold Leopold to his engagement against the Turks. In Borgomanero's view it was only the Poles who could profit from the war in the east. The council of state in Madrid had little understanding of the Hungarian scene, nor could the councillors appreciate the advantages Austria might win there. They also could not know that Borgomanero's continued opposition to the strong eastward thrust of Austrian policy was an anachronism in Vienna.

At the conclusion of a debate in the Spanish council on 2 December 1683 only the constable of Castile remained pessimistic about the prospect of assistance from the Empire. All the rest judged that the 'fabric of the state' was strong enough to hold France off for long enough to mobilize a coalition against Louis XIV.[2]

Leopold found himself faced by an old and familiar dilemma, one in which dynastic interests conflicted with the interests of his hereditary lands in central Europe. One thing only had changed significantly: for the first time it seemed that he had the opportunity to make himself absolute master in the east if only France would give him time. Louis VXI

demanded a high price for peace on the Rhine: recognition of the reunions and the incorporation of Strasbourg into France. This Leopold
had refused to consider for several years, yet now the east held greater
temptations. Another war with France meant giving up the momentum
in Hungary. Leopold avoided committing himself as long as he possibly
could, as he had done before when threatened on both sides of his
dominions. The tide was running strongly eastwards, however, and he
decided to leave the difficulties with France to his diplomats, let his
Spanish nephew's army fend for itself, and turn his own forces
eastwards into Hungary.

During the weeks after the battle for Vienna the allied forces had
cleared most of Royal Hungary of Turkish garrisons. Before they moved
to winter quarters they captured the important town of Gran (Esztergom),
seat of the Catholic primate of Hungary, which had been in Turkish
hands for nearly a century and a half. Even more might have been
accomplished had Sobieski not grown wary and suspicious of the Austrians, refusing to make more daring thrusts to the south and east which
would take him and his army ever farther from Poland and from their
proposed winter quarters in Upper Hungary. Sobieski's suspicion of
Leopold was returned full measure when the Polish king began to
meddle in the political affairs of Hungary, trying to set himself up as a
mediator between Leopold and the rebels still loyal to Thököly.
Sobieski's desire to become a 'saviour' in Hungary as he had been at
Vienna came to nothing; the scheme was ruined by the behaviour of his
troops who left behind them a trail of destruction as they moved through
Hungary. Thököly made a final, defiant proclamation of his allegiance
to the sultan, then suddenly disappeared from the scene, taking refuge
in Debrecen behind strong Turkish garrisons and leaving most of his
followers to their fate.

Leopold seized the moment to try to win back the remaining rebels
in Hungary. Seconded by Buonvisi and Innocent XI, he set up an
amnesty commission in Pressburg. On 12 January 1684 he published a
decree promising to abide by the decisions of the Sopron diet of 1681
and offering free pardon and security for the estates of all former followers of Thököly who presented themselves in Pressburg to swear
allegiance to him by the end of February. In western and central Hungary the response was good. Farther eastwards many magnates and
nobles held out against the crown, taking their cue from Michael Apafy
of Transylvania, who was still afraid of the Turks and unwilling to join
the Imperialists until they had driven the Ottomans beyond Belgrade.

In spite of the great hopes raised by the treaties renewing the Holy

League in March 1684 it soon became clear that John Sobieski had little further interest in enlarging Austria's control in Hungary. He continued to devise grandiose plans which he communicated to the papal nuncios, but nothing ever came of them. For the time being Charles of Lorraine was thrown back on what forces he commanded himself and the Bavarian elector's still loyal contingents.

Lorraine set as his objective for the summer of 1684 the great fortress at Buda, the centre of Turkish military and administrative power in central Hungary. His scattered units assembled slowly from their winter quarters, but once they took the field in June they moved quickly, clearing the Danube as far as Pest by the end of the month. The Turks abandoned the lightly defended market-city of Pest, retreating across the Danube to the fortress at Buda, and destroying the boat bridges that connected the two. After a difficult crossing below Buda the Imperial forces invested the fort on 14 July.

Lorraine clearly had superior manpower: some 34,000 men plus a reinforcement of 9,000 additional Hungarians raised by the Magyar nobility under Esterházy.[3] The fort itself was held by about 10,000 Turkish regulars, while the seraskier Mustafa stood south of Buda with another Turkish army of some 15,000, clearly not enough to relieve Buda. Ludwig Wilhelm of Baden, nephew of the war council president and now Lorraine's second in command, was optimistic. A week, he thought, should do the job. Ernst Rüdiger von Starhemberg, with somewhat more experience in siege warfare, opposed the whole operation, proposing instead that Lorraine destroy the seraskier's force first before worrying about a formal siege. The decision went against him, and the siege proceeded.

For a short time all went well, but sanguine overconfidence led Lorraine to make many costly technical mistakes in the operation. Days grew into weeks and Buda still held out. As time passed, Lorraine's war council lost its happy optimism. Violent arguments divided the command. The army itself, pounded by the heavy and accurate artillery of the fort, began to melt away. Losses were staggering. By mid-August, when the siege was but a month old, Lorraine could count on only two-thirds of his original force. A few weeks later disease and poor supplies, combined with the unrelenting bombardment from the fort, had reduced his force by half again: to only about 12,500 men – a force hardly equal to the garrison he was attacking. Lorraine himself fell sick just as word arrived that the seraskier was drawing near with his relief force.

Fortunately for Lorraine, Max Emmanuel of Bavaria arrived on

9 September with about 8,000 men. In October more troops arrived from the Imperial circles and from Moravia, but still there were not enough men to take Buda. On 1 November Lorraine gave up the siege and sent what was left of his army (which had suffered more than 20,000 casualties) into winter quarters.

While the main Imperial army had melted away before Buda, smaller detachments had fared better elsewhere. In the south, general Leslie had conquered valuable strongholds along the Croatian border, while in the north, the outcome of general Schulz's running duel with Thököly's guerrilla bands ended with the former's capture of the rebel's head-quarters in September: Thököly had fled once more into Turkish Hungary.

Taken as a whole, the Holy League's crusade of 1684 had produced no successes equal to the ambitious and optimistic plans laid for the campaign. The operations of Venice and Poland had been modest and done no more than harass the frontiers of the sprawling Ottoman empire. Leopold's decision to concentrate on his eastern frontier had borne little fruit, largely because he could not disengage himself entirely from the conflict with France over the reunions. The key to this situation lay not at Versailles, however, but in Berlin. Above all things the war council wanted the superb troops of the Great Elector to stiffen the Imperial army in Hungary, but had been frustrated by Friedrich Wilhelm's refusal to send his men until Leopold had accepted French conditions for a truce on the Rhine.

During a long reign filled with wars of aggrandizement and effective reform of his military and administrative structures, Friedrich Wilhelm made himself the strongest prince of the Empire after the Emperor himself. Though he was technically Leopold's vassal, he took full advan-tage of the diplomatic freedom guaranteed him by the treaty of West-phalia to build his position as a power in the north.[4] His army, though not large, was generally judged one of the best in Europe. The elector was sensitive to the fact that rival princely houses in Germany had won glory at Vienna while he sat by and looked on, but for the time being none of the blandishments of Habsburg diplomacy could induce him to join the crusade against the Turks until Leopold had assured peace in the Empire by accepting a truce on French terms.

In May 1684 the French bombarded Genoa, then on 4 June captured the supposedly impregnable Spanish fortress city of Luxembourg. Louis then sent his troops against the Imperial electoral city of Trier. With all his forces occupied in Hungary, Leopold had no choice but to give in and accept a truce with France, the Regensburg armistice of 15 August

1684, signed for a term of twenty years. Leopold has been widely accused by later German historians of betraying the Empire, of failing to take advantage of a wave of anti-French sentiment in Germany.[5] Pamphlets and public opinion had little to do with the matter, however, so long as they had no effect on the elector of Brandenburg. Even Max Emmanuel of Bavaria advised Leopold strongly against a war with France.

Leopold was again well served by his diplomats, who managed to avoid ceding outright all the territories France had occupied since 1679. The Regensburg pact included a formal French recognition of Imperial rights of suzerainty, but for the period of the armistice, Strasbourg and all reunions effected prior to 1 August 1681 were to remain under French administration. Spain's effrontery in declaring war on France was punished by the cession of Luxembourg. Innocent XI and cardinal Buonvisi rejoiced at the peace between the two great Catholic powers, loudly praising the restraint of Louis XIV, whom they now confidently hoped to win over to the crusade against the Turks, a move which was unthinkable at Versailles.

Leopold won his freedom to concentrate on the Turkish wars, but only at the cost of accepting the reunions, a price he had not been willing to pay in 1683. It was more immediately important to remove the last barrier to Brandenburg's collaboration. Leopold must have known that the face-saving formulae in the Regensburg truce preserved only the appearances while conceding the substance, and that twenty years of peace with France was unlikely.

Once he had decided to press the war against the Turks, whatever the disappointments along the way, Leopold held to his choice. Even before Charles of Lorraine lifted the siege of Buda, the war council was planning an ambitious campaign for 1685. There seemed many good reasons to press ahead in spite of reverses. The crusading spirit had caught on among young nobles all over Europe. Many volunteers flocked to the east to join the great battle, a number of them coming from France in spite of the fact that Louis XIV had firmly forbidden any of his subjects to fight under Imperial standards against the Turks. The German states promised more substantial forces than ever. There were now firm commitments from Hanover for 11,000 men, promises of another 8,000 from Bavaria, the same from the Rhenish circle, 4,500 from Swabia, and some 6,000 from the elector of Cologne.

By the end of 1684 Leopold's problem was no longer finding the men to fight, but rather putting his own household in order so that the army could be effectively supported and directed. While there were criticisms of the field commanders in 1684, most enthusiasts for the crusade saw clearly that the poor showing then had more to do with the organization of finances and military supply than it did with the quality of the troops or their leaders. Some of the sharpest criticism came from the remarkable man who had recently become Leopold's most intimate spiritual adviser, the fiery evangelist and faith-healer, Marco d'Aviano.

Like his fellow Capuchin, the now aged and frail bishop Sinelli, Marco d'Aviano had rejected the world of the petty bourgeoisie for a career in the Church. At seventeen he intended to set out to convert the Turks; instead he joined the Capuchins, perhaps the most intensely proselytizing and rigorous order of the day. Like many zealots who combine shrewd intelligence with deep dedication to the faith, he found himself constantly called upon, by the world of affairs, to perform administrative or diplomatic tasks for the Church, to travel everywhere as his reputation as a faith-healer spread. By 1682 he had become one of the few close friends in Leopold's intimate circle, perhaps his most constant confidant outside the Imperial family and the privy council, largely replacing Sinelli in this role. He did not, however, haunt the court perpetually, but followed the armies into the field, corresponding at length with Leopold,[6] inspiring even the German troops, so it was said, with the eloquence of his Italian sermons. After the victory at Vienna he became a sort of talisman to the troops, and to Leopold as well, who saw in d'Aviano the marks of divine inspiration. It is much to the Capuchin's credit that he never used his influence over Leopold irresponsibly, though in political matters he generally stood firmly for the point of view currently pursued in Rome.

Returning from the Hungarian campaign in November 1684, Marco d'Aviano gave Leopold a carefully worked-out critique of the operation with trenchant comments on the men who led it and the failings of the bureaucrats who had let them down. Buonvisi did much the same, adding many pithy remarks about economy measures the court itself could undertake as a modest sacrifice for the war effort. Both were convinced that the court chamber and the war commissariat were the centres of the trouble. Buonvisi urged that both Orsini von Rosenberg and the commissariat director count Siegfried Breuner be replaced.

It was strong medicine, and Leopold refused to take the whole dose. Count Breuner had proved himself a good man for routine work, but even his colleagues admitted that he could not deal with emergencies. Leopold solved this problem curiously, by appointing Breuner to the vice-presidency of the court chamber. Since Orsini von Rosenberg retained the presidency, Leopold thus concentrated incompetence in a single, critical department. The new head of the war commissariat, count Rabatta, proved more efficient at organizing supply and transport, but he was still limited by the increasing muddle in the central financial agency.

Buonvisi and d'Aviano continued for a time to argue for fiscal reform, but in the end they had to concede defeat. One more attempt to reform the court chamber came to an end because Buonvisi was forced to take the side of the treasury against the Austrian clergy, who resisted the pope's order to contribute cash and suffer further confiscations and forced loans for the crusade. The monarchy continued to survive financially, as it had done since the reign began, by living from one windfall to another.

In 1685 the money for war came almost entirely from the Church. The Hungarian primate Szelepcsényi died in January 1685. The court chamber, with Buonvisi's cooperation, seized the bulk of his large fortune and also Sinelli's estate when he died the following month. Then Innocent XI ordered the secular and regular clergy in Austria to sell one-third of all the property they had acquired in the past sixty years and give the money to the crown. Further papal appeals throughout Europe brought a variety of donations from often unexpected sources. The pope himself again sent substantial subsidies from his own revenues which he intelligently, and apparently at Buonvisi's advice, transmitted directly to the commanders in the field to provide supplies and pay for the troops. If the court chamber could not be reformed, at least for some purposes it could be circumvented.

The war council again determined to strike at Buda in 1685, but the mustering of the army as usual took weeks longer than anticipated in the plan. Then, to avoid having his supply lines threatened, Charles of Lorraine had to divert his attack towards a lesser fort, Neuhäusel (Ersek Ujvár), where for several weeks he held his main force of 40,000 men besieging a fortress held by 3,000 Turks. On 16 August he engaged a Turkish relief force near Táth, defeated it completely, and three days later Neuhäusel fell. The Imperial troops plundered the city and killed the remainder of the garrison. The remnants of the Turkish field army in Hungary pulled back to Belgrade, leaving behind a number of garrisons with little hope of relief.

In northern Hungary Thököly emerged for one more contest with the Austrians for possession of his Turkish-sponsored principality. This time, however, the Turks left him to fight alone, for they had more than enough to do elsewhere. On 11 September an Imperial detachment took the town of Eperjes, and Thököly again fled with a small band of followers into Turkish territory. He was at first received cordially, but when the Turks saw that his cause looked hopeless, they made him a prisoner and sent him in chains to Belgrade to await the sultan's pleasure. Deprived of its youthful leader, the Hungarian insurrection collapsed; the remaining bands in Upper Hungary hastened to capitulate to Imperial commanders.[7] The *Kuruczók*, some 17,000 strong, gave their allegiance to Leopold, whose commanders took their oath of homage. Leopold himself accepted their 'repentance' in good faith, even praising their fidelity to their former cause. General Caprara and Paul Esterházy now began turning them into a regular standing army.

The Turks apparently intended at first to use Thököly as a pawn in their efforts to make peace with Austria and detach the Emperor from the Holy League. In their innocence of western politics, they assumed that Leopold might find a rebel's head worth a province. To their chagrin they found that by removing the one capable leader from the insurrection, they had made it possible for the palatine to incorporate a large and experienced, if still primitive and ill-organized, corps of *Kuruczók* cavalry into the Imperial army and turn them against their former protectors.

In November 1685 the Sublime Porte indicated a willingness to negotiate peace with the Empire, their main concession being Thököly's person. The privy conference debated and agreed that the success of the campaign, though modest, was encouraging. The reply returned to Constantinople through the war council was vague but plainly a refusal to negotiate on any grounds other than the evacuation of all Hungary. This precipitated a sudden change of government in Constantinople and, as a sort of footnote, the liberation of the now useless Thököly from his Belgrade prison in January 1686. His old comrades did not flock to his banner again. Only his wife Helena and a small band of faithful followers now remained holed up in their fortress at Munkács.

Thököly's failure to revive the insurrection served as one more proof that the power relations in eastern Europe were shifting in Austria's favour. Nowhere did this shift have a greater impact than in the pivotal province of Transylvania, historically a dependency of the crown of St Stephen.[8] Since the sixteenth century it had existed in a state of semi-dependence on the sultan, following the movements of its larger neighbours and taking what advantage it could from the quarrels among them while retaining internally its strong diet and semi-republican character under an elected prince. In Transylvania, a land of mixed nationalities, a variety of confessions co-existed in relative harmony: Catholics, Lutherans, Calvinists, Unitarians and even some Orthodox peasants.

Under Turkish suzerainty it accepted a certain amount of interference in its political affairs and paid tribute in men and money to the Porte. Beyond these periodic gestures of dependence, the province had on the whole been left to itself, protected in part by the encircling mountains and above all by the mutual jealousies among its neighbours, Poland, Austria, the Ottoman empire. It was a haven for refugees from all these lands, and the one place where the Magyars at least could retain their sense of national identity, ruled by princes of their own choosing.

The collapse of Turkish power before Vienna fundamentally altered the delicate balance that had guaranteed Transylvanian independence. Prince Michael Apafy, whose election had been part of the background of the Turkish wars of 1663–64, did not yet dare to renounce his allegiance to the sultan, but with his adviser Michael Teleki he offered to mediate between the Turks and the Emperor. Early in 1685 Apafy sent an agent to Vienna with this proposal, only to find that the Austrian regime was thinking not of a mediated peace with Turkey, but rather of re-annexing Transylvania to the Hungarian crown. Leopold sent an agent of his own, the Burgundian Jesuit Antidius Dunod, to Apafy with an offer of a place in the Holy League if he would recognize Leopold's sovereignty over Transylvania.

The Transylvanian diet debated a variety of counter-offers which they hoped would preserve their independence. Teleki meanwhile signed a secret, private agreement with Dunod promising his personal support to Leopold. As the diet debated the future of the principality the successful Imperial campaign in Hungary in 1685 put Vienna in a position to increase its demands and its pressure on Apafy. In October Dunod came a second time to Karlsburg, this time with the demand that Transylvania break completely and openly with the Porte and provide support and quarter for Imperial military units. Fearing for their independence, and quite understandably convinced that their cherished confessional liberty would not survive under Austrian occupation, the Transylvanian diet sent a delegation of its own members to Vienna to deal directly with the Emperor. Leopold delegated the grand chamberlain count Dietrichstein, Hermann of Baden and chancellor Stratmann to negotiate with them. From the beginning the deputies from Karlsburg were outmanœuvred, for Imperial units were already moving into the principality pursuing stray Turkish patrols. The Imperial conferees offered protection of the land, a guarantee of confessional liberty and recognition of Apafy's princely title with his son to succeed him. Beyond that they demanded joint Imperial occupation of the province. This deeply offended the deputies, but there was little hope of resisting Leopold. They consented to a treaty conceding all the Austrian demands on 28 June 1686. Leopold ratified it the next day.

In Transylvania the diet did not see the situation as being nearly so hopeless as its deputies thought. If anything, they remained still more fearful of a break with the Turks, a move which would surely bring reprisals. Who, after all, could be sure how permanent Austrian successes in Hungary would prove to be? The change in sovereignty in itself posed few difficulties to so flexible a society, for the Transylvanians were practised in the ceremonial shifts of allegiance that their location made logical and necessary. Military occupation of their homeland was a different matter. For the moment fortune favoured Leopold over the sultan, but accepting Imperial garrisons could provide bait for a Turkish invasion if fortune turned the other way.

With the backing of his diet Apafy found a formula that seemed to offer him the time he wanted in order to wait out events in Hungary. With all the usual baroque courtesies he informed Leopold that he could not ratify the treaty his agents had agreed to until Imperial forces had taken Buda, Temesvár, Belgrade and a number of other major Turkish strongholds in southern Hungary: a very large order indeed. Then in the accepted tradition of Transylvanian politics, Apafy appealed to John Sobieski of Poland, Leopold's ally in the Holy League, for Polish support in his cause; and to cover all possibilities, he appealed to the grand vizier for Turkish protection as well.

Apafy's refusal to ratify the treaty ended Vienna's efforts to negotiate a peaceful accession of Transylvania. It took two more years for Leopold to win by force what he had hoped to gain by negotiation. Apafy and the Transylvanian diet assumed that Austria would prove too weak to protect all it had won from the Turks, an assumption which would perhaps have been valid a decade earlier. Events proved that this time the tide of power had turned decisively and permanently.

XII

The Conquest of Hungary

With each new victory in Hungary Leopold's ministers enlarged the scope of their policy in the east, daring now to dream of an empire far beyond what had already been won, even beyond what Leopold could legitimately claim as part of his inheritance. As early as 1685, with Buda still in Turkish hands, the privy conference began eyeing the lower Danubian provinces of Wallachia and Moldavia, whose Christian princes, like Apafy, were technically vassals of the sultan.[1] This optimism in Vienna increased Sobieski's suspicions, making him more willing to listen to the French, who were eager to detach Poland from the Holy League. Austrian efforts to bring Russia into the alliance seemed to disturb the Polish king even more.

Russia's last war with the Turks (1677–81) had shown that the tsar alone could not break the Turkish hold over the southern steppes, and the Holy League provided a convenient means for coordinating several offensives against Islam. Sobieski, however, found himself caught between two great powers who, though they were his allies in the crusade against the Turks, could not – he felt – be trusted to leave Poland undisturbed in the future.

Leopold had agreed to an armistice with France in 1684 largely to win Brandenburg's military assistance, but the elector Friedrich Wilhelm was in no hurry to transfer his allegiance. Even though he had many good reasons to regret his alliance with Louis XIV,[2] he knew the value of his army and would not sell it cheaply. French policy itself finally brought him to change his mind, mainly because Louis began to seem a greater threat to his co-religionists than did the Habsburgs. The French, finding Sweden a more reliable ally than Brandenburg, had frustrated the elector's attempts to annex Swedish Pomerania. The succession of a Catholic king in England coupled with Louis' persecution of the Huguenots in France alarmed the elector and in August 1685 he signed at Augsburg an alliance with prince William of Orange, ending the estrangement between them that had begun at Nijmegen. Just at the time when these two leading Calvinist princes formed what was to become the League of Augsburg, Louis XIV published the claims of his sister-in-law to substantial portions of the Rhenish Palatinate.

Perceiving this move as a challenge to the balance of power in Germany, Friedrich Wilhelm publicly expressed his gratification at Austrian successes in Hungary. Leopold's envoy in Berlin, Franz Heinrich von Fridag, appealed to the elector's Christian conscience and his duty as an Imperial prince. By September 1685 Friedrich Wilhelm was ready to send a contingent to Hungary. A French threat to stop subsidies made the elector pause, but when Louis XIV on 18 October issued the edict of Fontainebleau, revoking the edict of Nantes, the elector cut the last ties binding him to France. Within weeks his officers were planning their junction with the Imperial army in Hungary even though a formal treaty had yet to be worked out.

Friedrich Wilhelm still drove a hard bargain. His main demands concerned his claim to certain Silesian fiefs of the Bohemian crown, the same issue that later provided Friedrich II with his excuse for pouncing on Austria in 1740. Leopold, appealing to his oath as king of Bohemia, refused to compromise territorial rights he believed were his. The old elector refused to go ahead with the treaty without the fiefs. Fridag finally found a way out of the impasse by getting the elector to accept a compromise by which certain territories were ceded to Brandenburg 'for the life of the elector'.[3] With little difficulty, Fridag then got the electoral prince, a confirmed francophobe, to agree secretly to their return to Austria upon his accession. The treaty was signed on 1 April 1686 and 8,000 crack Brandenburg troops marched towards Hungary at once.

Brandenburg's example encouraged other German princes to follow suit. Saxony sent nearly 5,000 men, and even Sweden, as a member state of the Empire, sent a thousand men at its own cost. The Regensburg Reichstag had voted a contribution of fifty 'Roman Months', an archaic formula that translated into a sum of about two and three-quarter million Gulden, some two-thirds of which was actually raised and sent in the form of troops paid and supplied by the Imperial circles. In all, some 34,000 men from the Empire marched east to fight the Turks in 1686.

Austria and Bohemia had been induced to provide contributions of over three and a half million Gulden, Hungary was taxed another two million to keep the Emperor's own army in the field. These were large sums, but as usual they had been spent in anticipation of their approval for recruitment and winter quartering. Leopold appealed first to Rome, but found Innocent XI less generous than before. The pope's dwindling resources and Buonvisi's reports about the financial mismanagement in Vienna led Innocent to refuse another direct subsidy. Not until August did Vienna pry a new subsidy from Rome, and then it was a meagre 100,000 Gulden.

Indirectly, however, Innocent continued to provide Vienna with an important source of money through his 1685 order to the Austrian clergy. He named Buonvisi and Kolonitsch papal delegates to supervise the confiscation and sale of this property. By February 1686 their energetic and, to the clergy, dismayingly thorough pursuit of money for the war had produced 826,000 Gulden. When the action was completed by the beginning of the following year the total sum was nearly twice that.

To Leopold leadership seemed a greater problem than money. Three of his best generals were rivals for the supreme command: Charles of Lorraine, Max Emmanuel of Bavaria, and Ludwig Wilhelm of Baden. The war council president, margrave Hermann, still hoped to see his nephew given supreme command. Leopold preferred Charles of Lorraine, who had been married to Leopold's sister Eleanora since 1678, for the post. In July 1685 Max Emmanuel married Leopold's daughter, Maria Antonia. As the disputes among these three proud men grew more bitter, they spilled out of the war council to the court at large and even split the Imperial family into several factions. More was at issue than personalities. Lorraine wanted to concentrate all Imperial forces for another strike at Buda. Ludwig Wilhelm and Max Emmanuel each wanted to divide the army, giving themselves completely independent commands and the lesser tasks of sweeping up smaller Turkish garrisons first.

Leopold was very fond of Max Emmanuel, and inclined to allow him, at least, an independent command. Lorraine asked to be permitted to resign the supreme command if the Bavarian would not accept his strategy. Margrave Hermann tried to push his nephew's opinion in the war council. Leopold found the bickering intolerable and bolted from Vienna to Wiener Neustadt in order to work out his decision tranquilly, away from the uproar at court. He could not escape the furore entirely, however, for d'Aviano followed him there, where he presumed on his friendship by bursting into Leopold's presence uninvited, treating the Emperor to one of his thunderous, impromptu sermons. What, he demanded in essence, did secondary fortresses mean if for once, and possibly for the only time, Leopold was strong enough to take Buda and smash the sultan's power in Hungary?[4] Leopold gave in and agreed to follow Lorraine's advice.

With the angry sounds of the family squabble still fresh in his mind, Leopold shied away from the unpleasant task of facing margrave Hermann, Ludwig Wilhelm and Max Emmanuel. Instead he summoned Lorraine to Wiener Neustadt and told him his decision. Possibly at Lorraine's suggestion, Leopold ordered his chancellor Stratmann to go to field headquarters to read to the assembled generals Leopold's express commands for the campaign. This exercise of his sovereign will, even at a distance, had the desired effect. Everyone gracefully accepted his decision, even Max Emmanuel. Leopold probably never quite understood the terror his awesome office could evoke in other men, the genuine reverence that even haughty Imperial princes could feel when faced by the Emperor's decisive command to military subordinates. Such direct and outspoken orders were not Leopold's normal response to controversy among his subjects. To the frustration of many it was an exercise he seldom repeated.

Once Leopold asserted his authority the army moved rapidly against Buda, laying siege to the fortress city on 18 June. The vizier Suleiman assembled a Turkish relief force in southern Hungary, but refused to engage the Imperial army in an open battle.[5] On 22 July one of Lorraine's gunners hit a powder magazine in the citadel, blowing open a breach in the walls and killing or incapacitating perhaps a fifth of the defenders. Still the commander Abdurrahman Pasha refused to surrender, and the slow, bloody business of assaulting the fort went on while the vizier's army hovered near. In the Imperial war council tempers flared as the generals blamed each other for delays and failure, and argued heatedly whether to continue the siege or to strike at the vizier's relief force.

While it seemed clear in late August that Buda must soon fall, some of Lorraine's colleagues were unwilling to risk a costly assault with the vizier's army so near. Once again chancellor Stratmann hurried from Vienna, probably at d'Aviano's urging, to smooth over service rivalries with a display of Imperial authority. For three days, from 30 August to 1 September, he presided over the unruly war council until finally the generals agreed to make a final assault on Buda to be followed immediately with an attack against vizier Suleiman.

On 2 September the assault won through the inner defences and Buda was taken. Abdurrahman Pasha fell in the fighting; the remaining defenders surrendered. Marco d'Aviano's hastily written report reached Leopold the next day. The captured city was given over to plunder in the course of which a fire broke out in the residential quarter. By the time Leopold learned of the victory his prize lay in ashes.

When the grand vizier heard that Buda had fallen he beat a hasty retreat towards Belgrade, eluding Lorraine's pursuit. Most of the Imperial units began dispersing to winter quarters, though two corps remained in the field during the autumn. Ludwig Wilhelm, independent at last, won his marshal's baton as a reward for a highly successful sweep through south-western Hungary and Slavonia where he captured several fortified towns and destroyed a strategic bridge over the Drava. East of the Danube another corps led by general Veterani and Ferenc Barkóczy, a recent defector from Thököly, captured the important Tisza river town of Szegedin. Before winter brought operations to a halt the Imperial forces had reaped substantial rewards from the fall of Buda. Leopold's army pushed deep into southern Hungary, leaving only a few isolated Turkish outposts in the centre of the kingdom.

Once again the privy conference debated continuing the war in the east. Discouraged by a long series of defeats, the Turks were anxious to make peace, but none of the sultan's ministers was brave enough to advise concessions beyond the boundaries set at Vasvár. Convinced that Louis XIV was preparing yet another strike across the Rhine, the privy conference did not immediately reject the Turkish invitation to negotiate, though Leopold himself, strongly encouraged by d'Aviano and the papal nuncio, stood firm in his decision to continue the war which now promised the total 'liberation' of Hungary.

In January 1687 margrave Hermann of Baden sent a response to the Turkish peace proposals which indicated that negotiations might begin when the Turks indicated their willingness to return to the Emperor the lands they had robbed from him. The grand vizier's answer the following month hinted at the surrender of a few forts which the Imperialists already held, but remained firm on the Vasvár frontier. Since further negotiations were clearly useless, the privy conference voted on 19 April to continue the war in Hungary.

Once again the rivalry between Charles of Lorraine and Max Emmanuel of Bavaria threatened to wreck a vigorous campaign. Cardinal Buonvisi, anxious to preserve the hard-won unity of command that had proved so successful the year before, induced pope Innocent XI to suggest to the Bavarian elector that he should not expose his precious person on the field of battle. The pope's advice had precisely the opposite effect from its intention. In order to pacify the offended elector, Leopold had to give him an independent command east of the Danube covering Lorraine's army in the south and south-west. Ludwig Wilhelm of

Baden, on his own initiative, assumed a similar independence. From the beginning Lorraine had trouble with his stubbornly insubordinate colleagues, both of whom used every possible excuse to avoid coordinating their movements with the main force.

These delays and bad weather foiled Lorraine's attempt to seize Esseg and the Drava river before vizier Suleiman could reach them. Since duke Charles could neither attack the vizier's strongly entrenched force nor remain where he was, he began to retreat on 20 July. The vizier, urged on by his officers who were eager for booty and promotions, rashly moved out of his lines to pursue Lorraine. North of Baranyavar the two armies met. After a series of minor engagements a general battle began on 12 August near Mount Harsan. An Imperial cavalry charge split the Turkish force, striking the Ottoman cavalry which broke in flight and rode back through their own infantry lines. The result was a complete rout. The vizier fled from the field; his army scattered, having lost about a fifth of its number. Charles sent a contingent of about 10,000 men back to Esseg, which fell without a blow.

By October 1687 the whole of central Slavonia had been cleared of Turkish garrisons. Lorraine himself, with the bulk of his forces, moved eastwards towards Temesvár, intending to cut off Transylvania from its Turkish overlords. By 23 August he had crossed the Danube near Mohács and began marching eastwards when he received news of a great upheaval within the Ottoman empire.

The regime of Mehmet IV, corrupt and inept as it was, had endured four years of frustrating defeats in Hungary. In 1686 the loss of Buda and Slavonia produced a violent reaction. The troubles began with a general mutiny in the army, led by the elite janissaries, who were bitter about the defeats, arrears in pay and the incompetence of their commanders. After the defeat at Mount Harsan the mutiny turned into a bloody rebellion that cost the vizier his life and drove Mehmet IV from the throne. Mehmet's brother, Suleiman II, was installed as sultan.

These confusions offered Charles of Lorraine an irresistible opportunity. Turning north-eastwards, he sped quickly into Transylvania, demanding that Apafy provide provisions for his troops, fortresses to garrison and winter quarters for the Imperial army. When the Transylvanian diet stoutly rejected these demands, Lorraine took possession of Klausenburg and Bistritz. Apafy and his assembly fled to Hermannstadt, sending another deputation to bargain with Lorraine, who replied by moving his army deeper into the principality. Left without help from the Turks, Apafy and the diet had to capitulate. On 27 October the prince turned over twelve major forts, promised provisions for a large part of the Imperial army and a cash payment of 700,000 Gulden. Lorraine in his turn guaranteed Apafy security for himself and his family, religious liberty in the principality and respect for many of the local rights of the province. This political *coup de main* won for Leopold more than he had demanded of Transylvania the year before.

When Charles of Lorraine returned to Vienna, Leopold sent general count Antonio Caraffa as commandant to Hermannstadt with orders to bring the principality completely under the sovereignty of the Hungarian crown. With a cruel brusqueness that was later to make him deeply hated in Hungary Caraffa forced the diet's deputies to pay homage to Leopold as their king, increased their contributions and demanded they join the war against Turkey. On 9 May 1688 the diet, meeting in Hermannstadt acceded to the fateful document which returned Transylvania to Leopold's protection, designating him 'hereditary king of Hungary'. Leopold ratified the document on 17 June. In accepting the allegiance of Transylvania the Emperor formally guaranteed religious liberty in the province.

In four brief years the Turks had been pushed from the walls of Vienna nearly to the walls of Belgrade. This was not simply a border war against wild Asiatic hordes. The Turks had free access to European military technology through the French, who assisted them covertly, and also through a number of European refugee adventurers who took the turban and fought for Islam. The Turks took this advice freely, often with great success. In the conduct of sieges and the design of fortifications, one of the most complex and sophisticated military arts of the age, they often showed themselves the superiors of their presumed European masters. The real difference between the adversaries lay in the political and social organization of the two states. Constantinople was the centre of a military empire that depended for its survival on the army that created it. Its political power was so intimately bound up with the military establishment that mutiny was enough to bring about the virtual collapse of the state.

The Habsburg monarchy, for all its apparent inefficiency even by seventeenth-century standards, represented a more advanced level of organization than did the Ottoman empire. In spite of his innate conservatism and superstitious piety, Leopold reflected the increasingly rational views of statecraft associated with the growth of European absolutism, the systematic attempt to maintain a standard of civil obedience which placed the welfare of the commonwealth above all other considerations. The machinery of Austrian administration creaked and groaned under the burdens placed on it by large-scale wars in both eastern and western Europe, but unlike the Turkish system it did not cease to function when the army grew unruly. The dynastic principle itself, though it tied sovereignty to a single person governing by hereditary right, proved a source of strength, removing the central authority from the whims of barrack conspiracies.

Kara Mustafa's defeat at Vienna has often been predicted in retrospect by commentators who point out, quite reasonably, that Turkish power was strained beyond its capacities in 1683 and could move no farther into Europe. The important thing for the future, however, was not that Kara Mustafa failed to take Vienna: the great sultan Suleiman I had failed in the same enterprise in 1529. It was rather the astonishing speed with which the Imperial armies regained Hungary after a century and a half of Turkish occupation.

In this process Emperor Leopold's personal role was unspectacular but crucial, depending less on what he did than on what he stood for. He was no strategist; painful decisions had to be forced on him by stronger men around him. What he did was represent conscientiously the living focus of a network of sovereign rights which he alone, by virtue of his birth, could legitimately exercise through his chosen agents. While his generals won battles and took fortresses, Leopold prayed for their success and rewarded them generously when they achieved it. He lived in the conviction that God would reward his house if it pursued its legitimate rights and defended the Catholic faith. The reconquest of Hungary confirmed Leopold's view of his dynasty's place in the world. His ministers were well aware of the importance of the times as they set about the business of building an empire to the east of the old Reich, a Habsburg empire constructed on dynastic and monarchical rather than feudal principles.

XIII

Restoration and Royal Absolutism in Hungary

With the fall of Buda in 1686 the Austrian monarchy had to face the urgent need to reorganize the political system in Hungary and to provide organization for the new territories reunited to the crown. The war in Hungary produced great opportunities; the peculiarly brutal nature of warfare produced even greater problems.

Imperial troops from central and western Europe, locked in years of combat against the Turks and the Magyar rebels, used their enemies' techniques and gradually adopted their callous habits. For the innocent peasants caught between the two armies there was little to choose between them.[1] 'Liberation' from the 'Turkish yoke' by German soldiers seldom meant a change for the better. In much of central Hungary the movement of armies often forced those who survived to migrate or to join one of the outlaw bands living by violence and plunder.

Few villages or towns in Hungary were untouched by war between the *Kuruczók* rebellions and the capture of Belgrade in 1688. What the Turkish or Habsburg tax agents left untaken pillaging soldiers or brigands seized or destroyed. When the Imperial armies bypassed smaller Turkish garrisons to hit more important forts they systematically evicted the peasant population which might have supplied them. The farmers were herded with what they could carry to regions safely under Imperial control. What remained behind was destroyed.

These forced migrations destroyed the traditional social bonds of peasant communities, family ties were broken and customary habits of discipline disappeared as well. The loss of peasant capital in the form of dwellings, tools and livestock was enormous; it could not be replaced except by time, patience and more hard work. The rich plain between the Danube and the Tisza rivers lost most of its settled population in 1684 and 1685, when the peasants fled the war zone for the relative safety of Upper Hungary, leaving their fields untended. Their place was taken by roving bands of uprooted Poles, Ruthenians and Moldavians who lived more like the original nomadic settlers of the region.[2] This scene of waste and poverty extended as the war operations moved farther south into Turkish Hungary, the desolate picture made even worse by a crop failure in 1685.

Leopold could not ignore the troubles that beset Hungary, if only because he urgently needed to obtain from the reconquered lands the means for continuing the war. Armies could not be quartered in a desert. One of the major sources of trouble was the lax discipline in the Imperial army itself. At Leopold's command the war council made at least a beginning by tightening army regulations and encouraging officers to prevent the indiscriminate pillaging which made German soldiers universally hated in Hungary, authorizing commanders to make exemplary executions if necessary.

Such measures however, did not deal with the central problem of restoring civil order and a measure of prosperity to Hungary. The usefulness of that potentially rich kingdom to the Imperial cause depended on the Hungarians themselves. Leopold recognized this fact even though he could never sympathize with the extravagant nationalism of his Magyar subjects. Since the fiasco of 1681 he had followed a conciliatory policy which had on the whole paid handsomely. The large-scale defection of *Kuruczók* from Thököly's insurrection proved that in some quarters at least it was possible to build loyalty to the crown even after the excesses committed in its name by Kolonitsch and Szelepcsényi.

During the war years, as circumstances allowed, the chancellery had built a middle-level administration between the rudimentary administrative organs of local landowners' and village courts and the comitats on the one hand and the ministerial councils of the crown on the other. These intermediate agencies, largely concerned with overseeing the collection of taxes, also proved useful in organizing the building of roads and bridges and in directing resettlement of abandoned lands. After 1686 they proved their usefulness in the devastated area around Buda. Gradually the city was repopulated, new markets set up and more orderly communications slowly restored.

All the measures undertaken to cope with the problems of Hungary had one thing in common: the clear intention to subject the kingdom to the direct authority of the crown. While the intention was clear, in practice the attempt to centralize authority was continually interrupted by conflict and competition among the central organs of the monarchical government itself. So long as Hungary remained a war zone, there was conflict between the civil administration responsible to the court chamber for fiscal affairs and to the Austrian or Hungarian chancelleries for judicial matters, and the military commanders in the field who were responsible to the war council. The court chamber, the chancelleries and the war council all tended to support their own subordinates, with the unhappy result that coordination became increasingly difficult at all levels of the administration. Only the firm, decisive intervention of the monarch himself could have produced order amid the confusion. Leopold did not bestir himself, leaving his ministers to solve their problems by wrangling among themselves.

In matters touching on religion, however, Leopold could not in conscience remain indifferent. He openly supported the Catholics at every turn. While there was no returning to the massive persecutions of the hated special courts of 1672, the monarch's overt support for the Catholics led to complaints which served only to strengthen Leopold's deep suspicion of the Magyar Protestants. Each Protestant church closed, each Jesuit establishment founded in a Protestant town, became the basis for a new grievance against the crown and foreign rule, intensifying the underlying hostility towards the Austrian regime.

Leopold's military governor in Hungary, Caraffa, shared Leopold's dislike of the Magyars to a degree that seems almost pathological.[3] His naturally suspicious turn of mind made him see conspiracies and treason everywhere and made him believe even the most implausible rumours. As early as 1686 he was reporting to the Emperor his discovery of a wide network of conspiracy directed at Leopold's own person and against the Catholic faith itself. His evidence was singularly unconvincing, but his imagination filled in what the facts would not support. With the experience of Zrinyi and Thököly still fresh in their minds, Leopold and the privy conference at first accepted Caraffa's colourful reports.[4] In 1686 Leopold agreed to the establishment of a new special court at Eperjes, a town Caraffa believed to be the centre of the plot.

In February 1687 Caraffa personally took charge of the work of the court, which began a series of trials and 'investigations' using procedures reminiscent of the witchcraft trials earlier in the century. Confessions and accusations extracted under torture brought seventeen substantial citizens of the city to the scaffold in the course of the next few months. The same means used to extract 'confessions' from the condemned also produced additional accusations leading to further arrests of people mentioned by the earliest victims. These procedures quickly produced a state of hysteria in the city in which accusations were flung against even the highest officials of the regime, the palatine Esterházy and margrave Hermann of Baden among them. Many of the wealthier citizens fled to Poland to escape the atmosphere of distrust and suspicion; their flight served only to confirm Caraffa's insane suspicions. He forged ahead ruthlessly to root out every vestige of suspected treason or sympathy for Thököly.

The Hungarian magnates, led by their palatine, approached Leopold repeatedly, arguing that the special courts were illegal in Hungary. There was even a case for trying Caraffa himself, as they saw it, on the grounds that the governor's outrageous proceedings in Eperjes were destroying any faith remaining in the regime and undermining the loyalty of the Hungarian people to their elected king. Their arguments belatedly carried the day. On 21 August 1687 Leopold issued a decree suppressing the special court. The move came none too soon, but not before Caraffa's name had become a common curse in Hungary and Leopold's own reputation had been tarnished by his association with the sordid affair.

While Caraffa hunted for conspirators, Leopold turned to the important matter of assuring the succession to the Hungarian crown of his son the archduke Joseph. In April 1687 he appointed a commission of mostly Austrian and Bohemian courtiers to draw up a programme for political reform and to advise him on the succession. It was clearly his intention at this point to take advantage of his military success to transform the Hungarian kingship from an elective to a hereditary possession of the house of Austria.

The Bohemian chancellor, count Kinsky, and chancellor Stratmann were the leading figures in the commission's debates.[5] Kinsky, like his predecessor Lobkowitz, wanted to impose on Hungary an absolutist government on the Bohemian model. He saw no need to consult the Magyar estates or assemble the diet in order to accomplish this. Stratmann, though equally convinced of the absolute authority of the crown, considered it to be more politic to accomplish the same ends more gradually, without stirring up the embers of rebellion. Kinsky's arguments were cogent, thoughtful, almost academic in their appeal to theories of natural law. Stratmann was more concerned with tactics, with the possibilities of the situation as it existed. His arguments won in the end, possibly because his views were more comfortable to Leopold, who always preferred whatever seemed the safest, most prudent way to his objective. Leopold decided to use the constitutional proceedings of the Hungarian diet to secure Joseph's election as king.

The call for the Hungarian diet went out, summoning the deputies to meet in Pressburg on 18 October 1687. The crown of St Stephen, which had been safely guarded in Vienna since 1683, was ceremoniously returned to the old Hungarian capital. Esterházy and Stratmann prepared the ground well in advance, so that when Leopold came to Pressburg with Empress Eleanora and their son Joseph on 30 October the members of the diet had already declared it their will to crown Joseph as their 'hereditary king', a title not traditionally allowed by the Hungarian constitution.

In his formal reply to the diet Leopold took matters one step further, announcing his intention to give Hungary 'new laws'. While he re-affirmed his willingness to uphold the traditional freedoms of the king-dom, he demanded that the decree of Andreas II of 1222, containing the troublesome *ius resistandi* clause, be revised and the hereditary right of the house of Austria by primogeniture be expressly set forth by the diet as a constitutional provision. As soon as that was done, Leopold prom-ised, he would remain with the diet for two more weeks to hear their grievances. It was a firm address, even a challenging one. Leopold could confront the Magyar aristocracy as the restorer of the kingdom, a large part of which he held under military occupation by his German troops.

Apart from some heated comments about Caraffa's nasty work in Eperjes, the diet showed itself in a compromising mood. They 'elected and accepted' Joseph as their king, granting the house of Habsburg hereditary right to the crown by primogeniture in the male line in gratitude for their 'liberation' from the Turks. The question of the *ius resistandi* was not so easily settled. This constitutional embodiment of the ancient feudal right, which held that a man could defy the authority of his lord if he were denied justice or satisfaction of his just grievances, had become a symbol to the Hungarian nobles of all their liberties and privileges. To some magnates it seemed the very essence of their con-stitution; to Leopold's ministers it had become a sanction and encourage-ment for treason.

The diet at first offered a compromise which would modify the Andrean decree to interpret the *ius resistandi* as a right of the whole nation and not, as in the past, the right of any one person or part of the kingdom. Leopold seemed at first willing to accept this, but Kinsky and Stratmann together urged him to go the whole way and force the diet to expunge the offending article from the constitution. Stiffened by his advisers, Leopold held stubbornly to his position, while gracefully giving way to the diet on other matters, including some concerned with religious liberty.

The diet grumbled, but there was little the deputies could do short of trying to delay the question by creating confusion, a manœuvre Leopold experienced often when dealing with the various estates and assemblies of his realms. The crucial moment came when the diet took up the form of the coronation oath, or diploma, which Joseph would accept at his crowning on 9 December. In a series of last-minute conferences between Kinsky, Stratmann and the deputies, an acceptable document was prepared. Then at the last minute the diet produced a new form for the diploma just two days before the ceremony.[6] Since no agreement could be reached in the time remaining, Leopold ordered the coronation to proceed on schedule. The ninety-five-year-old George Széchenyi, primate of Hungary, placed the ancient crown on Joseph's head. The act was done, even though the diet continued to argue for over a month with the Imperial ministers about the form of the diploma and the coronation oath.

The crown had stolen a march on the diet, preparing the way for changes which could only end in strengthening royal absolutism. While Hungary remained a kingdom with a constitution setting forth a condominium between the estates and the crown, the crown had succeeded in placing itself above the constitution.[7] The fundamental law remained in part what it had been, a charter of the privileges and rights of the nobles who constituted the political nation, but these rights were now restricted and subordinated to the sovereignty of a hereditary king whose own authority was constitutionally limited only with respect to the processes he would use to govern his kingdom.

The situation created at Pressburg in 1687 did not completely satisfy the wishes of Kinsky and Stratmann; Leopold himself appeared content. Certainly the decisions did not represent the free will and consent of the Magyar aristocracy. They did, however, represent the current power relationship between the two adversaries at a moment when the crown held all the important instruments of coercion.[8]

The year 1688 marked the climax of Austrian power in the east. Never again would Leopold have the opportunity to concentrate all his resources against the Turks. With Buda cleared of the enemy and Transylvania subdued by military occupation, the goal for the next campaign was clear: Belgrade, the fortress key to the whole central Danube basin, the last great Turkish stronghold north-west of the Balkan mountains.

While the war council, the privy conference and the generals all agreed on the objective, controversy about who would lead the army became even more heated than it had been before. Max Emmanuel of Bavaria was in a position to demand a greater role in return for renewing his alliance treaty with Leopold which expired in January 1688. The marquis de Villars encouraged the elector to consider an alliance with France. Villars knew his man and dazzled Max Emmanuel with dynastic possibilities that even a prince less bloated with self-esteem might well have found irresistible. Villars suggested that with French assistance Max Emmanuel's son might one day become Emperor. Beyond that there was Spain itself, for the elector had married the only surviving child of Leopold's marriage with Margareta. If Max Emmanuel broke with the Habsburgs now, to what heights might his illustrious house not ascend?

Encouraged by Villars, Max Emmanuel demanded from Leopold the supreme command of the whole Imperial army in Hungary as the price for renewing his treaty. Once again the dispute between Max Emmanuel and Charles of Lorraine spread from the war council into the diplomatic corps and the Imperial family. When Max Emmanuel refused categorically to serve in any way subordinate to Lorraine, Leopold faced either dismissing his best commander and brother-in-law or the defection of his son-in-law and one of his principal allies.

Events rather than decisive action solved the problem when at the end of May Charles of Lorraine fell seriously ill. It was clear he could not lead the campaign. Leopold still hesitated to trust the supreme command to Max Emmanuel. Not until the beginning of July did Stratmann deliver to the elector his appointment to the post. By that time the chance for an easy victory at Belgrade was long past. Jegen Osman Pasha, one of the leaders of the mutiny against Mehmet IV, had established himself as commander in Belgrade and been confirmed by the new sultan. By the time the Imperial army was set in motion he had restored the great fortress and prepared it for a siege.

When Max Emmanuel began his march on Belgrade at the end of July he discovered that Ludwig Wilhelm of Baden, leading a detachment from Slavonia with the boat bridge essential to the planned attack, would not reach the Sava in time. Marco d'Aviano, again following the troops to battle, persuaded Max Emmanuel to push ahead in spite of the delay. Crossing the Danube at Semlin with great difficulty, the Imperial army appeared before Belgrade in mid-August. Despite a serious shortage of artillery, Max Emmanuel opened the siege at once. In strong contrast to the slower, more cautious and methodical manner of Lorraine, the elector conducted the siege with a bravura which took a bloody toll even among the general officers. On 6 September a general assault brought the attackers within the city, and the Turkish garrison quickly capitulated. Almost at once Imperial detachments moved far down the Danube, to the Iron Gates and westwards into Bosnia and Serbia, meeting little resistance and stopping only because their own supply lines would not let them go farther. Montecuccoli's dictum that control of the Danube meant control of Hungary was proved true. Leopold's army had won firm command of the whole Danubian plain.

Vienna's jubilation at this victory was muted, for the French had again struck at the Empire. Within a week of his triumph Max Emmanuel was speeding back to Vienna to consult with the war council. The crusade against Islam was over, but another great struggle with France was beginning, a conflict that was to dominate the rest of the reign. While the attention of the court and the military was now once again divided between the Rhine and the Danube, Leopold could use the security won by the capture of Belgrade to pursue the work of restructuring the Hungarian administration.

After Joseph's coronation Leopold instituted a new commission on Hungary led by prince Ferdinand Dietrichstein, charging it to draw up detailed proposals for the royal administration. There were no Magyars among its members, though the commission did seek advice from the palatine, the aged primate, and curiously enough from Caraffa, who had been removed from Hungary by the expedient of promoting him to the war commissariat. Beginning in July 1688 the commission worked steadily for nearly a near, presenting a preliminary report on the government of Hungary to Leopold in the summer of 1689.

Under the main commission Leopold set up several sub-commissions one of which was to deal with the *neoaquisten*, the newly-won lands in Hungary. This was a task of enormous difficulty, for it involved among other things restitution of lands to earlier proprietors' heirs, if such could be found after the long lapse of time. Simply finding, examining and verifying ancient records on lands that made up perhaps two-thirds of the kingdom would be a hard enough task in a settled society untroubled by the wars that had raged in Hungary. The complications caused by large movements of population throughout the region during the Turkish occupation, added to the physical destruction during the last phase of the war, made it virtually impossible. Yet order had to come from some source, and the Hungarian diet freely admitted that the old organs of government in Hungary were hopelessly inadequate to deal with the sudden increase in the territory of the kingdom.

As a rule the commissioners in both the main body and its sub-groups sought to preserve wherever possible existing legal and fiscal structures at the local level. Replacing local courts throughout the kingdom was clearly a physical impossibility. Rather than attempt that, the commissioners recommended introducing more uniform procedures and eliminating some of the medieval restrictions on access to justice, such as feudal laws forbidding vassals or subjects to make accusations against their lords. A criminal code similar to the one used in Lower Austria was to be substituted for the often contradictory body of traditional Hungarian law. The independent jurisdiction of the landowning nobility, the towns and the comitats was to be broken by establishing intermediate appellate courts in Kaschau, Buda and Zagreb, the Imperial court serving in all cases as the final court of appeal.

When it came to dealing with the tangled religious affairs of Hungary, the commission had to tone down considerably a report prepared for it by cardinal Kolonitsch, an energetic son of the counter-reformation, intolerant of heresy in any form, more often enthusiastic than reflective in his urge to homogenize belief among Leopold's subjects. While Kolonitsch would have had the crown sponsor salutary reforms of the Catholic clergy, he advocated the narrowest possible interpretation of Leopold's guarantee of religious liberty to other confessions. The Jews he wished to drive out of the kingdom. On all counts the commissioners recommended a more generous view. The military provisions of the recommendations were reasonable, indeed positively enlightened, given the character of warfare in eastern Europe and the passions stirred by events there since 1664. Some attempt was made to create a degree of local participation in decisions concerning quartering. The militia, however, was to be abolished; the commission saw no need to leave a large part of a volatile population armed to the teeth. Instead it proposed a standing army of 24,000 men, half Magyar, half German, but the whole organized and disciplined on the Austrian model.

Throughout the report the commission reflected the influence of the cameralist writers, Johann Joachim Becher, Philipp Wilhelm von Hörnigk and Wilhelm von Schröder.[9] The commissioners were sensitive to the intimate relationship between political authority and economic realities. This showed particularly in recommendations for reconstructing the economy of the *neoaquisten* by systematic repopulation and restoration of the depleted capital of the region. Colonists should be welcomed from all quarters, induced to settle by the promise of a given number of years free of both taxes and the *Robot*.

Taken all together the report represented the views of men like Kinsky, Stratmann and Kolonitsch, who saw in the integrating and centralizing power of the monarchy the promise of a better future for human society. In one sense, however, the report did not depart from tradition. In a section dealing with recolonization the commissioners could not resist indulging in an outburst of anti-Magyar prejudice. Germans, they argued, should be given preferential treatment in the new lands so that 'the kingdom, or at least a large part of it, will gradually be germanized, and Hungarian blood, with its tendency to unrest and revolution, will be tempered by German, and turned thereby to a steadfast loyalty and love of their natural hereditary king'.[10]

The tactless passage was perhaps the natural expression of the feelings of the Viennese commissioners, men who had spent much of their public lives dealing with the problem of Magyar insurrection and its attendant violent disruption of civil order. At the same time it was a blunder which led the Magyars to brand the whole programme and any detailed proposal in it as an attempt to destroy their national identity.

When it was made public the report drew the expected uproar from the Magyar magnates, led by their palatine. The 'germanizing' intent of the document rallied the Magyar nobles who feared even more other provisions concerning their legal relationship with the peasantry, restricting the *Robot* to three days, granting the peasantry greater proprietary and judicial rights, and, most obnoxious of all, subjecting nobles to taxation for their demesne lands.[11]

The Hungarian diet, assembled in Pressburg in October 1689, issued a strong protest against unconstitutional 'innovations' in the kingdom. Leopold himself was in Augsburg at the Imperial Diet when the commissioners presented the final report. There he discussed the report, and Magyar opposition, with Kinsky and some of the commissioners, deciding that it would be folly to try to enact all the recommendations at once. He was willing to take up only three of these provisions quickly and vigorously: administrative reform of the Hungarian chancellery and judicial system, the creation of new Catholic parishes, and the restitution or sale of land in the *neoaquisten*.

Though the work begun the next year bore some fruit, particularly improving the efficiency of the Hungarian chancellery, progress was painfully slow in other areas. The restitution of land in the *neoaquisten* to heirs of former owners proved a hopeless task, and the effort fell through almost at once. Some nobles who could move peasants from their own estates simply appropriated territory. The palatine began quite independently making land grants on his own authority. Since Leopold did not possess in Hungary an administrative apparatus capable of introducing some system into the muddle, he had little choice but to sell the remaining unclaimed land outright or to grant it as rewards to deserving commanders.

Colonization got underway quickly with settlers coming from the Sudetenland, Silesia and Moravia in such numbers that landowners in those regions complained about their loss of manpower. In 1699 Leopold had to declare a prohibition on emigration from Silesia and Moravia to protect the productivity of estates there. The largest flow of German settlers into Hungary did not come, however, until after the defeat of another Hungarian rebellion, in the early years of the reign of Charles VI (1711–40).

Leopold moved cautiously on the sensitive question of taxing the Magyar nobility. Not until 1697 did the court chamber induce him to appoint a deputation to negotiate with the magnates on the issue of regular contributions. In the face of the magnates' utterly intractable opposition, Leopold then tried to win the support of the more numerous lesser nobles by decreeing a contribution from the magnates of 250,000 Gulden, while exempting the lower nobles. Even this politically shrewd manœuvre failed to break through the resistance of the nobility as a caste. Only in 1715 did the diet make the regular contribution legal in Hungary, and even then this was done only by excusing the magnates from sharing the burden. In seeking to tax the nobility Leopold had struck, perhaps unwittingly, at the very core of aristocratic privilege, and the nobles defended themselves without respect to their standing within the aristocratic order. This much 'liberty' at least survived the onslaught of royal absolutism.

XIV

Two-Front War

In September 1688 the Viennese court had scarcely begun celebrating Max Emmanuel's victory at Belgrade when it learned that Louis XIV had sent the French army across the Rhine to invade the Palatinate. The Imperial circles immediately recalled their contingents from Hungary. Leopold's twenty-year armistice with France had run but a fifth of its course.

Louis' decision to invade the Empire was in part an act of overconfidence, but also in part one of desperation.[1] French influence in Europe had waned dramatically since 1683, particularly in Germany. The days of the League of the Rhine were over. Louis had tried several times to transform the Regensburg armistice into a permanent peace, threatening and cajoling the German princes while advancing his own dynastic claims to the Palatinate. Each of his attempts to terrorize the Empire merely weakened French influence in Germany and strengthened Leopold's hold over his German vassals. By 1688 only the Fürstenberg elector of Cologne remained firmly allied to France. When the old archbishop Maximilian Heinrich died on 3 June, it was crucial for France that another member of the same clan be elected to succeed him.

Emperor Leopold countered by supporting the candidacy of Joseph Clemens of Bavaria, Max Emmanuel's brother. The canonical election in Cologne produced a disputed result, neither candidate winning a clear majority in the cathedral chapter. Wilhelm von Fürstenberg seized the government, but when the election was examined in Rome, Innocent XI declared Joseph Clemens to have won. If the papal decree stood, France would lose its last firm ally among the German princes.

Events in the Palatinate further up the Rhine proved equally disturbing to Versailles. The old line of palatine electors died out in 1685. Leopold then granted the electorate to his father-in-law, Philipp Wilhelm of Pfalz-Neuburg, who, though a Catholic succeeding a Calvinist prince, clearly had the strongest legal and dynastic claim to the title. Louis XIV raised claims to parts of the Palatinate in the name of his brother, Philippe d'Orléans, who had married Elisabeth Charlotte, sister of the last elector of the old line. This claim, to be sure, did not extend to the sovereignty over the electorate itself, but to those parts which his lawyers persuaded him could legally pass through the female line. His purpose clearly was to use the claim as a counter in diplomatic bargaining with Vienna, which he hoped would finally produce confirmation of his hold on the reunions and Strasbourg; but Leopold refused to move beyond the agreement he had made at Regensburg in 1684.

It was not a propitious moment for France. Most of Louis' allies had left him. His interference in the Cologne election had cost him much of his influence in Rome, where Innocent XI remained disappointed at Louis' consistent refusal to join the crusade against Islam. The edict of Fontainebleau in 1685 lost him the support of his erstwhile Protestant allies Brandenburg and Sweden. In England, where the succession of James II had been seen from Versailles as a hopeful event, religious unrest had grown so great that Louis could scarcely count on strong support from that quarter. Even the Dutch, whom Louis had tried to neutralize with kindness at Nijmegen, inclined increasingly to listen to their Stathouder's militant advice. Prince William of Orange had already assured himself of the support of Brandenburg, Brunswick and Hesse for his plan to invade England, claim the throne for his wife Mary, and bring the English into a coalition against France. The League of Augsburg, as it came to be called from the city where William and the elector of Brandenburg cemented their friendship in 1686, had become a real force in European politics. William now sought to bring the Habsburg Emperor into the partnership.

Leopold remained as anxious as ever to check France, but the purpose of the League of Augsburg went beyond that, aiming at the seizure of the English crown. Leopold had grave objections to helping a Protestant unseat a Catholic monarch; to do so would affront his family's traditional attachment to Rome. Even more perplexing were the military considerations. Joining the coalition against France would almost certainly involve Austria in a new war on the Rhine. Once the issue had been raised, Leopold faced an old and familiar dilemma as his court divided once again between easterners and westerners.

Leopold was then forty-eight, nearly the age at which his father had died. The robustness of his youth was now long behind him, though he remained healthy and vigorous enough to continue hunting in one or another of the royal preserves around Vienna. Constant exercise on horseback kept his figure lithe and trim, but his face showed the marks of his years, the lines that etched his features exaggerating his protruding lower lip. The equable temperament and calm demeanour so admired in his youth had settled into a phlegmatic imperturbability that often perplexed those who had audience with him. The stiff ritual of court ceremonial had become so habitual that he no longer felt it annoying. He seldom showed much vivacity, not even at the court entertainments which so delighted him and for which he still busily composed music.

There was around Leopold little of the vitality and often brutal gaiety that surrounded Louis XIV at his new court at Versailles. By contrast, the conduct of the Emperor's entourage appeared to visitors more ecclesiastical than secular, as indeed in many ways it was. During the successful campaigns in Hungary a week seldom passed without a solemn *Te Deum* to vary the routine of masses, saints' days and processions. The sombre atmosphere of the Hofburg seemed out of keeping with the brilliant triumphs of his armies, yet this mode of life suited Leopold, and the court followed his lead.

The shadow that hung so long over the dynastic succession had lifted; there was a large and thriving family. Leopold's eldest child, Maria Antonia, had married the elector of Bavaria but still resided in Vienna while her husband went to the wars. Joseph, now king of Hungary, was lusty and vigorous at eleven. A second son, archduke Charles, seemed also to have passed through the worst dangers of infancy. Four daughters completed the family: Maria Elisabeth, Maria Anna, Maria Theresia, and a new baby, Maria Josepha. Leopold could look forward with confidence to the family's dynastic future.

Politically the future seemed equally promising. Probably not since the reign of Maximilian I had a Holy Roman Emperor received such general support from the German princes, Catholic and Protestant alike. Hungary had been reconquered from the Turks, nearly doubling the territory of Leopold's hereditary states. In spite of an empty treasury, Austrian military power had increased dramatically.

As Austria's strength increased, so did prince William's eagerness to harness that power to the League of Augsburg. In May 1688 he sent the Hessian treasurer, Johann von Görz, to Vienna to draw Leopold into the alliance. After a cordial audience with Leopold, Görz joined the indefatigable francophobe Borgomanero in secret negotiations with chancellor Stratmann. Görz explained William's claims to England, conveying a firm promise that if he won the throne he would permit no persecution of Catholics. In return for Leopold's adherence to an alliance, he offered a guarantee that any defiance of Leopold's claim to the Spanish succession would be a *casus foederis*, a promise reinforced by the States General's declaration of 20 July supporting William's stand. This appeal to the dynastic interest had its desired effect. On 4 September Leopold declared his intention to abide by his former treaties with the Dutch and his willingness to make a new defensive alliance.

News of Leopold's decision reached Versailles almost simultaneously with reports of the fall of Belgrade. Both events disturbed Louis, who now inclined to take Louvois' advice to deliver a 'healthy scare' to bring the German princes to reason and distract Leopold from the Turks. On 24 September Louis announced that before he could agree to a permanent peace based on the Regensburg armistice he would have to take back Philippsburg and be compensated in cash for his claims to the Palatinate. At the same moment his troops moved into the Palatinate to 'secure his rights', while other detachments attacked Mainz and Trier. The main French army under Vauban and Boufflers, with the dauphin nominally in command, attacked Philippsburg which capitulated at the end of October. By that time French forces had occupied the whole of the Rhenish electorates and the Palatinate, leaving only the cities of Cologne and Coblenz holding out against them.

These attacks were calculated to make the Imperial Diet come to its senses and force Leopold to accept Louis' terms for a peace treaty. The effect was quite different. French overconfidence had the immediate result of bringing virtually all the German princes together in the Concert of Magdeburg, which through Brandenburg and Hesse was linked with the League of Augsburg. German units returned swiftly from Hungary, followed shortly by Leopold's own Austrian and Hungarian detachments. By mid-winter the French had to withdraw to the Rhine.

By November Leopold felt secure enough in the east to accept the views of Borgomanero and the westerners at court, indicating his willingness to conclude peace with the Porte and send the whole of his now well-seasoned army west, leaving only nominal garrisons to protect Hungary. This near-decision brought the easterners and westerners into a noisy battle over priorities. Led by cardinal Buonvisi and d'Aviano, the easterners appealed to Leopold's sense of honour and his solemn promises to the Holy League, crying shame at the very thought of a separate peace with the Turks. On the other hand the Spanish ambassador, upheld now by the German princes and Görz, demanded that Leopold fulfil his equally solemn obligations as Emperor and come to the rescue of the Reich.

Charles of Lorraine argued strongly against attempting to fight on two fronts at once. Most of the privy conference members agreed with him, though not necessarily with his conclusion that the eastern war should take precedence. Innocent XI, still dedicated heart and soul to his crusade, supported Buonvisi but warned that his purse was empty.

With his court divided, Leopold had to make his own decision. He poured out his fears, his concern for the future, as he had often done, in a letter to Marco d'Aviano on 23 January 1689.[2] By that time he was already convinced that he would have to accept the challenge and fight on both fronts, whatever the cost. Peace with France was unthinkable now, however much his allies in the Holy League might want him to concede. The king of France, at least, could still move Leopold to anger. To the easterners at court he said that he could not possibly make peace with France because his cousin did not respect 'pacts, alliances or oaths'.

There was yet another factor at work inclining Leopold for once in his life to take the more dangerous course. The Imperial succession had still not been guaranteed to Joseph. From the dynastic viewpoint it was imperative that Leopold do nothing to discredit the house of Austria in the eyes of those princes who would elect the next king of Rome. Given the mood of Germany, if that king were to be Joseph then Leopold would have to fight France.

Leopold's decision to cast his lot with the Augsburg coalition against France, while at the same time continuing the war in the east if he must, represented his own firm resolve against the opposition of many of his closest friends and the hesitation of his advisers. In this decision the Empire stood behind him with uncharacteristic unanimity. For the moment he had little need to fear French influence in Germany. Indeed, with the Dutch and, after William's victory in February 1689, the English at his side, a way opened to achieve the main objectives of his dynastic policy: confirmation of Habsburg succession in Spain and in the Empire.

Alliance with Protestant William III to achieve these goals still unsettled Leopold's conscience, a difficulty made all the greater when James Stuart called on the Catholic princes of Europe to oppose the Calvinist 'usurper' in England. Marco d'Aviano, Leopold's most intimate spiritual adviser and an open partisan of the easterners, was opposed to the alliance from the beginning because it would dilute the forces available for the crusade in the east. To get more impartial advice Leopold put the problem to a group of theologians, six or seven Catholic scholars resident in Vienna.[3] Four of them spoke in favour of the alliance with William. Reassured by a majority of the consultants, Leopold took the final step on 3 April 1689, declaring war against France in the name of the Holy Roman Empire. A few days later he wrote the exiled James II that he could not heed his appeal, for no one had done greater damage to the Catholic faith than the Stuart's ally and protector Louis XIV.

During the winter of 1688–89 Leopold tried to disentangle himself from the Turkish war so that he could concentrate on the coming struggle with France. The Ottoman regime, however, was recovering rapidly from the internal troubles of the past years, even finding new strength in the reforms that followed in the wake of the mutiny. The French invasion of the Empire encouraged the *divan* to stiffen their terms for peace and make demands which Leopold could not conceivably accept. Negotiations in Vienna during February and March led nowhere.

Stratmann then negotiated an alliance with the Dutch, signed on 12 May 1689, a pact which went far beyond earlier agreements. It was an explicitly offensive alliance aimed at driving the French back to their frontiers of 1648 and 1659, restoring the duchy of Lorraine and all the reunions to their former sovereignties. For Leopold the most important parts of the treaty were secret articles signed only by Jakob Hop, the pensionary of Amsterdam, currently William's envoy in Vienna, and by chancellor Stratmann. These pledged England and the States General to assist Leopold in securing the Spanish succession should Charles II die without an heir, and to use their influence to secure Joseph's election as king of Rome.

While the coalition took form the French acted swiftly to keep the initiative in the field. Though pushed back to the Rhine by the swift dispatch of troops from Hungary in 1688, they still remained well within Imperial territory. In 1689 they undertook a deliberate, systematic campaign to waste and destroy the Palatinate, to make it useless to their enemies. In January they devastated Heilbronn and Heidelberg. In May the French dismantled the defence works of Speyer, Worms and Oppenheim, making the countryside around these cities as unproductive as their technology and ingenuity could contrive.

Charles of Lorraine, appointed supreme commander in the Empire, could not overcome the bickering among the other commanders swiftly enough to prevent the French from carrying out their programme of devastation. From July, when Lorraine finally mustered his army, until early September the Imperial army occupied itself almost entirely with the siege of Mainz. Once he dislodged the French from Mainz, Lorraine sent help to the Brandenburgers who had long been besieging Bonn, the residence city of the archbishop elector of Cologne. Bonn finally fell on 9 October. Both sieges were hailed as great victories, but in fact all Lorraine had managed to do was recover two bridgeheads on the Rhine.

He did hold the French behind the great river, but only after they had completed their destruction of one of the richest regions of Germany.

While the success of Imperial arms was far from dramatic, Leopold seized what seemed to him a propitious moment to secure his son's election as king of the Romans. Although Joseph was only twelve, Leopold felt compelled to move quickly to take advantage of the favourable political climate in Germany. Accordingly he summoned the electoral college to assemble at Augsburg, where he arrived with the Imperial family on the last day of August 1689. With his ministers he began the long, slow negotiations that preceded every such election. Not until 12 December were matters far enough advanced for Leopold to make his formal proposal to the electors. No one objected to Joseph's candidacy. What delayed the proceedings was Leopold's desire to get an electoral capitulation quite different from the humiliating and restrictive document he had accepted in 1658. All the restrictions concerning the future Emperor's relations with France were dropped as a matter of course, as were articles restraining his military role in Germany. Objections to Joseph's youth were circumvented by a provision which allowed that he could, if need arose, take the reins of Imperial government at the age of sixteen.

On 19 January 1690 the Empress Eleanora was solemnly crowned, a formality that had long been neglected. On 24 January the electors declared Joseph to be their choice as king. Two days later he was ceremoniously crowned and anointed in the Ulrichskirche in Augsburg. On 4 March the new king of Rome made the traditional ceremonial entry into Vienna, greeted by a city richly adorned for the occasion. Leopold was fully satisfied, and had good reason to write d'Aviano that 'things went wonderfully well in Augsburg'.[4]

Leopold had chosen his time well, for the coalition quickly ran into difficulties. The Viennese war council had assumed in its strategic planning that the English would participate in the continental war, sending land forces to operate with the Dutch and Imperial forces on the Rhine. William III, however, had other troubles closer to home. Ireland rose in rebellion under the deposed James II, who brought officers and arms from France. The threat of civil war combined with English reluctance to fight on the continent forced William to rely for the time being on English sea power against France. The Irish rebellion also provided a new source of friction among the allies, for Leopold felt compelled to speak out on behalf of William's Catholic subjects[5] just as the Dutch and English had interceded for Leopold's Protestant subjects during the Hungarian uprisings.

The hardest blow for Leopold fell on 18 April 1690 when duke Charles of Lorraine died suddenly in Wels as he was on his way from Innsbruck to Vienna. Leopold had come to rely heavily on his brother-in-law for military advice, in the process often ignoring or bypassing the war council president, margrave Hermann of Baden. Competition for Lorraine's command unavoidably meant trouble for Leopold. While Lorraine had contributed few men of his own to the Imperial forces, his reputation as the hero of Vienna gave him an undisputed right to command. Now the principal German allies, particularly Bavaria, Brandenburg and Saxony, demanded the honour of supreme command for themselves, while contrarily insisting that they have completely independent command over their own forces in the campaign. Leopold finally chose Max Emmanuel of Bavaria, but it was August before all had been settled and the new commander could take the field.

Militarily the year 1690 belonged to France, though the coalition against her was strengthened by the accession of Spain in July and of Savoy in October. Louis moved his forces into the Southern Netherlands before German units could muster to meet them, defeating a Spanish–Dutch force at Fleurus on 1 July. On 10 July the French navy defeated an Anglo–Dutch fleet off the coast of Sussex at Beachy Head. Even though William III won Ireland at the Boyne the next day, his victory over James II in Ireland had little immediate effect on the continental situation. When Max Emmanuel finally concentrated the Imperial army, he marched it about in utter confusion, heading first this way then that as ever more urgent demands for help came from different directions. Both the French and the Imperial armies went into winter quarters without once having engaged each other.

What had seemed like a ray of hope early in the year, the defection of duke Victor Amadeus II of Savoy from his alliance with France, turned out in the end to be another unhappy interlude.[6] Leopold sent one of his youngest generals, prince Eugene of Savoy, Victor Amadeus's cousin, with a small Imperial detachment to join the Spanish and Savoyard forces in Italy. The war council hoped in this way to create a second front which would draw French forces south from the Rhine. Unluckily Eugene's small contingent could not offset the incompetence of the Spanish forces and the inexperience of the Savoyards. The French quickly mastered most of Piedmont and began treating Savoy as they had the Palatinate the year before.

The year was equally disastrous for Leopold in the east, where the Turks retook Belgrade and threatened Transylvania. The Maritime Powers had little patience with the problems of Hungary, just as the

Holy League had no interest in Leopold's struggle with France. England and the Dutch Republic both wanted free commerce in the Levant, preferably to the exclusion of French competition, but in any case with as little interference from others as possible. In March 1691 William III and the States General went so far as to suggest that Leopold should renounce his sovereignty over Transylvania in order to induce the Turks to grant an armistice. Leopold pointed out rather sharply to his allies that it was after all France who encouraged the Turks to continue the war and to demand unacceptable terms for peace.

The campaigns of 1691 were little more encouraging, though Ludwig Wilhelm of Baden's victory at Slankamen kept the Turks out of Hungary for another year. On the Upper Rhine the Imperial generals spent more time fighting among themselves than fighting the French, who held firmly to their gains in the Empire. After a few weeks of futile movements the Imperial army was stopped in its tracks by an epidemic that produced complete inactivity on both sides. Prince Eugene won modest gains in Italy, but neither he nor the allies could engage the French or lure them from their strong positions in Piedmont.[7]

The strain of conducting large-scale war on two fronts at once proved as difficult to manage as Charles of Lorraine had predicted in 1689. An attempt to get a reasonable peace or at least an armistice with the Turks based on *uti possedetis*, an effort firmly seconded in Constantinople by the Maritime Powers, came to nothing when the French successfully encouraged the *divan*'s resolve to go on fighting. Leopold despondently began to contemplate a separate peace with France.

In the midst of this seemingly catastrophic situation, France scored a diplomatic victory in Germany that threatened to destroy the unanimity of the Reich. A French diplomatic offensive accompanied by the usual generous subsidies succeeded in detaching duke Ernst August of Hanover from the coalition. Hanover's defection not only cost the Imperial army a large and valuable contingent of troops, but raised the possibility that Ernst August would attract a party of German princes around him which would revive that perennial 'third force' in German politics: a coalition of princes independent of both the French and the Emperor, but by their very neutrality weakening the Empire's capacity to wage war.[8]

Duke Ernst August, ambitious and clever as well, was the key to the situation, and Leopold understood how to manipulate him. The Hanoverian duke coveted the electoral dignity for his house, and only the Emperor could grant it. Even though the duke had deserted the coalition against France, it remained possible that he could be won for the Turkish war, and so it proved to be. The privy conference was cool towards a bargain that would elevate Hanover to the electoral college, fearing that this would offend Brandenburg and Saxony, but Leopold himself favoured the move in spite of the opposition of the other electors. The Emperor acted with unusual speed, finally bringing a majority of his own conference around to his view.

A decree conferring the electoral dignity on Ernst August and his successors was published in April 1692. Hanoverian troops marched to Hungary and the court chamber profited from the 750,000 Gulden Ernst August paid for his new title. Even though the college of electors grudgingly accepted Leopold's new protégé, the move had been politically dangerous, attacked by some as a threat to the Imperial constitution, and feared by the Catholic princes as a threat to the political balance among the confessions. For once Leopold did not seriously trouble his conscience over the confessional problem and held firm to his decision; it paid off handsomely. The formal installation of the new elector took place on 19 December 1692. Within weeks Hanover rejoined the coalition against France.

While Leopold dealt with the defection of Hanover, a second of his German allies, Saxony, threatened to desert. The old elector Johann Georg III, in spite of all his touchy Protestant doubts about the Habsburgs, had been a faithful ally until his death in September 1691. His successor, Johann Georg IV, believed himself the only person fit for the supreme command, and demanded the post as his price for continued support of the coalition. His chief military adviser, field marshal Hans Adam von Schöning, who was secretly taking a pension from the French, encouraged his master in his obstinacy. The privy conference, well aware of Schöning's tie with France, dealt with the problem dramatically. On 4 July 1692 Schöning was seized by Imperial officials at Teplitz where he had gone to take a water cure.[9] He was quickly hustled off to the fortress at Brünn (Brno) and imprisoned. This summary action horrified the elector, but as proof of Schöning's treachery was very clear, he won no sympathy elsewhere. Even more than the freedom of his field marshal, Johann Georg IV coveted a noble title for his mistress, and for this he discovered that he needed Leopold as much as Leopold needed him. The treaty was signed on 2 March 1693, and Saxony again marched with the Imperial columns.

Such were the means Leopold had to use to hold together the fragile ties that bound his German 'vassals' to their Emperor. These troubles, a source of constant complaint by the Maritime Powers, were in part the legacy of the Thirty Years War which had left the German princes sovereign in their states. French attacks against Germany had, however, overcome to some degree the selfish independence of many of the princes. The real core of Leopold's difficulties in 1692 and 1693 was the issue of leadership and command. No one appointed after Lorraine's death had been able to win the confidence of the other generals, many of whom were sovereign princes leading their own armies into battle.

Max Emmanuel of Bavaria was a splendid warrior, but he lacked duke Charles' skill in handling subordinates and had no head whatever for strategy. He was out of the running in 1693 in any case, having been appointed governor of the Spanish Netherlands. His first successor, count Caraffa, the scourge of Hungary, proved equally inept. Among the able young commanders, Ludwig Wilhelm of Baden was needed in Hungary, and Guido Starhemberg was not only pinned down with the Imperial garrison in Trier but lacked the necessary princely rank. Prince Eugene, who stood out among the Imperial generals for his good judgment and his ability to handle troops, was employed in Savoy.

The Maritime Powers and some of the German allies pressed Leopold to appoint Ludwig Wilhelm of Baden, whose brilliant victories over the Turks had won him a heroic reputation. Leopold was reluctant to transfer the most successful of all his generals away from the scene of his triumphs, but finally agreed to name him commander in the Empire in February 1693. Ludwig Wilhelm, in Hungary the master of brilliant tactics and impulsive manœuvre, became in Germany a cautious administrator-commander, taking the most prudent posture in the field and concentrating his energies on building up a standing German force drawn from the Imperial circles and the Rhenish states. Over four years he built such an army, but he conducted no campaigns to match those that had won him fame in the east. He held the French west of the Rhine, a substantial success by the military standards of the day, but it was not enough to win a war.

Louis XIV had begun the war in 1689 striking out north and east in several directions, but after his first surprise attacks he found himself brought to a standstill. His expensive armies held more or less stable positions in the Netherlands, along the middle and upper Rhine and in Italy. In May 1694 he thrust in the opposite direction, invading Catalonia. Spain immediately demanded aid from its allies. Leopold's military power, an imposing force when it could be concentrated on a single front, was already divided among three: Hungary, the Rhine and north Italy. Louis' invasion of Spain added a possible and distant fourth. Every political and dynastic consideration urged a prompt Austrian response to this new challenge, but the limits of Leopold's power had been reached, perhaps exceeded.

XV

The Treaties of Ryswick
and Carlowitz

As Imperial commitments to the war expanded, Leopold once again faced the crisis with new ministers. Hermann of Baden was replaced by the ageing defender of Vienna, Ernst Rüdiger von Starhemberg, as president of the war council in January 1692. While no one doubted his merits or personal worth, Starhemberg was a man of action, not an administrator. In the privy conference his ignorance of diplomatic affairs quickly became evident and his voice carried little weight in policy discussions.

In October 1693 chancellor Stratmann died. In February 1694 Leopold finally appointed as his successor count Julius Bucellini, who had served many years as vice-chancellor. Bucellini knew the routine of the chancellery, but possessed none of the brilliance that distinguished his predecessors: the chancellery continued to function more or less as it had done in the past, but the new chancellor could never become a first minister. When the Imperial vice-chancellor count Königsegg died in 1694 Leopold lost the last strong personality in the conference except for the Bohemian chancellor count Kinsky, who now took undisputed leadership of the regime.

From 1694 until 1703, when events forced Leopold against his will to appoint several of his son and successor's adherents to the highest offices, the privy conference was made up largely of ageing men rewarded for long service in subordinate positions. With the notable exception of Kinsky, who was himself in failing health, it was not a ministry of great talent. Most of the men who came and went in these years were seasoned courtiers and old associates of the Emperor, like the grand chamberlain prince Dietrichstein, men who shared Leopold's conservative outlook and his excessive prudence. They had to face momentous challenges to the house of Austria; their response was for the most part halting, weak, irresolute, confused. From these years more than any other period in a long reign comes the familiar view of the Viennese court as a lazy, slow, indecisive and generally incompetent regime, a picture made vivid in diplomatic reports from Vienna and by the complaints of ambitious younger men gathering around the heir to the throne.

The declining quality of leadership manifested itself in a number of ways. Debates in the conference grew longer, diplomatic moves slowed perceptibly. Even more frustrating to the younger men, especially the army officers, was a growing muddle in military organization and supply. There were vigorous complaints, but Leopold merely listened with his accustomed calm and did nothing.

It is said that in modern bureaucratic regimes 'the squeaky wheel gets the grease'. Leopold's regime offers an interesting exception to the rule. The Emperor's personality made him virtually impervious to the grumblers, possibly because over the years he had become used to hearing the same insistent complaints from all sides. A good illustration may be seen in Leopold's relations with the most brilliant of his younger commanders, Eugene of Savoy, a man destined to become known as the 'Atlas of the Austrian monarchy'.

Eugene, brought up in France, had come to Vienna to fight in the battle for that city in 1683. With strong support from his Savoyard cousin and the patronage of Borgomanero, he won favour at court and rose rapidly in the officers' corps. He combined the best qualities of Leopold's greatest generals: the political instincts of Charles of Lorraine, the personal bravery and magnetism of Starhemberg, the tactical brilliance of Ludwig Wilhelm of Baden. He had also developed to a high pitch the art of being a squeaky wheel.

In 1693 court intrigues delayed planning for the campaign Eugene was to direct in Italy. As time passed Eugene grew fretful, making a nuisance of himself in antechambers, demanding swift decisions from the war council, and sending his colleagues bitter accounts of the lassitude and timidity he encountered everywhere in Vienna. His temperamental criticism of the whole system did not even spare the Emperor's august person. 'The business of the Empire somewhat disquieted His Imperial Majesty today', he wrote to Ludwig Wilhelm in June 1693, 'but, thank God, there was a religious procession and everything was forgotten'.[1]

To Eugene's intense frustration, Leopold responded to his criticism with calm praise for Eugene's brilliant work and promoted him to field-marshal. The Emperor wrote a few notes, gave vague promises, as he had done to all importunate commanders, and did nothing more. Since neither he nor the war council could find the necessary money and reinforcements for the Italian campaign, much less get them where they were wanted, Leopold could do little but express his gratitude for Eugene's services, an attitude that did not waver even when Eugene's cousin Victor Amadeus II turned coat again and deserted the coalition.

*

The war proved as hard on France as it was on the coalition. Louis XIV found himself still master of what he had seized at the beginning of the war, but he was now held firmly along a static front that cost as much to maintain as a victorious campaign: more, in fact, for there were no new territories to plunder. The surplus money and the credit stored up by Colbert had disappeared; the Anglo–Dutch blockade of French ports added to the rising cost of the military machine and accelerated the growing inflation.[2] Other problems, particularly the question of the Spanish succession, loomed in the future. Louis needed to make peace. Detaching Savoy from the coalition improved his chances. His problem now was to find another weak link that would allow him to detach one of the senior partners from the alliance.

Secret diplomacy between opposed belligerents was as much a part of warfare in the period as was siegecraft. Most monarchs indulged in confidential, often personal, conversations with agents of the enemy, discussions frequently unknown even to the most important official advisers of the crown. Leopold was no exception to the rule, and even seemed to enjoy his own little secrets, along with the excitement and intrigue that accompanied them.[3] Leopold's confessor, Father Menegatti, offered a good channel for backstairs diplomacy, one which Leopold now used to build a network of secret contacts with French agents.

Leopold's secret discussions with the French began as early as 1692, though little came of them except for some remarkably romantic intrigues. In 1693 the new Imperial vice-chancellor count Windischgrätz discovered the informal contacts and remonstrated with Leopold for leaving such an important matter in the hands of political novices like Father Menegatti and amateur adventurers like the Vicenzan count Giambattista Velo.[4] Rather than break the contacts, Leopold brought Windischgrätz into the intrigue and gave him the task of keeping open the secret ties with Versailles. Windischgrätz induced Leopold to entrust the correspondence to Johann Friedrich von Seilern, formerly a secretary to the privy conference, currently Imperial commissioner at the Diet in Regensburg, the diplomatic crossroads of Germany. Seilern was already privy to the most secret official business of the conference, and understood both the general interests of the monarchy and the inner workings of the Imperial government. He had a certain ponderous quality, a pedantry combined with touchy sensitivity that made him a difficult person to negotiate with. Even this worked to Leopold's advantage, for he did not necessarily want to enter into secret negotiations with Louis XIV in a spirit of *bonhomie*.

These initial discussions produced nothing in 1694, for Leopold remained adamant on the subject of Strasbourg and the reunions. Then, in spite of all precautions, London and Amsterdam learned about the negotiations. Faced with clear evidence of his own duplicity, Leopold ingenuously declared that it was all the work of adventurers, that he himself knew nothing at all about the whole affair. Father Menegatti had a difficult task soothing the Imperial conscience after that, for Leopold hated the lie direct, even though he knew that his allies were engaged in similar activities. The French were already negotiating with William III through agents in Amsterdam, and they may have been the source for William's knowledge of the Austrian discussions.

The changes in Leopold's ministry during these years also increased the difficulty of keeping open his secret contacts with the French. Windischgrätz died in December 1695. His disappearance from the scene afforded Leopold little choice but to trust all his diplomatic affairs, both confidential and public, to Kinsky, the only man left who had the knowledge necessary to allow him to pick up the strands of Leopold's adventurous intrigue.

Fortunately for the coalition and for Leopold's delicate relations with France, William III remained as stubborn as the Habsburgs, demanding *ab initio* French recognition of his right to the throne of England. Louis, quite naturally, hoped to keep that concession as a bargaining counter in the formal peace talks later.[5]

Frustrated in his private negotiations with France, William III then proposed that all members of the coalition draw up together a 'basic position' for future negotiations with France. Surprisingly Leopold refused to approve such a procedure, even though Kinsky produced a draft statement admirably setting forth Imperial and dynastic interests and priorities. Leopold may have held back because of his indecisiveness or lassitude, though it seems more likely that he acted out of distrust both of France and of his Protestant allies. In any event his refusal to begin formal discussions with England and the Dutch at that point proved a great mistake. The Maritime Powers began negotiating more openly with France and events moved at a pace that far outstripped Vienna's ability to respond.

Louis XIV agreed to William's proposal that a conference be opened with the treaties of Westphalia and Nijmegen as a basis of discussion.

Kinsky misread Louis' quick acceptance of William's preliminary proposals as a sign of French weakness and had Leopold respond with unrealistically severe demands. Both count Auersperg in London and count Kaunitz at The Hague were told flatly that the Austrian conditions could not be met. The Empire now found itself diplomatically isolated from the coalition. Even the privy conference expressed second thoughts, fearing that the allies would desert the Empire and leave Leopold fighting alone, but still Leopold held back.

In 1696 Leopold's delaying tactics had a strong motive: his desire to arrange matters in Madrid so that the Spanish succession would be guaranteed to his second son archduke Charles before he had to conclude peace with France. Leopold deliberately played for time, though the gamble was a dangerous one. The same considerations that held Leopold back from the peace conference urged Louis XIV to settle quickly with the Maritime Powers. Versailles knew about the secret articles in the coalition treaties concerning Spain. Delay in making peace could mean that Leopold would indeed get his way in Spain with Dutch and English support. Louis XIV could well afford generous concessions to some of his opponents if only the coalition could be broken before Charles II of Spain died.

The Maritime Powers wanted peace, but their will to resist was not broken. Late in 1696 Louis tried to intimidate William III by withdrawing all his concessions and appearing ready to continue fighting. In this he badly misjudged William's strength in England, for Parliament promptly voted another £5,000,000 for armaments. At this point Louis backed down and promised to recognize William's claim to the English throne as soon as peace was signed. On 8 January 1697 the Maritime Powers agreed to a general peace conference meeting under Swedish mediation even though Vienna and Madrid remained stubbornly adamant in their unrealistic demands.

Once France split the coalition, the Habsburg position was no longer tenable. Leopold clearly could not hope to fight France alone without weakening his defences in the east. Spain was utterly helpless, unable even to defend Catalonia against French invasion. Reluctantly Leopold delegated envoys to represent him at the conference when it opened at the castle of Nieuwburg near Ryswick on 9 May 1697, willing now to participate in the conference if only to delay a formal treaty of peace.

The Imperial envoys were all seasoned diplomats: count Kaunitz, Imperial vice-chancellor and envoy to The Hague, count Henrich Stratmann, son of the late chancellor, and Johann Friedrich von Seilern.

All three had been involved in the secret preliminaries; in most cases they were acquainted with the men they would have to deal with at Ryswick. Kaunitz, who enjoyed the trust of the Dutch grand pensionary Heinsius, had the task of soothing the Dutch and English delegates while Seilern did what he could to delay the final treaty. Seilern was a recent convert to Catholicism who, like many of Leopold's servants, rose to high office through the patronage of the house of Pfalz-Neuburg. While his knowledge of German affairs was second to none, his Catholic zeal bordered on fanaticism and made him widely distrusted by the Protestants. His pedantic legalism made him a wearisome bargaining partner.

From the beginning of the conference Seilern used every trick he knew to slow the proceedings. He lectured the delegates tediously about the complex legal issues concerning Strasbourg, Luxembourg and the reunions. With ponderous exactitude he pursued every precedent, every dynastic link, every antecedent treaty touching not only the great towns and fortresses in the disputed region, but villages and small fiefs as well. He kept the conference bogged down in minutiae for week after week while the Maritime Powers chafed in frustration. At one point William III began separate negotiations with the French at Halle near Brussels, but even this did not serve to speed the conference towards a settlement.

What Louis XIV could not win at the conference table he finally gained on the battlefield. On 11 August 1697 his army took the city of Barcelona. The Spanish council of state in panic and confusion instructed its envoys at Ryswick to sign a peace at any price. It was precisely the break Louis had waited for, and he exploited it cleverly, offering the Spaniards very generous terms. Barcelona and Catalonia he returned to Spain, retaining only Luxembourg, which he had held since the beginning of the war. This restraint delighted the Spanish envoys who eagerly signed a separate peace at once. Leopold found himself without diplomatic support and with little purpose in delaying further. Not only had his optimism about Spain been proven wrong; the prospect of a Habsburg succession appeared more remote than ever. The Maritime Powers signed articles of peace in the night of 20–21 September 1697. Leopold was granted an armistice until 1 November to permit the necessary communication between the Imperial envoys and Vienna. Seilern tried to delay matters once again by inserting some strongly pro-Catholic articles in the treaty, but even this could not postpone the deadline. The Imperial envoys signed the treaty on 30 October, ceding to France all of Alsace and the city of Strasbourg. Louis restored Lorraine to the nominal sovereignty of its duke and gave up most of the reunions along the

Rhine, though he continued to occupy the majority of the strongpoints he had taken.

*

The war in the east ended on a more triumphant note. In 1689 Leopold ordered his commanders in Hungary to stand on the defensive. In spite of the vociferous objections of the easterners at his court, he did not adopt the optimistic, expansionist views that prevailed in his privy conference, but rather held to his conviction that France, not the Turk, was for the moment the more dangerous enemy. With most of the German troops already back on the Rhine and the Austrian forces pared down to provide troops for the west, Ludwig Wilhelm of Baden faced the campaign of 1689 with only 24,000 men to protect the vastly extended eastern frontier.

Austrian expansion into the Balkans brought troublesome political problems in its wake, as the German Catholic Emperor extended his dominion over large populations of Orthodox Slavs. As early as 1687 the Serbian Metropolitan of Üsküb (Skoplje) went to Moscow to seek Russian support against both the Austrians and the Turks.[6] The following year other leading Balkan churchmen begged the young tsars Ivan and Peter to liberate the Balkan Christians before the Roman Catholic powers of the Holy League beat them to it. The Russians, now partners in the Holy League, treated the emissaries politely but promised nothing. The Balkans were still far from the Muscovite frontiers, and Russia's immediate ambitions centred on the Crimea. Even so, the appeals from southeastern Europe laid the groundwork for future Austro–Russian rivalry in the Balkans which brought forth bitter fruit well before 1914.

By the early summer of 1689 Guido Starhemberg had done much to set Belgrade in defensive order, but lack of money made it impossible to provision the city for a siege. Artillery to strengthen the garrison was still far up the Danube awaiting transport, while floods in the Tisza valley, lasting well into July, cut off the detachments quartered over the winter in Upper Hungary and Transylvania. In desperation Ludwig Wilhelm mustered his small force south of Belgrade, where he intercepted the main Turkish army and defeated it on 30 August, pursuing the remainder to Niš where it scattered. This bold move contradicted the defensive strategy dictated by the war council, but Ludwig Wilhelm's supplies would not permit him to stand above Belgrade and still hold that key fort. His boldness paid off handsomely, but the same shortage of supplies that dictated his move also made it impossible for him to march on Sofia where the sultan and grand vizier were encamped.

With his field army reduced to only 16,000 men, Ludwig Wilhelm divided the force, sending general Aeneas Sylvius Piccolomini with some 6,000 men to eject Turkish outposts from Serbia. Piccolomini led his troops across the Midar plain to Pristina and the famed field of Kossovo. The Turks fled before him, usually leaving ample booty and provisions behind. From Pristina he marched on to Üsküb, which he found a city of corpses struck down by the plague before they could flee. By 6 November Piccolomini had moved on to Prisren in northern Albania, where he was well received by the patriarch of Ipek, Arsen Cernojević.

This remarkable campaign reached a tragic end at its zenith when Piccolomini, apparently exposed to the plague at Üsküb, died on 9 November. His command fell to duke Georg Christian of Holstein, who continued to extend his forces around the region of Prisren, but who had neither the military ability nor the tact of his predecessor. His mismanagement of the military occupation led quickly to a strong reaction against the Austrian forces among a population Piccolomini had tried so hard and at first so successfully to win for the Emperor.

The Austrian victory in Serbia produced another convulsive move-ment for reform in Adrianople where the sultan appointed as his new vizier Mustafa Köprülü, brother of the famous Ahmed. Köprülü quickly sent a detachment of well-trained regulars to Albania, pushing Georg Christian back to Niš by January. The patriarch of Ipek had little choice but to flee from his homeland. He gathered nearly 40,000 Serbian families and led them north into Hungary where many of them settled on the Maros, others scattering farther north and west seeking refuge and settling in abandoned villages. Leopold accepted the immigrants gladly. On 21 August 1690 he formally granted them freedom to prac-tise their Orthodox faith, the right to elect their own patriarchs and to use their old calendar.

At first Piccolomini's astonishing success produced another wave of overconfidence in Vienna. Ludwig Wilhelm tried to inject a note of realism into the war council's deliberations, pointing out the impossi-bility of extending military operations south of Belgrade so long as the resources of the Empire were concentrated on the Rhine. He made little headway, however, against the illusions of men who had become accus-tomed to reading glowing accounts of great victories won against over-whelming odds. Ludwig Wilhelm proposed drawing the defensive line back from Niš to Belgrade to prevent the Turks from thrusting at Transylvania and again endangering Upper Hungary. Leopold chose to take the more optimistic view of the war council and the military amateurs in the privy conference. He expressly ordered Ludwig Wilhelm not to speak further of any retreat from the lands won beyond the Sava.

At the same time, during the late winter months of 1690, Mustafa Köprülü worked hard to set the sultan's house in order. He removed many incompetent local pashas and built up a new army. Imre Thököly, now a pensioner of the Porte, was given another chance to carve himself a princedom in Hungary. Michael Apafy died on 15 April 1690; the sultan, still claiming his right as suzerain, named Thököly prince in Apafy's place and sent him off a few months later with a mixed force of Moldavian and Wallachian irregulars, a few irreconcilable *Kuruczók*, and some of the dreaded Crimean Tatars.

Once he had mustered this motley army Thököly struck north into Transylvania, defeating several Austrian garrisons in August 1691. The governing council and part of the Transylvanian diet fled to Klausenburg, sending desperate pleas to Vienna for help. Gambling on his reputation, Thököly called the estates to meet him. Many of the deputies appeared and on 22 September elected him their prince. For the moment much of Transylvania was lost and Upper Hungary, as Ludwig Wilhelm had predicted, again faced civil war and Tatar raids.

Debates in the war council about eastern strategy kept Ludwig Wilhelm away from his command until mid-August 1691. Once he heard of Thököly's victory he quickly marched northeast, leaving Niš and Belgrade to fend for themselves against the Turkish forces moving up the Danube supported by a strong river fleet. Guido Starhemberg held out in Niš for three weeks, but wisely chose to surrender with safe conduct and free passage for his garrison, saving his irreplaceable troops at the cost of abandoning the last Imperial outpost south of Belgrade. The Turks invested Belgrade on 28 September.

Count Aspremont, whom Ludwig Wilhelm left to defend the great river fort, refused to believe that the enemy would begin a siege so late in the campaign season, and took few precautions to prepare for it. Once aroused from his comfortable illusion, he found it was too late for him to make up the deficiencies. On 8 October a Turkish projectile hit a tower of the citadel, touching off a fire which spread rapidly to the powder magazine. In a moment the whole fortress blew asunder. Amid explosions, falling walls and towers, collapsing and burning houses in the city, a universal panic seized soldiers and civilians alike. The Turks entered the burning city; Aspremont saved himself by fleeing in a skiff on the Danube. Most of the 8,000-man garrison was killed.

Ludwig Wilhelm reached Transylvania on 3 October to learn that only the German minority in the region remained loyal to the Emperor, the rest of the population having accepted Thököly as their prince. Ludwig Wilhelm immediately began to pursue the usurper, who moved freely around the province avoiding a pitched battle. In the midst of these manœuvres word arrived that Belgrade had fallen. Ludwig Wilhelm then made the hard decision to abandon Transylvania in order to cover the central Danube. Thököly, encouraged by the same news, determined to use Ludwig Wilhelm's dilemma to extend his own control over Transylvania. Gathering his forces, he set out on a rapid march towards the Iron Gates. Ludwig Wilhelm, seeing his chance, sent a strong cavalry detachment in pursuit. Thököly was trapped and completely defeated. The Hungarian rebel withdrew again to safe Turkish territory while Ludwig Wilhelm returned to the Danube with Transylvania safe behind him. It was the one real success in an otherwise disastrous year.

The misfortunes of 1691 on both fronts served to sober the optimists in the privy conference. Caution dominated strategic planning for 1692, when the Imperial and the Turkish armies approached each other warily north of Belgrade. Again Ludwig Wilhelm decided, in spite of his restraining orders, to stake his chances on a direct engagement. After a series of brisk manœuvres in intense August heat he caught the main Turkish army at Slankamen where, on 19 August, he fought one of the bitterest and bloodiest pitched battles of the long war. For hours the Turks held the advantage until Ludwig Wilhelm led a desperate cavalry charge at the Turkish flank, breaking through their solid position. In a few more hours of murderous fighting the Turkish army was destroyed. The vizier Mustafa Köprülü and most of his commanders lay dead on the field among thousands of their best troops.

The victory at Slankamen, hailed in Vienna as another miracle of the house of Austria, was crucial in the sense that defeat might well have meant Turkish reoccupation of central Hungary. The cost was staggering: almost a third of the whole Imperial force were dead or wounded. There was little Ludwig Wilhelm could do to take advantage of his position. Indeed, Slankamen proved to be the last great battle against the Turks for five years. As Vienna turned its attention to the expanding war against France, the Danube–Sava line and the positions won in 1688, Belgrade excepted, became a more or less stable battlefront of a war in which sickness proved to be the greatest enemy of both belligerents.

When Leopold sent Ludwig Wilhelm to Germany to command the Imperial forces there he was left without a competent replacement in Hungary. In 1693 the duke de Croy quickly proved his lack of ability and was replaced for the following year by the ageing field-marshal Caprara, who promptly fell seriously ill and did not reach his command post until the end of August. These two years of inactivity allowed the Turks once again to recruit and equip a new army.

Sultan Ahmed died in February 1695. His successor, Mustafa II, proved more competent than either of his predecessors, and was filled with a yearning to restore the old glory of the Ottoman empire. Soothsayers declared the omens to be propitious: the Venetian fleet was defeated at Chios, the Tatars again raided far into Poland. Sultan Mustafa II himself took to the field with his troops, leading his army from Adrianople to Belgrade where in early August his war council decided to attack a string of fortresses guarding the approaches to Transylvania.

Leopold could find no more soldiers for Hungary, and had to turn again to the German princes for help in the east as well as in Germany. In the young elector of Saxony, Friedrich August, who succeeded his brother in April 1694, he found a potential ally anxious to win fame for himself in battle against the infidel. He offered Leopold 8,000 Saxon soldiers, demanding in return supreme command over the entire Imperial army in Hungary. The price was high, but Leopold had no able commanders to spare. He reluctantly appointed the twenty-five-year-old Saxon Hotspur to the post, leaving Caprara as second in command to act, it was hoped, as a seasoned adviser and moderating influence. From the moment they met Friedrich August and Caprara fell to fighting among themselves rather than against the Turks.

The Turks took the initiative by default, crossing the Danube near Páncsova and taking Lippa by storm on 7 September. Friedrich August marched his army east to intercept the invasion, then changed his mind without informing general Veterani, whose Transylvanian corps was moving south to join him. This criminal blunder led Veterani into a trap. A Turkish force five times his superior fell on him on 20 September. Veterani, the best and most experienced commander left in Hungary, fell mortally wounded into the hands of the Turks, who ended his pain by beheading him. Some 2,000 Imperial soldiers were killed; the remnants fled back to Transylvania. Content with his victory, sultan Mustafa returned in triumph to Constantinople.

Friedrich August had needed only one campaign to make himself thoroughly disliked by the whole officer corps, if not for his incompetence alone, then for his pretentiousness and rudeness. He was a man of great physical strength, whose sexual exploits were already the talk of the continent. A few weeks of campaigning made his incompetence equally legendary. Leopold quickly admitted his mistake in giving the elector supreme command, but it was not easy to extricate himself from his bargain. At one point he considered bringing Ludwig Wilhelm back from Germany and sending Friedrich August to the western front in his place, but the need for pretentious incompetence was no greater on the Rhine than on the Danube. Without a clearly superior alternative, Leopold left the elector with his command after Friedrich August promised to bring 12,000 more Saxons for the 1696 campaign.

For once the Hungarian campaign began more or less when it was planned, the elector taking the field in June 1696. This hopeful beginning achieved little. Friedrich August first marched towards Temesvár, then turned back when word reached him that Mustafa II had crossed the Danube at Semlin, threatening to cut the Imperial army from its supply base where the elector had left behind half his artillery. In the midst of this counter-march the elector learned that the rumour was false, so he reversed direction once more, turning back towards Temesvár. In the meantime the Turks had in fact crossed the Danube at Páncsova and were themselves marching towards Temesvár. In the confusion the Turks got behind the Imperial army, forcing Friedrich August to engage them on the banks of the Bega. After a bloody but inconclusive engagement, the two armies withdrew. Nothing was won by either side, and the campaign came to an end.

By avoiding defeat, Leopold's eastern armies provided the time needed to complete the incorporation of Transylvania into the Habsburg monarchy. In 1691 the Emperor had issued the Leopoldine Diploma which in the following years provided the basis for the Transylvanian constitution. In some respects it was a model of moderation, particularly with respect to the traditional freedoms of the four recognized churches: Catholic. Lutheran, Calvinist and Unitarian. It placated the nobles by recognizing and guaranteeing existing property rights. The Emperor's sovereign authority was to be represented by a governor, elected by the estates but requiring confirmation by the monarch. Fixed permanent contributions were set forth amounting to 50,000 Thaler in peacetime and 400,000 per year when the Emperor was at war. In return Leopold agreed not to introduce extraordinary taxes. A special chancellery bureau was created in Vienna to deal exclusively with Transylvanian judicial business.

For several years Leopold recognized Michael Apafy's heir as successor to the princely title, while the rich revenues of that office flowed into the court chamber. In 1696 the young Apafy heir was brought to Vienna and there induced to renounce his claim to the title. With moderation and a certain amount of deliberate deception Leopold had put himself gradually into a position as direct ruler over one of the largest and richest of his dependent provinces. By creating a separate chancellery he raised the status of the province to near equality with the kingdom of Hungary. This affronted the Hungarians, but strengthened Leopold's own hold over the eastern bastion of his growing Habsburg dominions.

Leopold had affirmed his political control in both Hungary and Transylvania by 1696, but these realms still faced the threat of Turkish invasion. It was clear to him and to his advisers that retaining the Saxon elector in command of his relatively small forces in Hungary meant courting disaster. The war council president Ernst Rüdiger von Starhemberg and several members of the privy conference advised Leopold to recall Friedrich August and send in his place prince Eugene of Savoy who, with the end of the Italian operation in 1696, was free to take an assignment elsewhere. Leopold agreed heartily with this advice, but could not bring himself to get rid of the elector if it meant losing his valuable Saxon troops.

Unexpectedly, a royal election in Poland provided the solution. When John III Sobieski died in 1696 the Polish nobility gathered to elect his successor. As usual many of the candidates were foreigners, supported by Poland's neighbours. France favoured the prince Conti, Brandenburg supported Ludwig Wilhelm of Baden. The Austrians at first supported Sobieski's unpopular son Jákob, then considered supporting Max Emmanuel of Bavaria who had married Sobieski's daughter in 1694 after Maria Antonia's death.

During the early weeks of negotiating no one in the privy conference seemed to have been aware that Friedrich August of Saxony was quietly working for his own election. When the elector's first tentative efforts to win support in Poland proved fruitful, he approached Kinsky who immediately offered him Austrian support. Nothing could better serve Habsburg interests than to have the Saxon elector vacate the Hungarian command, convert to Catholicism, and ascend the throne of Poland indebted to Vienna for Leopold's support.

Leopold and Kinsky did everything they could to smooth Friedrich August's path to the Polish throne, and the elector himself responded quickly. On 1 June 1697 he went to the town of Baden south of Vienna where, with a minimum of hasty instruction, he converted to Catholicism. By 25 June he was in Breslau; two days later he was elected king of Poland. The happy news reached Vienna on 5 July. Leopold promptly named prince Eugene Imperial commander in Hungary.[7] Within a week Eugene reached the Imperial encampment at Kolluth.

Eugene faced a situation of remarkable disorder, yet almost at once the presence of an experienced and forceful commander made itself felt. By commanding and threatening, wheedling and bargaining, Eugene gathered storehouses of supplies along the Tisza and brought together the scattered Imperial units in time to march with his whole force to meet the invading Turks. Mustafa II did not reach Belgrade until 10 August, by which time Eugene had brought the Austrian forces into a position to threaten any move beyond the Danube. The Turks again crossed at Páncsova, then divided their army, sending one detachment with the river fleet towards Slankamen, while the main force under the sultan's command marched towards Transylvania. Eugene swiftly moved ahead to secure the Tisza river crossings. Mustafa II, finding the river barred against him, turned southwards to strike at Peterwardein.

While on the Tisza Eugene drew the Transylvanian corps into his own force, so that he commanded an army actually up to its intended strength of 50,000. In a series of forced marches he led his men in a long arc around the Turks to get between them and the fort at Peterwardein. The move succeeded, but he was denied the battle he so ardently wanted. The Turks, finding themselves outflanked a second time, reversed their march, thinking that the Tisza line was now clear. Once again Eugene pursued them, pushing his tired units back towards Transylvania. On 11 September he caught up with Mustafa's main army just south of Zenta.

The Ottoman army had already begun to cross the river on an impromptu bridge strung across the hulls of boats. The sultan and a large part of his cavalry were on the east bank; most of the infantry remained west of the river waiting to cross in their turn. Eugene decided to attack at once, even though it was late afternoon and his troops were tired after the long march.[8] His cavalry made quick headway against the ill-protected Turkish infantry which crowded behind hastily erected earthworks close to the bridgehead. Sultan Mustafa, seeing his infantry helpless against the heavy Imperial cavalry, sent his *spahis* back over the bridge to reinforce the foot soldiers. This countermove jammed the makeshift bridge, blocking the retreat of fleeing infantry, who, finding their retreat cut off, fell into panic in the narrow and crowded space they occupied west of the river. The battle became a massacre as the Imperial forces hacked their way through the formless mass of men that was all that remained of the Turkish infantry. Many of the Turks were pushed into the river to drown. The grand vizier fell among his men, along with most of the officers. The sultan watched helplessly while his army was destroyed before his eyes. While the butchery still went on west of the river, he turned with his cavalry and fled to Temesvár, leaving his entire supply train and war chest as booty for the Imperial army.

The battle of Zenta, which cost the Imperial forces only 2,000 casualties, most of them wounded, proved to be the decisive victory in the long war against the Turks. On 17 November 1697, after a sweep through Bosnia with a select corps of 7,000 men, prince Eugene returned to Vienna where he placed in Leopold's hands the great seal of the Ottoman empire which had been found hanging from the neck of the grand vizier on the field at Zenta. The remaining campaigns were only an epilogue. In January 1698 the sultan accepted the mediation of Lord Paget, Britain's ambassador to the Porte. Serious negotiations between Vienna and Constantinople began within months.

By the spring of 1698 all conditions seemed right for concluding a victorious peace with Turkey, though the Holy League allies were not united in their demands. Venice agreed to work with Austria on the basis of *uti possedetis*, but Poland and Russia still held out for territories they had not yet reconquered or conquered. Tsar Peter, who was touring western Europe and storing up dazzling impressions to bring home to his puzzled subjects, cut short his sojourn in the Dutch Republic and hurried to Vienna to postpone, if he could, a separate peace between Turkey and the Empire.

Leopold delegated count Kinsky to deal with the tsar. The Bohemian chancellor handled his large and unpredictable guest very firmly. Peter wanted a Black Sea port for the fleet he dreamed of floating there. Kinsky sympathized, urging the tsar to conquer it quickly because Austria was in no position to continue an aggressive war in the east. Having failed to make his point, Peter left the Imperial capital on 29 July.

On his hasty journey back to Russia to deal with the *streltsy* uprising, he stopped in Warsaw to discuss his Baltic plans with Friedrich August. Lured by the prospect of more conquests in the north at the expense of Sweden, the Poles and the tsar agreed, reluctantly, to send plenipotentiaries to negotiate with the Turks.

Late in October 1698 all the delegates, translators and the mediator Lord Paget arrived at the town of Carlowitz near Peterwardein. The treaty between the Empire and the Porte was quickly drawn up along the lines of *uti possedetis*. No land changed hands, though the Austrians had hoped to get Temesvár in return for a payment of 200,000 Gulden. As negotiations with the other Holy League partners, Poland, Russia and Venice, dragged on week after week, the privy conference instructed the Imperial envoys to sign without them if necessary. This proved not to be necessary, though Russia refused to sign a treaty of peace, accepting only an armistice. The chief Ottoman plenipotentiary, Rami Reis Efendi, having consulted his astrologers for the most favourable moment, signed the resulting documents at precisely 11.45 a.m. on 26 January 1699.[9]

The peace of Carlowitz confirmed all Leopold had won and held in sixteen years of war against the Turks. The new frontiers settled by that treaty lasted with only a few modifications until 1918. Behind the fortified frontier along the Danube–Sava rivers the Habsburg monarchy slowly built an empire vastly different from the loosely federated hereditary sovereignties Leopold had inherited in 1657.

XVI

The Spanish Succession

Leopold had assured the dynastic succession in his hereditary states and in the Empire, but he remained obsessed with the problem of the Spanish inheritance. Since 1665 he had lived in constant anxiety about his nephew-cousin Charles II of Spain, who feebly held title to the rich empire in Europe and overseas. Contrary to all expectations Charles II lived on in spite of his doctors and his own physical and mental weakness. His mother, Leopold's sister Mariana, acted as his regent, holding together for more than a decade a court and government which she managed to dominate despite her own unpopularity and the intense distrust aroused by her German advisers.[1]

Only once did her hold over the government slip. During the Dutch War the opposition to her at the Madrid court rallied behind the bastard son of Philip IV and the actress María Calderón, don Juan of Austria, a susceptible, foppish young man who allowed himself to be put forward as leader of a faction friendly to France. Mariana had to leave the court for a time while the council of state under don Juan's influence contracted a French marriage for the king. In November 1679, as part of the peace settlement at Nijmegen, Charles II married Louis XIV's niece Marie Louise d'Orléans.

Don Juan of Austria died suddenly in September 1679, even before Charles II married his French princess. Mariana returned to the court more influential than ever. Supported by Leopold's ambassador, count Mansfeld, she defeated the French faction, completely isolating the unfortunate young queen and her French entourage from affairs of state. None of these manoeuvres could offer more than temporary reassurance, however, so long as Charles II failed to provide an heir, and the rudimentary medical knowledge of the time was sufficient to discern that he was unlikely to do so.

Each passing year made it seem more evident that Spain would pass to a foreign prince at Charles's death, probably to either a Habsburg or

Bourbon claimant. In 1685 the dynastic question was complicated even further when Leopold married his daughter Maria Antonia to Max Emmanuel of Bavaria. In due course Maria Antonia gave birth to a son, who as a greatgrandson of Philip IV of Spain had in many ways the soundest claim to Spain. What was even more important, he offered an excellent choice to those powers, especially England and the Dutch Republic, who preferred that Spain be neither Habsburg nor Bourbon.

Leopold had tried to anticipate this complication by having Maria Antonia join him and her husband in a secret, solemn renunciation for herself and her children of any right to the crown of Spain, transferring claims to the male heirs of Leopold I. Max Emmanuel, in return for his renunciation on his children's behalf, was promised full sovereign possession of the Spanish Netherlands should Austria inherit Spain. Leopold further engaged to try to secure the Netherlands for the elector while Charles II still lived.

Within a year the French discovered the general terms of the Bavarian bargain and promptly made them known to the Spanish government. Knowing well the Spaniards' sensitivity about the integrity of their empire, they assumed that Madrid would view Leopold's agreement as another attempt to partition the inheritance. The reaction in Madrid was not at all what the French expected. The council of state refused to recognize Maria Antonia's renunciation, and instead welcomed the prospect of a Bavarian prince, who would be a descendant of Philip IV, inheriting the entire empire. 'All my states', wrote Charles II to Leopold in 1687, 'are firmly convinced that the archduchess should unquestionably succeed me in all my territories.'[2]

Leopold's desire to secure the succession for his second and favourite son Charles came nearer to fulfilment in 1689 when Spain joined the coalition against France. In the treaties binding Spain to the alliance were included secret articles guaranteeing the succession to Leopold's heirs in the event Charles II died without issue. This new pro-Austrian stance, largely the work of English and Dutch diplomacy, was confirmed the following year when, after the death of Marie Louise d'Orléans, the Spanish council of state sanctioned the king's marriage with Maria Anna of Pfalz-Neuburg, Leopold's sister-in-law.

This marriage and the treaties of 1689 temporarily settled the Spanish question to Leopold's satisfaction. Contrary to all expectations Charles II had lived to maturity and an heir was still theoretically possible. Max Emmanuel of Bavaria, however, became increasingly impatient to reap the rewards he had been promised in 1685. In December 1691 Leopold, with Mariana's help, forced Charles II to sign the document appointing the elector governor of the Netherlands, though the council of state had strongly opposed the nomination of a 'foreigner'. Bavaria's continued support of the coalition was thus secured, but personal difficulties continued to cloud Max Emmanuel's relations with the Habsburgs.

Maria Antonia, though perfectly sane and competent, had all the blandest qualities of her insipid mother. Her headstrong husband tired quickly of her quiet ways and openly sought gaiety amid a stable of lively mistresses, conduct which deeply offended Leopold's sense of propriety and his affection for his first child. Leopold and the Spaniards were still more offended when Max Emmanuel did not take his wife to Brussels upon assuming the office of governor. Left behind in Vienna, Maria Antonia produced a second son in October 1692 and died two months later. In her final testament Maria Antonia again affirmed her renunciation of Spain, but no family agreements or treaties could change the fact that her newborn son, Joseph Ferdinand, was widely regarded in Spain as the rightful heir in preference to Leopold's second son of his German marriage. Even Leopold's sister, Mariana, ignored her brother's wishes and family tradition in giving her powerful support to the Bavarian candidacy. Over the years Mariana had adapted herself to her adopted country, coming more and more to feel herself a Spaniard. Like many of her courtiers she began to see that the close tie between Spain and Austria had in the past brought only disaster to Spain. This change in her attitude further dimmed archduke Charles's prospects in Spain, for her influence over the king remained unchallenged until her death in May 1696.

Mariana's death left the young queen Maria Anna of Pfalz-Neuburg the most influential person at court. As Leopold had expected she proved faithful to the Habsburg interest. What Leopold had not anticipated was that her silly intrigues and political stupidity would do his cause more harm than good. The queen quite unnecessarily made an enemy of cardinal Portocarrero, the leading figure in the council of state and perhaps the only political figure in Spain with the experience and ability to lead the monarchy through years of deepening crisis.

Since the cardinal could not work with the queen, he decided to work around her. Without the queen's knowledge Portocarrero induced the king to sign a will naming the electoral prince Joseph Ferdinand his heir general. When Maria Anna discovered this she forced Charles to tear up the will with his own hands and without informing the council of his act. This instability in the court at Madrid encouraged foreign powers to meddle in Spanish affairs.

In 1697, during the months of negotiations preceding the treaty of

Ryswick, Leopold sent count Ferdinand Harrach as his ambassador to Spain. The elderly Harrach had already represented Leopold in Madrid from 1674 to 1677 and knew most of the men he would be dealing with there. At one point he succeeded in having Charles II write to Leopold intimating that he intended to name archduke Charles as his heir, but Harrach accompanied the royal letter with his own warnings that the political climate in Spain was most unfavourable to the Austrian succession.

In spite of Harrach's warnings, Leopold and his privy conference chose to be more optimistic than they had reason to be. In a sanguine mood they let slip the one opportunity remaining in 1697 to make a tangible gesture that would win adherents in Spain. The council of state sent urgent requests for assistance in the defence of Barcelona, and Leopold promised to dispatch Imperial regiments from Italy. Unfortunately other matters seemed more pressing. Decisions were postponed and precious time sped by while the Imperial troops waited for their orders and transport. Barcelona fell to the French and Spain accepted French terms for peace.

Louis' generosity had its intended effect. Opinion at the Spanish court turned decisively against the house of Austria. Harrach did his best, but even he could not handle the queen, who further offended the court by inducing the king to banish count Oropesa, a powerful figure in the council of state. The Austrian privy conference aggravated the situation by haggling over troop commitments in Italy, the governorship of Milan and other matters, conduct which served only to alienate Spanish opinion and further dim the archduke's prospects. Count Harrach brought his thankless mission to an end, leaving Madrid in October 1698 and placing Leopold's affairs in the hands of his son Alois.

The marquis d'Harcourt, French envoy to Madrid after the peace of Ryswick, found little opposition. Oropesa returned to favour and resumed leadership in the council. Even Maria Anna could not hold out against him and Harcourt.

Once it was clear that Leopold could not accomplish his designs in Madrid, he turned to the Maritime Powers, which had given him secret guarantees for the Spanish succession in the alliance treaties of 1689. Here again he found little encouragement. The Maritime Powers refused to do anything until Charles II made a will expressly naming archduke Charles as his heir.

This response was in fact a blind to obscure efforts by William III to settle the Spanish succession without a general war. In a series of secret discussions, about which Vienna surprisingly learned nothing, William worked out a treaty with French diplomats partitioning the Spanish empire. The agreement was signed on 11 October 1698 in Het Loo palace. The Bavarian prince was to get Spain, the Indies and the Netherlands; Leopold would be given Milan, and the dauphin of France Naples, Sicily and a substantial part of the Spanish Basque provinces.

Max Emmanuel, who quickly learned of the partition treaty, had his six-year-old son Joseph Ferdinand brought from Vienna to Brussels. Leopold failed completely to see the threat in this move and let his grandson join the elector with warm expressions of family affection.

Madrid learned of the partition treaty from the Bavarian court in Munich. Stung by the arrogance with which the Protestant Maritime Powers and France had carved up Spain's European dominions, the council of state prevailed on Charles II to sign a new will naming Joseph Ferdinand, for the second time, his heir general and invalidating the claim if any part of the inheritance was separated from the whole.

Leopold's privy conference did not get detailed information about the partition treaty until December 1698, just as Harrach returned from Madrid with his pessimistic view of the situation there. News of Charles II's new will favouring Joseph Ferdinand came to Vienna as a considerable relief. When Leopold learned of it he remarked: 'Well, after all he is my grandson.' In a letter to Marco d'Aviano on 31 January 1699 the Emperor made it clear that while he regarded the Spanish will as an injustice, contrary to all the treaties and agreements he had made, now that it was done it remained only to keep the peace and protect the electoral prince from other claimants.[3] So far as he was concerned the issue was settled.

Just one week after Leopold wrote d'Aviano the electoral prince died suddenly in Brussels on 6 February 1699. In his short life Joseph Ferdinand had been a hope for peace and compromise. His death raised the possibility of another general war. Archduke Charles's candidacy stood without any legal challenge, provided that all of Europe would respect the treaties and renunciations on which it rested. At the Hague, Heinsius expressed his belief that not even a new will could alter the situation and Charles would succeed as a matter of course. The fact remained, however, that the duke of Anjou, Louis' second grandson, was descended from Philip IV and Charles of Austria was not.

Unfortunately for Europe the Spanish empire was too vast to be treated simply as a matter of treaties, family law and contracts. The association of any substantial part of the inheritance with either France or the Austrian Habsburg dominions deeply concerned other powers. Dynastic right had to give way before realistic international politics, and Leopold agreed with his privy conference when it advised him to begin direct discussions with France in order to preserve the peace.

The marquis de Villars had represented France in Vienna since August 1693. Even before Leopold agreed to direct conversations about the Spanish inheritance several court officials approached Villars informally, giving their private opinions that war was unnecessary. France had its troops on the Pyrenees and could easily take possession of Spain. Austria, they intimated, was mainly concerned with Italy. Leaving aside the importance Leopold placed on the dynastic tie with Spain, and more and more of the leading political figures in Vienna were able to do this, the central political question for Austria was precisely that. Spain still ruled Milan and Lombardy, the crossroads of northern Italy, and Naples and Sicily as well. French occupation of any of these Italian states clearly threatened Austria's security.

These informal talks with Villars made the French aware of Leopold's intentions even before he had agreed to open formal discussions with France. The death of Kinsky in late February 1699 further delayed negotiations with Villars, who on instructions from Versailles used every opportunity offered by etiquette and baroque ceremonial to delay substantive discussions.

Leopold found himself in an unusually strong position not only legally but militarily as well. The peace of Carlowitz, signed in January, left his eastern frontiers secure. His army, now freed from the long war in the east, was available for employment elsewhere. Louis XIV recognized Leopold's advantages and concluded that he would get a better bargain from the Maritime Powers than he would from Austria. While Villars delayed in Vienna Louis XIV reopened negotiations with William III, transmitting to London a plan for a new partition treaty which was surprisingly generous to the Habsburgs. Archduke Charles was to become king of Spain and receive the colonial empire, the dauphin was to receive Naples and Sicily, plus the Tuscan ports, ceding Milan to the duke of Lorraine, or, if he should refuse this in exchange for his own duchy, to either Max Emmanuel or Victor Amadeus II.

After some shrewd bargaining William III signed a partition treaty on these terms with France on 11 June 1699. It was also stipulated that the crown of Spain should never be united with the Austrian hereditary lands or the Holy Roman Empire. Louis' envoy convinced William that the only way to accomplish the partition without a war was to present Leopold with a *fait accompli*. With some pangs of conscience about the ill-usage of his old ally, William III agreed.

Meanwhile, after Kinsky's death Leopold turned to his two favourites in the privy conference, Harrach, now the grand chamberlain, and Kaunitz, elevated to the Imperial vice-chancellorship since his return from The Hague. Both were experienced diplomats, but they were also, like their Imperial master, cautious, punctilious, rather old-fashioned gentlemen, unlikely to act hastily. They took up the discussions Kinsky had begun with Villars, but made little progress. Leopold wanted to reach an agreement with France as quickly as possible, but at the same time he had to exercise great caution for fear of offending Madrid, where any talk of partition was an abomination. This was made evident late in June 1699 when Madrid learned of the latest partition agreement between William III and France, responding with a burst of outrage against the signatories.

When the second partition treaty was formally conveyed to Leopold, it came accompanied by a demand from Versailles that the Emperor accept it without alteration. Through the summer months the privy conference met frequently to debate the Spanish question, often with both Leopold and his elder son, Joseph, present. In October the conference finally decided unanimously that the treaty was unacceptable as it stood, though the ministers differed widely in their views on what sort of partition Austria could accept.[4]

Count Kaunitz, the most realistic and, as it turned out, the most far-sighted member of the conference, urged Leopold to give up Spain itself. Austria, he argued, could not hope to protect it against France. The same he thought was true for the Netherlands, which would be a constant source of trouble for the monarchy and produce little tangible increase in Habsburg power. The best solution would be to give them outright to Max Emmanuel, in return annexing Bavaria to Austria. Italy, however, and especially Milan, must be held by the house of Austria. On this there could be no compromise.

All Kaunitz's best arguments could not overcome Leopold's ambitions for Charles nor convince him to accept a solution so much at variance with Habsburg dynastic tradition and Leopold's sense of responsibility to the family enterprise. In a formal statement to Jakob Hop, the Dutch ambassador, Leopold wrote that he could not accept the partition treaty and trusted that 'the Lord of kings and armies' would deal justly with 'those who would divide and tear apart foreign kingdoms'.

The note of firm defiance in Leopold's letter was interpreted as another example of Austrian selfishness, though in fact Leopold had tried to reach a direct agreement with France through Villars. It was also intended for public consumption, particularly for Madrid where he hoped his firmness might advance his cause. Certainly Spanish resentment against the partition treaty had made the Austrian cause seem more hopeful.

Leopold was right, however, in intimating that only armies could settle the issue unless the Spaniards could be brought to accept partition. Alois Harrach wrote repeatedly from Madrid that no testamentary disposition of the kingdom by Charles II could provide the troops and money needed to defend the country from France. Spain was disorganized, demoralized, insolvent and helpless after its last war with its powerful neighbour.

Leopold could be firm about his rights, but he was not capable of decisive and bold action to protect them. Growing more lethargic and at the same time more stubborn as he aged, he was content to share the unrealistic optimism of his old advisers, particularly Harrach, Dietrichstein and Mansfeld, in spite of the activists on the conference led by Kaunitz. When Villars presented the ratified partition treaty on 18 May 1700 demanding a prompt decision, Leopold's response was the same: a firm refusal to be party to the partition. In this mood, Leopold let himself be deceived by false optimism and to misjudge the state of opinion in Spain.

Charles II, to the extent that he was capable of independent judgment, and even this was overestimated in Vienna, probably intended the Spanish empire to go entire to a member of his own dynasty. Queen Maria Anna saw the danger to herself should a Bourbon succeed to the throne. Both, however, agreed with the council of state, and in so far as it is possible to judge such things, the temper and opinion of the nation at large, that the empire must be maintained in its totality with no territories whatever alienated from the Spanish crown.

The integrity of the empire became above all other considerations the driving motive of Spanish policy in the last months of the king's life. Harcourt, realizing this, had all along advised Versailles against a new partition treaty, believing that the threat of partition would force Spain to choose Habsburg over Bourbon. Louis XIV thus became increasingly aware that Spain's choice was either partition and war with France if it chose archduke Charles, a war Spain could not hope to win, or accepting a Bourbon heir who would bring with him the might of France to defend the integrity of the empire. He calculated, and was proved right, that there were a few important men in Madrid who could rise above the passions of the moment and see that only France could hope to protect the whole Spanish inheritance.

Cardinal Portocarrero used all his influence and persuasiveness to convince the council of state that a Bourbon succession was the only reasonable course for Spain. By May 1700 a majority of councillors agreed with him in spite of Louis' ratification of the partition treaty. It remained only to convince the king. Portocarrero appealed to Charles's deep piety and superstitious nature, raising the spectre of the Protestant English and Dutch getting a foothold in the colonial empire and destroying Spain's work for the true faith. In June 1700 Pope Innocent XII, long sympathetic to France, advised Charles to follow the advice of his council. Charles informed Leopold of the pope's advice, but suggested vaguely that in spite of everything he still intended to hold his crown intact *pro domo austriaca*. Leopold and the privy conference again were lulled into believing that their cause would triumph in Madrid if only they did nothing to upset the present state of affairs. Charles II was still in relatively good health in August.

The next month, however, the Spanish king fell ill again and weakened rapidly. His sickbed became the centre of a dramatic battle over his will. On 29 September the queen and Alois Harrach, with the help of Charles's confessor, induced him to sign a will naming archduke Charles his heir general. Cardinal Portocarrero learned of this at the last moment, and on the evening of 3 October made the now half-conscious king write his '*yo el rey*' on another will naming the duke of Anjou the heir. Charles hovered between life and death for another four weeks and finally died on 1 November. Portocarrero promptly published the will of 3 October and sent couriers hurrying to Versailles, setting in motion the events that plunged France, Austria and eventually all of Europe into yet another war.

XVII

The Coalition Reassembles

For two years after Carlowitz the Habsburg monarchy was at peace; the fortunes of the house of Austria seemed to have reached their zenith. Leopold's prestige remained high in Germany in spite of losses to France;[1] Hungary had been reunited after a century and a half of Turkish occupation. Archduke Joseph was crowned king of the Romans to succeed Leopold as Emperor. Vienna, recently besieged by the Ottoman host, was now the capital of a monarchy second only to France, the greatest power on the continent. Leopold's forty years of rule had produced phenomenal results.

Even the physical aspect of Leopold's realms changed remarkably in the decades after 1683. When the Turks fell back from Vienna, among the earliest decrees to go out from the Imperial government were orders to restore churches, monasteries, roadside shrines and monuments. Throughout the hereditary lands, but particularly in the Vienna basin, Lower Austria, parts of Styria and Moravia and above all in Hungary, there was an unparalleled wave of new construction that forever stamped the region with the architectural style of the high Austrian baroque.[2] The triumph of cross over crescent called forth an architectural celebration in the rich, elaborate, highly decorated Italianate style, now adopted enthusiastically by native builders throughout the Austrian dominions.

The building mania could be seen everywhere; in market towns and villages parish churches were stripped of their gothic altars to make way for flamboyant baroque structures. Isolated rural monasteries raised immense new churches, libraries and ceremonial halls to receive visiting royalty. Nowhere was the transformation so evident as in Vienna itself. The Hofburg was renovated and enlarged, a magnificent chancellery built across from the remodelled Leopoldine *Trakt*. Great nobles vied with each other in building anew or renovating town palaces, donating elaborate altars to their favourite churches and chapels. Outside the city walls suburban villages rebuilt their churches. The Emperor himself ordered work begun on a magnificent summer palace at Schönbrunn which would rival Versailles in beauty and charm if not in grandeur.

The opulence of the Austrian baroque seems astonishing in view of the chronic poverty of the public treasury. Much of the work was done, of course, by *Robot* labour, but vast sums of money were poured into the hands of contractors, skilled craftsmen, painters and sculptors. Most of it came undoubtedly from aristocratic or ecclesiastical revenues which increased somewhat with higher commodity prices, privileged money which still eluded the tax collectors. Few in or out of office complained that the magnificence it purchased was too dearly bought. Least of all the ageing Emperor, who saw in each new altar a votive offering in thanksgiving for God's abundant favour to his house.

Approaching sixty, Leopold had already outlived the span allotted to most of his predecessors. His mind remained clear, but his physical vigour had declined; it became ever harder for his ministers to rouse him to participate actively in crucial public business. He tried to share these burdens with his successor, bringing Joseph frequently to meetings of the privy conference, but so long as he lived and reigned, only he could make the final decisions on important matters and give official force to decrees by his signature. While the activists who gravitated to Joseph's informal court demanded reforms, Leopold grew ever more cautious, 'prudent' he would have called it, turning to his old, familiar companions in the conference, men whose optimism he found congenial and undisturbing.

The inner circle of the Imperial court now split into two clearly defined factions. Around Leopold stood the majority of his privy conference: prince Dietrichstein who died in 1698 to be replaced as grand chamberlain by old count Harrach; count Kinsky, who died in 1699; the ancient warrior Ernst Rüdiger von Starhemberg who died in January 1701 to be replaced by another of Leopold's contemporaries, prince Mansfeld. It was, as Oswald Redlich termed it, a 'council of ancients'[3] stalked by death. Of the men appointed to the privy conference in the 1690s only one, the chancellor Bucellini, survived to the end of the reign. When a great office fell vacant, Leopold chose by preference someone from his own generation to fill the post. Most of these were men who had once served diligently and well, but who regarded high office as a reward to be enjoyed, a kind of distinguished retirement.

Within the privy conference only Kaunitz spoke up for the growing opposition. He was not young, but his political outlook led him into Joseph's faction. Joseph's supporters were for the most part younger men like prince Eugene, the victor of Zenta; count Wenzel Wratislaw,

an unusually brilliant diplomat; Joseph's tutor prince Salm, and count
Jörger, governor of Lower Austria. Most of them were warhawks who
did not find the prospect of war for the Spanish inheritance unwelcome.
Their immediate concern was to force the regime to undertake a
thorough reform of finances and begin building up the military forces
to prevent Austria from being caught, as it had so often been in the
past, a helpless victim of French aggression. On the whole these were
men who did not share Leopold's dynastic outlook, but took a more
pragmatic view of Austria's interests in central Europe and above all in
Italy. Their hopes centred quite naturally on the heir to the throne.

Joseph was unlike his father both in appearance and in manner. From
childhood he had been mercurial, over-lively, audacious. He showed
some flashes of brilliance, but completely lacked his father's patient,
thorough, scholarly temperament. He was easily bored, often unpredictable. Leopold saw to it that he was trained for the position he must
inherit and that he received all the ceremonial honours due his high
station, but the bonds between father and son arose from duty, not from
affection.

Joseph's governor, his *ajo*, prince Karl Theodor von Salm, was an
intelligent and pious gentleman who quickly won Joseph's affection (as
Portia had Leopold's), learning in the course of time to handle his hotheaded young charge. Interestingly enough there were no Jesuits among
Joseph's teachers, and Salm, though pious, was no stranger to the new
rationalist thought stirring in western Europe. The most interesting of
Joseph's tutors was his instructor in history and politics, Dr Hans Jakob
Wagner, a lawyer, master of the liberal arts, a much-travelled writer
and *raconteur*, the author of flaming patriotic pamphlets that sought to
stir the Germans against Louis XIV.[4] His *Ehrenruf Teutschlands*, written
in the 1680s and published in 1692, the year after he became Joseph's
tutor, was a strong protest against everything French, a scathing attack
on German imitators of French taste and manners, a call to national
rejuvenation. Johann Georg von Buol, another lawyer, had charge of
teaching Joseph the elements of 'public and private law', in which Joseph
proved an apt pupil. Leopold expressed his great satisfaction with Buol's
accomplishments by making him secretary to the privy conference in
1699.

By 1700 a new regime in embryo already existed in Joseph's entourage.
His *ajo*'s son, the younger prince Salm, Buol, Kaunitz, prince Eugene
and Wratislaw all shared the notions Joseph had derived from his education. Since their political experience began after 1683, they took the
Danubian monarchy for granted. Except for Kaunitz none of them had

any substantial memories of a time when the Turkish frontier was still only a short march from Vienna. Their conception of the interests of Austria, which they began to think of more as a single state than a collection of sovereignties, reflected neither the dynastic presuppositions that governed Leopold's political maxims, nor the militant Catholicism that had for nearly two centuries been the hallmark of Habsburg policy.

Joseph had been educated to believe that it was his patriotic, German duty to use the absolute power delegated to him by God to pursue the interests of the state for the common good. Nationalist German historians have repeatedly tried to cast Joseph in the mould of a Frederick the Great, seeing in his short reign a brief flicker of hope for the German national idea. In fact Joseph remained throughout a Habsburg in his political ambitions, intensely conscious that he was king of Hungary and Bohemia, that his state centred around Austria and the Danube, not in the Empire and on the Rhine. His temperament was not that of an enlightened monarch of a later generation, but a full, passionate baroque temperament.

In 1699 Joseph married, partly at his own impatient insistence, the charming princess Wilhelmine Amalie, daughter of duke Johann Friedrich of Brunswick.[5] She was five years older than her husband, but the match seemed a good one and the young couple fell in love. Leopold especially appreciated Wilhelmine's calming influence over Joseph, and the fact that she quickly produced children.

During the months before the death of Charles II of Spain the privy conference worked more or less harmoniously to assure as much support as possible for Austria's claim to Spain. As in the past, one of the main objectives was to win the military support of Brandenburg, which had been so important both on the Rhine and in Hungary. Elector Friedrich III, who succeeded his father in 1688, had from the beginning been favourably disposed to the house of Austria. He also longed for Imperial recognition of the royal title for his possessions in Prussia, making that the central issue in his negotiations with Vienna. The privy conference at first opposed the concession, for it meant elevating a prince of the Empire to a status equal to that of the king of Bohemia, a title now hereditary in the house of Habsburg. Leopold, on the other hand, saw no danger either to himself or to his dynasty now that he had secured Joseph's election (in 1690) as 'king of the Romans'.

With the signing of the second partition treaty, Leopold lost any faith he still had that England and the Dutch Republic would support his claim or defend his interests in northern Italy. By the end of July 1700 the privy conference had come to believe that a royal title was not too high a price to pay for the assurance of Brandenburg's support. After some further negotiation about the size of Brandenburg troop commitments and the subsidies to be paid for their maintenance, the treaty was signed on 16 November 1700. Two days later Leopold learned that Charles II had died, naming the duke of Anjou his heir.

Leopold responded to the unexpected news from Spain with unusual firmness and haste.[6] Even before he learned that Louis XIV had accepted the Spanish crown in the name of his grandson, Leopold ordered the war council to send Imperial forces into northern Italy to secure Milan. He named Eugene of Savoy supreme commander on 21 November, at the same time ordering military authorities in the Tyrol to prepare for the army's march over the mountains into Lombardy. In making this unusually hasty decision neither Leopold nor the war council seem to have thought beyond a quick strike to seize a crucial portion of the Spanish inheritance, which could then be used in negotiating a partition directly with France.

The Spanish will had been a blow to Leopold's expectations, but it was equally a disappointment to Louis XIV who had all along seen partition as the only politically reasonable solution to the disputed succession. Portocarrero's will, however, passed the throne to the duke of Anjou only if he and the king of France accepted the principle of the empire's integrity. Should they not pledge to maintain the whole, the right to inherit passed automatically, and within a specific, short space of time, to archduke Charles. No matter what his decision, Louis faced a war against the Empire. He accepted the challenge and began arming.

Once this decision was made, Louis pursued it with his customary aggressiveness, spreading through Europe a new fear of 'universal monarchy' on the continent. This fear was fed by Louis' decree of 31 December in which he expressly reserved Anjou's right to succeed to the throne of France, though such a union of the two crowns would have been a direct contradiction of the terms of the Spanish will. From this moment the old coalition between Austria and the Maritime Powers began to revive. William III and Heinsius started negotiations at once, though neither could move public opinion in England and the Republic quickly enough to aid Austria in its first campaign in Italy.

Leopold sent Wratislaw to London to urge William III to greater haste. Once he reached England, however, Wratislaw found himself in a frustrating position, for William had decided shrewdly to wait and let events bring Parliament around to his viewpoint. Sooner or later, William calculated, the French would do something so resented by the English that Parliament would force him to do just what he wanted.

Meanwhile Wratislaw had the difficult job of explaining English parliamentary politics to the Austrian privy conference.

Louis XIV moved quickly to secure the Bourbon succession by occupying the Spanish Netherlands. The States General, with French troops now on their own frontier, hastily made the best of a bad situation and in February 1701 recognized the duke of Anjou as Philip V of Spain. This panicky move to appease France convinced the deputies to the Dutch general assembly that the new regime in Madrid had little or no independence from France. Dutch agents were now sent to begin serious negotiations with England and the Empire for renewal of the coalition.

Leopold for once negotiated from strength. His alliance with Brandenburg had already taken effect, and both elector Georg Ludwig of Hanover (the future George I of England) and the Palatine elector Johann Wilhelm of Pfalz-Neuburg, Leopold's brother-in-law, were strong and unconditional supporters of the Habsburg claim. In January and May 1701 Leopold secured the alliance of the powerful Schönborn family and of Saxe-Weimar. The only serious disappointment was Leopold's erstwhile son-in-law Max Emmanuel of Bavaria.

Max Emmanuel had been forced to choose between France and Austria the moment the Spanish will was published. He threw his lot in with France and opened the forts of the Spanish Netherlands to French troops. In return for French confirmation of his post as Spanish governor, he signed an offensive-defensive alliance with Louis XIV. His brother, Joseph Clemens, elector of Cologne, who owed his election initially to Leopold's support, followed Max Emmanuel's lead, so that by the end of 1701 some 85,000 Franco–Spanish troops were able peacefully to take up positions in the Netherlands and within the Empire.

Just as Leopold manœuvred to counter the French, a new war broke out in northern Europe. Tsar Peter of Russia, freed from his Turkish war by a truce in the summer of 1700, turned towards the Baltic and his struggle for a 'window to the west'. Poland's new king Augustus found himself drawn in the same direction. Both Poland and Russia coveted parts of the sprawling Baltic empire of Sweden, whose young king Charles XII seemed to both a suitable sacrifice. In August 1700 Saxony-Poland and Russia, allied with Denmark, invaded Sweden's Baltic provinces. Almost at once what began as a quick raid to steal territory from a supposedly weak neighbour turned into a collective disaster for the deluded allies. Charles XII first broke the Danes, then defeated the Russians at Narva on 30 November 1700. This left Saxony-Poland alone to face Sweden's new Alexander.

The eruption of war in the north brought a very mixed reaction in

Vienna. In one way it was a blessing, for it preoccupied the powers on Austria's northern and eastern frontiers, states that in the past had often proved susceptible to French influence. With the defeat of Peter at Narva, however, Vienna had to face the possibility that the war would spread into the Empire, for the crowns of Poland and Saxony were united. As the war against France spread to engulf the powers of Europe and much of the New World as well, Vienna had constantly to keep one eye on the north. Not the least of Austria's diplomatic victories in these troubled years was its success in isolating the northern war from the conflict in the west.

Leopold's bold move to secure northern Italy began well. Prince Eugene moved his forces across the Alps and descended into northern Lombardy unexpectedly early, in May 1701. Although his army was small and constantly drained by the need to leave garrisons behind as he advanced, he scored two important victories over the Franco–Spanish forces at Carpi on 9 July and at Chiari on 1 September. Milan itself was still held for Philip V, but Eugene had won a firm foothold in Lombardy and proved that Leopold would and could fight to protect his interests. This gave Wratislaw the arguments he needed to push through the alliance with England and the Dutch.

Wratislaw had been instructed to seek a treaty which in effect renewed the alliance of 1689, guaranteeing the house of Austria the Spanish succession *in toto*. William III remained convinced, however, that partition was the only workable solution. Wratislaw concurred in that judgment, as had his mentor Kaunitz, but he pointed out firmly that Leopold must publicly defend his claim to the entire inheritance in order to appease Spanish sensitivity to partition. In fact the privy conference as early as January 1701 had advised Leopold not to demand the whole inheritance, and to instruct Wratislaw that the Emperor would be content 'if only some equality or proportion is maintained, so long as the balance of power is not wholly upset'. Italy was the main concern, and Leopold reluctantly agreed that this was so, provided that the treaties of alliance did not mention partition.[7]

The Maritime Powers could not share Leopold's concern with Italy. The English Parliament put Spain itself and the colonial empire first, while for the Dutch the primary issue was the line of barrier forts stretching along the frontier between the United Provinces and the Spanish Netherlands.[8] The English wanted Leopold to fight for Spain, the Dutch wanted him to concentrate on winning the Netherlands. Leopold wanted the Spanish throne for archduke Charles, but neither he nor his ministers had much interest in the Netherlands, a province too distant ever to become an integral part of the Austrian hereditary lands.

In March 1701 Leopold indicated to Wratislaw that he would consent to accept the Netherlands if the Dutch would agree to his incorporation of all Spanish territories in Italy.[9] The English reluctantly agreed, but the Dutch resisted, hoping that by reserving Naples and Sicily for France they might yet induce Louis XIV to accept a peaceful compromise and avoid having to go to war at all. Prince Eugene's victories in Italy and the duke of Marlborough's intervention on Wratislaw's behalf finally brought the Dutch to agree. The tripartite treaty was signed on 7 September 1701 at The Hague. Leopold ratified it the moment it arrived in Vienna on 19 September. As many had feared, the Spanish succession had produced yet another European war centring around the dynastic ambitions of Habsburgs and Bourbons.

XVIII

The Opposition takes over

The possibility of winning Spain for the house of Austria seemed remote in 1701. The privy conference at first planned no more than to secure Spain's Italian possessions; Milan and Lombardy because they were the southern key to Austrian security, then Naples and Sicily to protect growing Austrian interests in the Adriatic. When Eugene moved over the Alps even this modest partition of Spain seemed beyond the resources available, but Eugene's ingenuity and excellent knowledge of the terrain quickly made him master of events. When he defeated Villeroy at Chiari it seemed that nothing could hold him back from Milan. His victory led the privy conference to indulge in more optimistic plans for the future, while at the same time they ignored the difficulties that beset the small Imperial army in Lombardy.

A group of émigré Neapolitan nobles opposed to the Bourbon succession had sought refuge in Vienna where they reported widespread disaffection against the Neapolitan governor, who had declared for Philip V. They promised a popular uprising which would eliminate any opposition to Austrian occupation. Such uprising was in fact planned and set in motion, a small group of nobles proclaiming archduke Charles king of Naples. The incompetence of its leaders and the distrust of the populace they thought they could command produced a complete fiasco, whose main result was to bring to Vienna another, larger group of émigré Neapolitans hatching new schemes to restore themselves to their former prosperity in the wake of an Austrian victory in southern Italy.

The Emperor and his court listened optimistically to these tempting projects, debating plans for a campaign against Naples, but they underestimated the size of the army they needed to realize their objective. Leopold had sent about 40,000 men to Italy. By the end of 1701 the force had been seriously reduced by desertions and casualties. Eugene had already begun sending urgent pleas for reinforcements to make up his losses in battle, losses now increased several fold as disease ravaged his troops through the rainy winter months.

Eugene did what he could to keep the initiative he had won. In February 1702 he led a daring night attack on the French headquarters in the city of Cremona, capturing marshal Villeroy but failing to take the city itself.[1] All Europe laughed at the exploit, but the blow to French morale proved only temporary. Villeroy, even with his superior force, was no match for Eugene; but his successor, marshal Vendôme, was a commander of much greater ability.

So long as Starhemberg had remained president of the war council the interests of the military were firmly, if gruffly, represented in the privy conference. His successor, prince Mansfeld, had little understanding of war, and what experience he had was a generation out of date. Between him and prince Eugene there was a gap of age and temperament which could not be bridged. Eugene's adventurous raiding tactics he found distasteful, smacking of the *Kuruczók*. Mansfeld was convinced that Eugene exaggerated all his troubles merely to make his victories seem the more glorious. As Eugene's demands for money, men and supplies grew ever more strident, Mansfeld became increasingly impatient, passing them on through bureaucratic channels of the war council where they were filed and forgotten.

Prince Eugene quickly discovered that normal procedures could not serve him. In desperation he sent his dismal, complaining reports to anyone he could think of who might penetrate the wall of silence in Vienna, including Leopold's confessor Father Bischoff. Unfortunately for Eugene the 'opposition' to the old men in the privy conference was scattered in the summer of 1702. Wratislaw was either in London or following the duke of Marlborough on his travels. Joseph went campaigning with Ludwig Wilhelm of Baden, observing the Imperial capture of Landau on 10 September. There seemed to be no one at the Imperial court who could break through the conspiracy of indolence that protected the Emperor from a pessimistic view of the military situation. Even the Empress Eleanora, possibly from a personal dislike of Eugene, did her best to filter the news from Italy to keep the truth from disturbing Leopold.[2]

By midsummer 1702 Eugene was in real danger of being cut off from Austria by Vendôme's growing forces. In desperation he pulled out of his strong defensive positions and offered battle at Luzzara on 15 August. It was a bloody, enormously costly engagement, but successful enough to induce Vendôme to withdraw and offer no serious challenge to the Austrians for three months. Vienna rejoiced at another 'victory', but the war council did nothing to improve the desperate situation of its miserable army. Eugene requested that he be allowed to come in person to Vienna, after an absence from the court of nearly two years. Mansfeld saw in the request only a domestic, political danger and held up Eugene's petition as long as he could. Finally in December 1702 Leopold himself gave Eugene leave to return to the capital. This proved the first step towards bringing the opposition into power.

Seen from Vienna, the events of 1702 reinforced the optimism of Leopold's ministers. On 14 October Ludwig Wilhelm defeated Villars at Friedlingen, preventing for another year a junction of the French and Bavarian armies. Luzzara, Landau and Friedlingen were proof enough to the old councillors that the situation was far from hopeless. When Eugene arrived in Vienna on 8 January 1703 he found the situation worse than he had imagined. He had intended to cause just enough stir among the officials in the war council to get the reinforcements and money he needed in Italy, prior to his return to his command in February. In Vienna he discovered that his troubles were not unique. Equally urgent appeals for money, material and recruits poured in from all sides; from Ludwig Wilhelm in Germany, soon thereafter from the Tyrol and then from Hungary where rebellion broke out once more. Still the ministers, above all Mansfeld and the indolent court chamber president count Salaburg, did nothing, while isolating the Emperor behind misleading reports of Imperial successes.

Prince Eugene's judgment that the military problems resulted from incompetence and hostile personalities in the privy conference has been widely accepted. In some measure this was certainly the case, particularly with respect to Mansfeld and Salaburg. Yet the troubles went much deeper. Strategic planning on a global scale demanded a fundamentally new outlook, one foreign to the narrow vision of the war council. The court chamber was equally at a loss to understand the complex financial operations of the Maritime Powers whose loans and subsidies were essential. As the winter months of 1703 passed by it became clear that the whole structure of the monarchy faced a general crisis.

As usual the root of all the problems was money. Only ready cash in hand could pay the troops and their officers, buy ammunition, weapons, clothing, food, draught animals, and then transport all these to where they were needed. Military officers and bureaucrats alike needed money to buy intelligence, to pay secretaries and servants – in short, to transform plans, promises and intentions into reality. Without this money the system was little more than a hierarchy of officials transmitting orders downward and sending excuses back up the chain of command. By 1703 operations of the war commissariat had come virtually to a stand-still, lacking both money from the court chamber and firm decisions from the war council. While Eugene fretted the court by making noisy scenes and denouncing Mansfeld, all the problems of the regime came to rest in the court chamber, which Leopold thought he had set in order with the *Hofkammerordnung* of 1681.

The shortcomings of the treasury had been disguised in part by the operations of the 'Court Jew' (*Hofjude*), Samuel Oppenheimer, an astute banker and the main military contractor for the war commissariat. Although he was constantly the target of antisemitic criticism by courtiers, his collaboration with the treasury had been profitable to both; over the years he became the monarchy's major source of credit.[3] At the end of April 1703 Oppenheimer died, and with him died the confidence in his banking firm which his personal prestige had kept intact in spite of the very large sums he had advanced to the crown. The collapse of Oppenheimer's business left the regime literally penniless and without an alternative local source of credit. This misfortune, even more than the military disasters that began to crowd in upon him, forced Leopold to act.

Reluctant as he was to abandon his old friends, Leopold had no choice but to yield to strong pressure from his creditors and allies alike. On 28 June 1703 he dismissed Mansfeld from the war council and removed Salaburg as president of the court chamber. Two days later he named Eugene of Savoy president of the war council, and to head the treasury count Gundaker Starhemberg, a man known for financial acumen, and a younger brother of Ernst Rüdiger (president of the war council until 1701). Both men began cleaning house as best they could, but as Eugene wrote on the eve of his appointment, 'I have little hope of success in a situation these gentlemen have so badly mishandled.'[4]

The most immediate change was apparent in the privy conference, where the Josephine party now had a majority with Kaunitz enthusiastically joining Starhemberg and Eugene in pursuing reform. Wratislaw, though still away on diplomatic missions in England and on the Continent, began to exercise the function of virtual foreign minister, receiving in London or The Hague copies of the most important despatches, sending back his advice to the privy conference and to Eugene. Leopold received from his new ministers a realistic view of the situation which seemed to give him new resolve. Having been forced by circumstances to take new men into the conference, he gave them their way and supported their decisions firmly.

These changes came just as a new set of dangers beset the Empire. Franco–Bavarian troops invaded Upper Austria in March 1703, then marched into the Tyrol in June. Troubles arose in the east as a party of warhawks took control of the Ottoman regime in Constantinople and prince Ferenc II Rákóczy raised the standard of rebellion in Hungary. In the midst of these problems, the Maritime Powers demanded that Leopold join with them and Portugal to claim the entire Spanish empire for archduke Charles.

William III, the original exponent of partition, had died in March 1702. Since then queen Anne's ministers, prodded by a more aggressive parliament, evolved more expansive war aims. English policy had long aimed at breaking Spain's trade monopoly in its colonial empire. Setting up archduke Charles as claimant to the throne appeared to be a good means to achieve this. This shift away from the idea of partition towards support for Leopold's original claim for the Spanish inheritance *in toto* emerged clearly during the negotiations that led to Portugal's joining the coalition against France.

With the blessing of queen Anne's council and parliament the English merchant-diplomat John Methuen and his son Paul, used their influence in Lisbon to turn Pedro II away from his alliance with France. After long negotiations in 1702 and 1703, during which there was often much heated disagreement between the Methuens and Leopold's crotchety ambassador count Waldstein, a treaty was worked out. Pedro II agreed to break with France and make war against Philip V, provided the Maritime Powers did most of the fighting and compensated Portugal handsomely (in money and future conquests) for its modest participation. Pedro also demanded that the archduke Charles come to Portugal to give the cause a leader in whose name the 'liberation' of Spain could be undertaken. The first article of the treaty signed in Lisbon on 16 May 1703 bound Leopold to proclaim Charles king of Spain, and then to send him immediately to Lisbon.

Waldstein had serious misgivings about the treaty. He knew that the ambitions of England and the Dutch went far beyond Leopold's immediate goals, even though they coincided with the Emperor's wish to see Charles on the throne of Spain. When the text of the treaty reached Vienna, the privy conference at first objected to ratification. In the end, however, the conference concluded that Austria could not risk losing the support of England and advised ratification. Leopold finally accepted this advice, but with many pangs of conscience and well-founded misgivings about sending his favourite son to Spain with a Protestant fleet, surrounded by Protestant soldiers.

Before Charles could leave Vienna there were serious family matters to deal with. Leopold made both his sons sign an agreement which in effect ceded the Spanish holdings in north Italy to Joseph as king of the

Romans. Joseph himself had insisted on this; the privy conference made Leopold see the necessity of protecting Austrian interests, even though the agreement annoyed Charles and led to tension between the brothers. The family compact signed on 5 September 1703 reflected the new ministers' view of Austrian interests and the domination of those interests over dynastic considerations. At the same time it forced Charles to accept in advance a partition of a kingdom he had yet to win.

Just one week later, on 12 September, two more ceremonial acts were performed at the Favorita palace. First Leopold and Joseph renounced their claims to the Spanish crown. Following that the Emperor and his sons went to a meeting of eleven counsellors, a slightly enlarged privy conference, where Leopold read aloud a secret pact which would determine the succession in the house of Austria in the absence of male heirs to Joseph. This *pactum mutuae successionis* reserved Charles's right to succeed Joseph in Austria, Hungary and Bohemia, and provided that in the absence of male heirs the succession would pass to the eldest daughter of the last male to occupy the throne.[5] Leopold, Joseph and Charles formally swore to uphold this agreement with the counsellors as witnesses. This done, Leopold then went to another chamber where, before a larger gathering of his courtiers, he made a brief announcement about the renunciations and formally proclaimed Charles king of Spain. Count Harrach then went to the antechamber and announced the elevation of Charles to the throne of Spain to the assembled diplomats and dignitaries. The pact governing the succession remained secret until 1713.

With the future of his dynasty provided for as well as was possible, Leopold bade an emotional last farewell to Charles, who set out from Vienna on 19 September. Leopold hoped that a way could be found to convey Charles to Spain by way of Italy, with a Catholic rather than a Protestant escort, but it was not to be. Charles and his entourage had to be sent instead on a long northern detour around Bavaria to Hanover, the northern Netherlands and England, to a future that seemed as uncertain as the fortunes of the Habsburg dynasty.

French strategic planning for 1703 centred on Bavaria, whose location astride the upper Danube offered tempting prospects for a direct strike at Vienna. Villars was ordered to join Max Emmanuel for a thrust into Austria, while Vendôme marched his army from Italy to join them by way of the Tyrol.[6]

For once the war council anticipated the danger and sent a force under general Schlick to invade Bavaria. Max Emmanuel defeated Schlick in two engagements near Passau, then rushed into Upper Austria where he scattered other units before they could concentrate to oppose him. Secure on his Austrian frontier, Max Emmanuel then sped west to rendezvous with the French before Ludwig Wilhelm of Baden could move his German units beyond their defensive lines. By mid-May 1703 Villars had passed the Black Forest and joined with Max Emmanuel on the headwaters of the Danube. Villars brought with him the French plan for an attack on Vienna. The moment seemed a good one, for the war council had moved most of the Austrian garrison forces east to Hungary. Vendôme was already preparing to march a large part of his Italian force over the Alps to join the invasion.

Max Emmanuel surprisingly rejected the French plan, protesting that the men at their disposal would be too few to take Vienna. He may have suspected that the French wanted to trap him into taking action that would forever ruin his chances of a reconciliation with Leopold. In any event he proposed that the Franco–Bavarian units first attack the Tyrol and cut Leopold's communications with Italy. Villars accepted this, for it still left a role for Vendôme's units which he could hardly hold back once they were in motion.

The Tyrol, spared from war for over a century and a half, found itself suddenly the scene of a full-scale invasion by over 12,000 Bavarian and French troops. The Tyrol had been directly incorporated into Austria only in 1665 and still enjoyed a greater degree of independence from Vienna than the rest of the Habsburg dominions. Internal administration and local defence relied on a popular militia (*Landaufgebot*). It was an archaic system subject to endless complaints from the individualistic mountain farmers about the seemingly senseless exercises in which virtually all men in the province had to take part. At the same time the Tyroleans were perhaps more widely acquainted with the rudiments of military science than any other people in Europe. What was even more important, they could be quickly armed with weapons they knew how to use.

With ample warning of a possible invasion, the Tyrolean diet began to activate the defence system as early as May 1703. The system, so long in disuse, did not function as it was meant to do. The commanders knew war largely from the parade ground and firing range; they had little notion about how to mobilize and direct forces in a real emergency. With almost criminal negligence the commander, general Gschwind, failed to guard the passes leading into the Tyrol from Bavaria.

Max Emmanuel therefore marched into the Tyrol unopposed and took the fortress of Kufstein on 18 June 1703. Peasants fleeing in confusion before the Bavarians scattered through the Inn valley, then crowded into Innsbruck where they vented their disgust on the estates and particularly on general Gschwind, who narrowly escaped from the mob with his life. Taking advantage of this confused scene Max Emmanuel entered Innsbruck on 2 July, receiving the homage of the Imperial officials who were caught in the city. Reinforced with fresh units from Bavaria, the elector seized the Brenner Pass and sent units out from Innsbruck to take the other fortresses in the Inn valley.

The Bavarians' easy conquest turned to a nightmare when the Tyroleans recovered from their confusion and slowly began to organize their defence. Loyal units in the South Tyrol assembled to protect Brixen, where a provisional government was set up to represent the Emperor. Other Tyrolean units recaptured the Brenner Pass. In the upper reaches of the Inn valley militia units fought back a Franco–Bavarian contingent, then virtually annihilated it with a carefully planned landslide, the mountaineer sharpshooters picking off survivors as they fled.

Max Emmanuel tried to retake the Brenner Pass on 17 July, only to have the whole Inn valley, which he thought he had subdued, rise up behind him as soon as he removed his heavy units from Innsbruck. Town after town rid itself of the occupying garrisons and the elector faced the possibility that he would be cut off from Bavaria. 'If you only knew', he wrote to his wife on 28 July, 'what it is like fighting an armed people in the mountains!'[7] On 21 August he fled back to Munich having experienced perhaps the ultimate humiliation that could befall an aristocratic prince who imagined himself a great general: defeat at the hands of peasants.

This did not end the threat to the Tyrol, however, for Vendôme, following orders from Versailles, was marching into the Alps from the south. Encouraged by reports of Max Emmanuel's early successes he sent his columns north along both shores of Lake Garda on 19 July at the very moment the elector faced disaster on the Brenner. Before Vendôme reached Trent he found regular Austrian units hastily dispatched by prince Eugene barring his way, while the 'armed people' threatened every step along his route.

By this time it was clear that Max Emmanuel's invasion had failed. Vendôme spent the first week of September bombarding Trent, then turned south again to deal with Victor Amadeus II who was preparing to desert France and ally himself with the coalition. For the moment the Tyrol was free save for the fort at Kufstein which the Bavarians held with a strong garrison. Max Emmanuel occupied Augsburg and Passau, then moved the remnants of his army into Upper Austria where he quartered his troops on the helpless peasants.

★

The troubles in the east were even more disturbing. Hungary had been 'pacified' in 1687, but it was hardly tranquil. The lassitude and ineptness of the Viennese regime during the years after Zenta kept alive the old competition between the comitat authorities and representatives of the central government, raising again all the old Magyar grievances without winning the support of any powerful faction in the kingdom save that of the respected archbishop Széchenyi, whose own efforts to keep the peace were constantly undermined by the highhanded, uncompromising behaviour of Austrian officials sent to collect the new, and from the Hungarians' point of view, unconstitutional war contributions. Peasant uprisings along the Tisza sounded a warning which Vienna ignored. All that was needed was a leader.

Ferenc II Rákóczy, unquestionably the most attractive figure in the long history of Hungarian rebellion against Austria, seemed to have been born to his role. A grandson of a prince of Transylvania and of Peter Zrinyi, he grew to manhood in the household of his mother, Helena Zrinyi, and his stepfather, Imre Thököly. He was twenty-seven in 1703 when his friend Nicholas Bercsényi persuaded him to lead his compatriots in winning back the nation's freedom. Rákóczy raised his standard in May, but the privy conference was so distracted by the invasion of the Tyrol that it did not take the uprising seriously until July, when a rebel army of 8,000 men was roving freely throughout Hungary, attacking royal officials and effectively disrupting the whole Austrian administrative apparatus. The French were understandably pleased to see the old rebellion revive under an attractive new leader, and sent subsidies which, as in the past, proved a good investment.[8]

The *Kuruczók* bands rose again, raiding along the Danube as far as the Vienna basin, where the Imperial garrisons were unable to stop them. The war council and the municipal authorities in Vienna hastily ordered new fortifications built around the capital. Within the city there were seditious grumblings; rumours spread that Leopold and the court were preparing to flee to safety in Carinthia. The Dutch ambassador, Hamel-Bruynincx, wrote to Heinsius on 16 January 1704 that matters were so desperate in Vienna it seemed the house of Austria was near its end.

Such pessimism is hardly surprising given the events of the preceding year, though the strength of the regime was vastly underestimated both by its enemies and by its more anxious well-wishers. Leopold's steadiness in supporting his new ministers had a good effect. There was no doubt anywhere that prince Eugene had become the most important political as well as military figure in the Empire. Working in close collaboration with Wratislaw, who remained at the centre of the coalition's international operations with the peripatetic entourage of the duke of Marlborough, Eugene was able to develop the kind of large strategic plans which had long been lacking in Austrian military operations.

It was Wratislaw who convinced Marlborough that he should make Bavaria the object of the campaign of 1704, and Wratislaw again who persuaded Eugene to leave Vienna to lead the Imperial forces in person. Eugene and Marlborough found in each other a genuine meeting of minds; from their mutual respect grew that very rare phenomenon, an effective partnership between supreme commanders of different nations.

Eugene lured the French into sending marshal Tallard with a major force to join the Bavarians; then Marlborough, shaking off the troublesome Dutch field deputies, rushed his splendidly equipped English army eastward to join with Eugene on the Danube, where they agreed to risk a major battle. The resulting engagement, known to the Austrians as the battle of Hochstädt, to the English as Blenheim (Blindheim), was a brilliant and decisive victory. The allied Franco–Bavarian army was smashed, Tallard and some 9,000 of his men taken prisoner along with their entire baggage train and '34 carriages of French women'.[9]

The political consequences of the victory were immediate. The French evacuated all of southern Germany. Max Emmanuel appointed his wife regent in Munich and fled to Brussels and his mistresses. Joseph hurried from Vienna to watch prince Eugene besiege Landau, which the French had retaken in 1703. The regency in Bavaria sued for peace on terms which amounted to surrender. While Max Emmanuel's Polish consort retained titular sovereignty and the income from the elector's personal patrimony, the Bavarian state itself and its revenues fell under Imperial administration.

Hochstädt-Blenheim was another 'miracle of the house of Austria', the last Leopold was to see. Growing fragile with age and illness, he retired more and more from the affairs of state which were, after all, already in the hands of the men who would serve his successor. Even the ceremonies celebrating the triumphs of his arms wearied him, and he retreated to the intimacy of his close family circle, to his music and his books, his curiosities and his faith. To the men who had saved his Empire he expressed as usual his deep and sincere gratitude. He invested Marlborough with the dignity of a prince of the Empire. To Eugene of Savoy, now his most powerful minister and one of the richest men in Europe, he could only give his confidence and the troubles that remained to vex the monarchy.

XIX

Epilogue

On 17 April 1705 the grand chamberlain, count Harrach, noted in his journal that the Emperor had yielded to the advice of his physicians and cancelled a hunting expedition to Laxenburg. Later that day he showed the symptoms of one or a series of mild heart attacks: painful pressure on his left side, heavy breathing, loss of appetite. Still he met his chief advisers in the morning and gave audiences in the afternoon. Three days later, to relieve the persistent troubled breathing, the court physicians administered a purge which worked with quite unexpected vigour. The next day Leopold seemed better, joining some of his musical friends in accompanying the Italian singer Angelo Grimaldi. The relief was of short duration; within three days Leopold had grown so weak, his breathing so troubled, that he sent for his confessor to confer about his testament. Churches throughout Vienna offered prayers for his recovery; the court resigned itself to the inevitable.

Having been taught all his life to expect death, Leopold prepared himself for it now with his usual calm acceptance and ceremonious piety. Count Harrach's journal record of these last days dwindled to terse, hasty scribbles as he and his regiment of underlings busied themselves to provide for the Emperor's physical and spiritual comfort.[1] On 26 April Leopold signed his last testament, a document prepared for him by Seilern. Two days later he turned over to Joseph all affairs of state. The Emperor lingered on another week, at times in great pain, then died quietly early in the afternoon of 5 May, fully conscious to the end, taking leave of his family and his servants with a calm, clear voice.

The quiet end of Leopold's long reign produced no political surprises. No couriers stood by their mounts to carry the news to men waiting for their call to power; Joseph's men had already won the highest offices, or had been placed in the line of succession to them.[2] The few changes that did take place during the following weeks were almost entirely confined to the more ceremonial offices of the household which customarily went to the personal favourites of a new monarch. The Emperor's death shocked no one.

While the court performed the lengthy, prescribed mourning rituals[3] for the Emperor who had outlived at least three generations of ministers, the European war went on. Those who expected startling results from the new monarch were disappointed. The new ministers, having chafed in opposition, were learning humility in office. Eugene of Savoy heard of Leopold's death in Italy where he was trying to direct simultaneously the Italian campaign and the complex affairs of the war council. His energy and painstaking attention to detail made military administration function more smoothly than usual, but fundamental reform of the system itself had to be postponed until quieter days. The same was true for Gundaker Starhemberg in the court chamber, where no reforms, however well-reasoned, could transform overnight the tangled financial affairs of the monarchy.

Improvement in military and financial administration depended on careful attention to detail; on the painfully slow process of discovering incompetents, removing them and replacing them with more competent officials; it also required devising new procedures which these men could adopt. Even in normal times this is the work of years, not weeks. In the midst of a war fought on many fronts at once Joseph's ministers were forced, as his father's had been, to fall back on expedients and to make the best they could of the situation as they found it. Loans and subsidies from England and the Dutch remained the main bulwark against disaster.

The French openly encouraged Rákóczy's uprising in Hungary, while the long history of Habsburg persecution there made it easy for the Maritime Powers to believe that all the rebels were victims of religious intolerance, even though Rákóczy himself and many of his closest advisers were in fact Catholics. Joseph had more sympathy for the Magyars than his father had ever shown, but the meddling and interference of his own allies nullified his best intentions, weakening his hold on the kingdom and at the same time poisoning his relations with the allies whose money alone kept his armies in the field.

The Austrian occupation of Bavaria, one of the main fruits of the victory at Blenheim-Hochstädt, quickly turned into a costly, wasteful operation. The Austrian governor could not control the poorly paid occupation troops who began exacting their back pay from the villages where they were quartered. On top of these informal exactions, Vienna imposed special 'contributions' to help fill the perennially depleted war chest. At the end of July 1705 the war council ordered a special recruitment of Bavarians which amounted to impressment in the Imperial army. The young men of Bavaria fled to the mountains or hid in the forests to escape the 'recruiters'; soon they organized in guerrilla bands whose terrorist attacks forced the Austrians to commit even more units to the occupation. By October the Bavarian irregulars pinned down over 7,000 soldiers who were badly needed on several other battlefields.

During the six brief years of Joseph's reign his ministers gradually proved themselves able to master the situation. What could be extracted from the potentially rich monarchy was organized to make good Austria's claim to the status of a great power. With unstinting help from the British parliament, and more grudging but equally welcome support from the Dutch, Marlborough and prince Eugene held at bay and nearly brought down the military might of France. Archduke Charles held court in Barcelona behind English bayonets now enthusiastically pledged to place him on the Spanish throne.

The imposing success of the coalition banished for the moment any thought of partitioning Spain. 'No peace without Spain' ran the patriotic slogan in London and Amsterdam. Louis XIV sued for peace in 1709, promising negotiations at the The Hague concessions which would give each of the allies as much as they could hope to win from a humbled France: Spain for Charles of Austria, colonial and commercial concessions for the English, an impregnable barrier of fortresses to protect the Dutch. But Louis balked at joining the coalition to drive his grandson from Madrid. When the allies refused to compromise on that issue, Louis withdrew from the discussions and settled down stubbornly to fight for the preservation of his own frontiers.[4]

The opportunities the allies missed at The Hague disappeared forever. In spite of economic exhaustion and the most severe winter in memory, the French fought on as the allies themselves grew weary. In England voices were heard begging for a prompt end to the carnage. By the beginning of 1711 the coalition was already in disarray when the sudden death of Joseph broke it apart for good. In April 1711 Joseph contracted smallpox, seemed to recover, then – without warning – died on 17 April. Joseph had two daughters, but no surviving sons, so according to Leopold's family pact of 1703 his brother Charles inherited the Austrian, Bohemian and Hungarian crowns along with the dynastic claim to the Imperial throne. The Maritime Powers quickly reconciled themselves to the Bourbon succession in Spain. That biological good luck that had so often sustained the Habsburg dynasty had at last run out.

In 1713 the Maritime Powers made peace with France at Utrecht, sanctioning the Bourbon succession in Spain. After one more inconclusive campaign Eugene of Savoy negotiated peace at Rastatt in 1714, ending the long dynastic struggle for Spain. Charles VI, bitterly disappointed, surrounded himself with refugees from his former Spanish court and dreamed of the golden days of his youth in Barcelona, never understanding why a country he loved so much loved him so little.

Leopold I died still hoping that the global empire of his illustrious predecessors would survive the onslaught of France and remain a great Habsburg patrimony. Yet when his favoured younger son Charles entered Vienna as Emperor seven years later the ties with Spain were already being cut by the treaty provisions worked out between his allies and France. It is difficult to imagine a different conclusion to the great war for the Spanish succession even if Leopold had lived on to its end. In general outline the events of 1709 to 1714 repeated on a larger scale Austria's experience with earlier coalitions against France. Joseph's death in 1711 was a dynastic misfortune, but it offered only an occasion and an excuse for the Maritime Powers to complete the disengagement they were determined to make before the costs of global war could further damage their commercial power.

The final partition of Spain closely resembled the design worked out in 1701 between Wratislaw and William III. Austria reluctantly took over the Spanish Netherlands, providing a political barrier of sorts between France and the United Provinces. Austria also received the coveted Italian states. The treaties of Utrecht and Rastatt confirmed a long-delayed victory for the 'easterners' at the Viennese court, that faction which, whatever its current cause or composition, favoured consolidation of the monarchy on the Danube, if necessary at the expense of old dynastic ties to Spain.

Leopold had sided consistently with the 'westerners' who stood for the family enterprise, the union with Spain and implacable enmity against France. It had been his good fortune that the English and Dutch found him a convenient, if expensive and often uncomfortable, ally in their struggle against French preponderance on the continent. Their loans and subsidies disguised the imbalance between the economic and military power of France and the corresponding poverty of the Habsburgs.

In 1664 and again in the months before 1683 it took the prospect of total disaster in the east to divert Leopold's attention from France. While he wholeheartedly espoused the Christian crusade against Islam, he was convinced that God would favour his cause in that contest in the long run. France, a Christian power, was the greater danger, a great power whose king offended God by encouraging the Turks to fall upon their Christian neighbours while he unjustly seized provinces God had entrusted to the rule of others. The Holy League reflected Leopold's crusading piety. The League of Augsburg represented that same piety but also his dedication to the Habsburgs' Imperial mission and his own determination to defend all that was his by right of inheritance.

Leopold has often been characterized as an indecisive monarch, yet there is a certain consistency in his political decisions. Until the last years of his life, when old age and physical infirmity left him little inclination to keep abreast of public business. Leopold had worked steadily at his job, keeping himself well informed. He had strong views about his duties as a Christian Emperor and a Habsburg ruler, responsibility for decisions which he knew he could not delegate. Yet when none of the visible alternatives clearly favoured the interests of his house or of his faith, he often hesitated. If events seemed to allow him no choice, he could act firmly and quickly, but it was not his usual mode of operation. His deep faith in Providence encouraged his ingrained prudence, while the striking success of many of his undertakings confirmed it. He saw the events that forced him to act not as the working of blind chance, but rather as the unfolding of God's design.

While Leopold's Catholic piety clearly dominated his political outlook, this fact does not necessarily confirm the traditional view of a man dominated by his Jesuit confessors and nis intimates among the clergy.[5] Emmerich Sinelli, cardinal Buonvisi, and above all Marco d'Aviano had enormous personal influence over Leopold, but they were all very able men, strong and compelling personalities who served the same ideological goals Leopold had set for himself. They were also honest men, careful to avoid abusing their influence, more conscientious in this respect than were many of Leopold's lay advisers or even members of his own family. Yet Leopold did not appoint clerics to ministerial positions. The churchmen at court, following the lead of Rome, were usually 'easterners', lacking that strong sense of dynastic mission so fundamental to the house of Austria. All their influence could not induce the Emperor to appease France and concentrate on the Turkish crusade.

The confessors present a more difficult problem, for the secrecy of the confessional leaves no evidence of what was said there. That Leopold separated official matters from his personal confession, however, seems evident from the public manner in which he dealt with his scruples about allying with Protestant powers. Many courtiers sought to use the confessor as a means to get Leopold's ear secretly, and at times they succeeded in doing so; yet it is hard to find any instance where this clearly influenced state policy or appointments to the privy conference. It is just as likely that the confessional served as a useful link between the Emperor and the popular masses he ruled but seldom saw, a channel through which common grievances and rumours reached the monarch's ears.

After 1683 Leopold was not free to pursue his singleminded anti-French policy. The southeastern plains, the lower Danube and the Balkans drew Austria eastward with a promise of power few governments could resist. Once reclaimed, Hungary had to be governed, even in the face of stiff opposition from the Magyars themselves. Gradually the demands of the east changed the political outlook in Vienna and in the end they transformed the monarchy itself.

Leopold sensed this shift and resisted it, often against the urgent advice of his most intimate spiritual advisers, Sinelli and d'Aviano. His distrust of the Hungarian nobility, fed by their repeated rebellions against him and by their questionable loyalty to the Christian cause against the Turks, turned into a deep dislike and prejudice. Among the many men who served in his privy conference there was not a single Magyar, though there were many Bohemians, some of whom were, like Lobkowitz, avowed 'easterners'. For the most part, however, Leopold's ministers were Austrian or Italian nobles and German lawyers. The empire they built on the ruins of reconquered Hungary began its political life with an unhealthy legacy of prejudice and national passion which no amount of political or economic rationality could ever completely overcome.

The Habsburg imperial tradition was adaptable and very cosmopolitan, but it could not easily adjust to the task of governing a large, virtually landlocked conglomeration of eastern nationalities as diverse in their religious confessions as they were in language and cultural traditions. When the western imperial ambitions of the house of Austria were shattered by the loss of Spain, it still took the dynasty half a century and more to adjust to its new identity, and even then the recollections of its Roman imperial past lived on to haunt it.

Leopold's long reign encompassed both the end of the old Habsburg family enterprise and the creation of a new great power on the Danube. The dynasty failed, but Austria itself succeeded astonishingly. By 1705 the monarchy had both health and vigour enough to carry it through a long war and yet another violent rebellion in Hungary. Survival itself, though not necessarily a virtue, is at least an advantage.

Driving the Turks out of the central Danube region brought a new level of security which contributed to the general improvement of life for all in the hereditary lands. By 1700 colonization and migration into the *neoaquisten* extended the rural population, the base upon which all traditional societies rested. In spite of periodic violence and disastrous plagues it is clear that by the beginning of the eighteenth century the rural population was increasing in numbers, if not always in prosperity. New construction during the last decades of the reign, encompassing not only the great ecclesiastical buildings and noble palaces, but also humble *Bauernhöfe*, market towns, roads and bridges, was not produced by a society on the verge of starvation whose every Groschen was claimed by a rapacious government.

Emperor Leopold's personal role in this large process of empire-building was in many ways modest, yet at the same time absolutely fundamental. With few exceptions he was well served by the men he chose to do the routine work of government, most especially by his soldiers and diplomats. He knew how to value dedication and loyalty, even at the expense of rewarding the undeserving. His own gentle trust and his profound ignorance about money made him an easy mark for the professionally corrupt; it is surprising that he was victimized by so few.

Leopold's approach to public affairs was not practical in a modern, materialist sense; subsequent observers tend to agree with his contemporary critics who found that the structure and procedures of his government defied the rational precepts of statecraft. But Leopold believed that Providence ordered human affairs, that the 'process of government' was, in decisive moments, more a matter of God's direct, miraculous intervention than a question of bookkeeping procedures in the court chamber.

To the despair of posterity, Leopold was not the apostle of a *Drang nach Osten*, of German nationalism, nor even of a 'United States of Europe'. Yet it was in his name that the Austrian monarchy extended its power as far into the Balkans as it was ever to reach: as far as Albania, central Serbia, Bosnia and Wallachia. It was around the Emperor Leopold that the German publicists, smarting under humiliating French defeats, united in an outpouring of wounded national pride, rallying to the *Deutscher Kaiser* in a moment of common peril. Then, too, it was Leopold himself, speaking through his diplomats, who argued for harmony and unity against the ambitions of Louis XIV, while at the same time representing what remained of Christian unity in the epic struggle against the Turks.

Empires are not usually created during moments of absentmindedness. Leopold's territorial expansion in eastern Europe was produced by military conquest, success more striking to contemporaries even than the

French expansion towards the Rhine. By systematically eliminating alternatives to Habsburg rule he acted not unlike his grandfather Ferdinand II, who had subdued Bohemia between 1620 and 1627 in similar fashion. In 1705 there were only tentative plans for transforming the fact of conquest into the reality of a new allegiance. It remained for Leopold's children and their descendants to try to create a system within that new empire.

Bibliographical Note

Bibliographical Note
For brevity, the following abbreviations are used both in the notes to the text and below:

HHSA   Haus- Hof- und Staatsarchiv, Vienna
AGS   Archivo Simancas, Valladolid
ÖNB   Österreichische Nationalbibliothek, Vienna
FRA   *Fontes rerum austriacarum*, published by the K. u. K. Akademie der Wissenschaften in Vienna
AÖG   *Archiv für Österreichische Geschichte*
MIÖG   *Mitteilungen des Instituts für Österreichischen Geschichtsforschung*
MÖS   *Mitteilungen des Österreichischen Staatsarchivs*
Feldzüge: *Feldzüge des Prinzen Eugen von Savoyen*, published by the Abteilung für Kriegsgeschichte of the K. und K. Kriegs-Archiven (20 vols, Vienna, 1876–92)

An analytical bibliography of this period would require a substantial volume in itself. In most instances the works selected for citation here, particularly the more recent ones, contain extensive guides to the published literature and to the archival sources. In cases where works are translated into English, I have cited only the English version.

Bibliographies; The most comprehensive listing of sources is Karl and Mathilde Uhlirz, *Handbuch der Geschichte Österreichs und seiner Nachbarländer Böhmen und Ungarn* (4 vols Vienna-Graz-Leipzig 1927–44). Unfortunately only the first volume, which does not extend to Leopold's reign, has been brought up to date in the last decade. Since 1965 the American Bibliographical Center in Santa Barbara, California, has published *Österreichische Historische Bibliographie*, which, though somewhat behind schedule, still offers a thorough annual review of recent publications. The *Austrian History Yearbook*, edited by John R. Rath at Rice University, Houston, Texas, is an invaluable guide to publications, dissertations in Austria and the U.S., and research in progress. Alphons Lhotsky, *Österreichische Historiographie*, gives a survey of Austrian historical writing in all periods. For Leopoldine historiography see Anna Coreth, *Österreichische Geschichtsschreibung in der Barockzeit* (Vienna 1950) and Nana Eisenberg, 'Studien zur Historiographie über Kaiser Leopold I', MIÖG, 51 (1937).

Published documents; Of Leopold's own correspondence only bits and pieces have been deciphered and published. The best collections are Onno Klopp (ed.), *Corrispondenza epistolare tra Leopoldo I imperatore ed il P. Marco d'Aviano Capuccino* (Graz 1888), A. F. Pribram and M. L. von Pragenau (eds.), *Privatbriefe Kaiser Leopold I an den Grafen F. E. Pötting, 1662–1673*, FRA, Second Series, vols 56–57 (Vienna 1903–04), and Max Dvórak (ed.), 'Briefe Kaiser Leopold I an Wenzel

Euseb Herzog in Schlesien zu Sagan, Fürsten von Lobkowitz, 1657–1674', AÖG, 80 (1894). The indispensable Venetian ambassadorial reports have been edited by Joseph Fiedler, *Die Relationen der Botschafter Venedigs über Deutschland und Österreich im 17. Jahrhundert*, FRA, Diplomataria et Acta, 26–27 (Vienna 1867).

Austria; The two best recent histories of Austria are Erich Zöllner, *Geschichte Österreichs* (2nd edn, Vienna 1961) and Hugo Hantsch, *Die Geschichte Österreichs*, 2 vols (3rd edn, Graz 1962); both contain excellent bibliographies. Adam Wandruszka's *The House of Habsburg* (London 1964) is an interesting essay on the ruling dynasty. Most American and British historians of the Habsburg monarchy have concentrated on later centuries, treating Leopold's reign superficially if at all. Friedrich Heer, *The Holy Roman Empire* (New York/London 1968), is a fascinating, if eccentric, study of the whole history of the Empire. The chapter on Leopold is brief, but the discussion of Imperial baroque style is well worth reading.

Two of the most satisfactory recent works on the monarchy are by the French historian Victor-L. Tapié: *The Rise and Fall of the Habsburg Monarchy* (New York 1971) is particularly useful for its extensive reference to Czech literature on the period and the attention it gives to the demographic, social and economic structures. Even more appropriate to Leopold's reign is Tapié's *Les États de la Maison d' Autriche de 1657 à 1790* (2 vols, Paris 1961).

Leopold I; The cornerstone for any study of this reign remains Oswald Redlich, *Weltmacht des Barock, Österreich in der Zeit Kaiser Leopolds I*, published originally in 1921 as a continuation of Alfons Huber's monumental *Geschichte Österreichs* (5 vols, Vienna 1885–96) and reprinted several times since (4th edn, Vienna 1961). This volume covers the period 1648 to 1700. The last years of Leopold's reign are dealt with in Redlich's *Das Werden einer Grossmacht, Österreich von 1700–1740*, (3rd edn, Vienna 1942). In both books the emphasis is on Austria's role in Europe; Redlich died before completing another volume devoted to internal developments. Reinhold Baumstark's *Kaiser Leopold I* (Freiburg i.B. 1873) is over a century old, but remains the only attempt at a full 'life' of Leopold since the eighteenth century.

Government; An ambitious project begun in 1907 by Thomas Fellner and Heinrich Kretschmayr provides the basic reference work on governmental structure in this period: *Die Österreichische Zentralverwaltung von Maximilian I bis zur Vereinigung der österreichischen und böhmischen Hofkanzlei (1749)*. The first volume (Vienna 1907) gives a general historical survey and very useful lists of office holders. More general, but still useful, is F. C. Helbling, *Österreichische Verfassungs- und Verwaltungsgeschichte* (Vienna 1956).

Alfred Francis Pribram's 'Die Neiderösterreichische Stände und die Krone in der Zeit Kaiser Leopold I', MIÖG, 14 (1893) is a model study of the interaction between the crown and the estates. Unfortunately the other estates of the hereditary lands have not been given the same attention. There is a greater abundance of writing on some of the agencies of the crown: Henry F. Schwarz, *The Imperial Privy Council in the Seventeenth Century* (Cambridge 1943); Oscar Regele, *Der österreichische Hofkriegsrat 1556–1848* (Vienna 1949); Adam Wolf, 'Die Hofkammer unter Leopold I', *Sitzungsberichte der philosophisch-historischen Classe der kaiserlichen Akademie der Wissenschaften*, 11 (Vienna 1854); and L. Gross, *Die Geschichte der deutschen Reichshofkanzlei 1559–1806* (Vienna 1933).

On financial management see Eduard Holzmair, 'Geld und Münze unter Kaiser Leopold I', MIÖG, 60 (1962); Josef Fischer, 'Die Neueinrichtung des innerösterreichischen Kammerreferats in Wien im Jahre 1665–1666', MIÖG, Additional vol. 11 (1929), and Theodor Mayer, 'Das Verhältnis der Hofkammer zur ungarischen Kammer bis zur Regierung Maria Theresias', MIÖG, Additional vol. 9 (1913–15). Alfred Francis Pribram assembled a mass of raw economic data: *Materialien zur Geschichte der Preise und Löhne in Österreich* (2 vols, Vienna 1938), which has yet to be adequately analyzed. For a survey of economic trends, see Stanislas Hoszowski, 'Central Europe and the Sixteenth- and Seventeenth-century Price Revolution', an article originally published in *Annales*, included in Peter Burke (ed.), *Economy and Society in Early Modern Europe* (New York 1972).

The court and its personalities; Jürgen Freiherr von Kruedener, *Die Rolle des Hofes im Absolutismus* (vol. 19 of *Forschungen zur Sozial- und Wirtschaftsgeschichte*, Stuttgart 1973), offers a general overview of European courts as social institutions. The best contemporary views of the Viennese court are in the Venetian ambassadorial reports and Alfred F. Pribram (ed.), 'Aus dem Berichte eines Franzosen über den Wiener Hof in den Jahren 1671 and 1672', MIÖG, 12 (1891), and Esaias Pufendorf, *Bericht über Kaiser Leopold, seinen Hof und die österreichische Politik 1671–1674*, edited by Karl G. Helbig (Leipzig 1862). Heinrich Ritter von Srbik, 'Abenteurer am Hofe Kaiser Leopold I, Alchemie, Technik und Merkantilismus', in *Archiv für Kulturgeschichte*, 8 (1910), should be consulted together with Herbert Hassinger, *Johann Joachim Becher 1635–1682* (Vienna 1951).

There are many biographies of Leopold's servants, with the generals, as usual, best represented. Among the finest are Alfred F. Pribram's *Franz Paul Freiherr von Lisola 1613–1674* (Leipzig 1894); Max Braubach's monumental life of *Prinz Eugen von Savoyen* (5 vols, Vienna 1963–65); Grete Mecenseffy, 'Im Dienste dreier Habsburger, Leben und Wirken des Fürsten Johann W. Auersperg, 1615–1677', AÖG, 114 part 2 (1938); and Adam Wolf, *Fürst Wenzel Lobkowitz, erster geheimer Rath Kaiser Leopold I, 1609–1677* (Vienna 1869).

Cultural life; One of Oswald Redlich's late essays: 'Über Kunst und Kultur des Barock in Österreich', AÖG, 115 (1943), offers a good introduction. Ann Tizia Leitich's *Vienna Gloriosa* (Vienna 1947) is superbly illustrated. Robert A. Kann, *A Study in Austrian Intellectual History from Late Baroque to Romanticism* (New York 1960), devotes the first two sections to Leopold's reign and to Abraham a Sancta Clara. On art and architecture see Emerich Schaffran, *Kunstgeschichte Österreichs* (Vienna 1948). On music: Guido Adler, *Einleitung zur Ausgabe der Compositionen Kaiser Ferdinand III, Leopold I, Joseph I* (Prague 1892), and *Musikalische Werke der Kaiser . . .* (Vienna 1893).

The Church; The Austrian Church has not received the attention it merits, although the graceful study by Anna Coreth, *Pietas Austriaca, Ursprung und Entwicklung barocker Frömmigkeit in Österreich* (Vienna 1959), is an excellent introduction to the ritual and symbolism of the age. On Leopold and the Church see S. J. Miller and J. P. Spielman, *Cristóbal de Rojas, Irenecist and Cameralist 1626–1695* (Philadelphia 1962). Max Immich, *Papst Innocenz XI 1676–1689* (Berlin 1900), is good on papal policy. The reports of the papal nuncios were edited by Arthur Levinson, 'Nuntiaturberichte vom Kaiserhofe Leopolds I', AÖG, 103 (1913) and 106 (1919).

Hungary and the Nationalities Question; The problem of national consciousness in the seventeenth century is widely debated. An excellent statement on the subject is Jean Béranger, 'La question des nationalités dans l'Autriche du XVIIᵉ siècle', in *Bulletin de la Société d'Histoire Moderne*, 4th Series, No. 9 (1974). Most general histories of Hungary have been written from a national viewpoint, with little attention to the problems of the ruling dynasty or to the non-Magyars within the kingdom. C. A. Macartney, *Hungary, A Short History* (Edinburgh 1962), and Denis Sinor, *A Short History of Hungary* (London 1959) are both useful, but better on the period after 1740 than on the earlier epochs.

For the Zrinyi rebellion see E. Lilek, *Kritische Darstellung der Ungarisch-Kroatischen Verschwörung* (4 vols, Celje 1928–30), and Georg Wagner, 'Der Wiener Hof, Ludwig XIV, und die Anfänge der Magnatenverschwörung', MÖS, 16 (1963). Literature on the Rákóczy rebellion is vast and tendentious. The best recent work is Béla Köpeczi: *La France et la Hongrie au début du XVIII⁰ siècle: Étude d'histoire des relations diplomatiques et d'histoire des idées* (Budapest, Akademiai Kiadó, 1971).

On Transylvania see Ladislas Makkai, *Histoire de Transylvanie* (Paris 1946). An excellent monograph on Austria's eastern frontier is Gunther Rothenberg's *The Austrian Military Border in Croatia, 1522–1747* (Urbana, Illinois, 1960).

The Turks and the Siege of Vienna; For a guide to the literature see Walter Stürminger, *Bibliographie und Ikonographie der Türkenbelagerungen Wiens, 1529 und 1683* (Graz 1955). For the English-speaking reader there are two good studies: John Stoye, *The Siege of Vienna* (New York 1964), which concentrates on the year 1683, and Thomas M. Barker, *Double Eagle and Crescent, Vienna's Second Siege in its Historical Setting* (Albany, N.Y., 1967), which covers a wider range of topics and the long train of events leading up to the siege. For the years from 1683 to Carlowitz see Otto Brunner, 'Österreich und die Walachei während des Türkenkrieges von 1683–1699', MIÖG, 44 (1930). William B. Munson, *The Last Crusade* (Dubuque, Iowa, 1969), details the diplomacy of the Holy League in these years. The best study of John III Sobieski is Otto Forst-Battaglia, *Jan Sobieski, König von Polen* (Zurich 1946). Though it is old, Onno Klopp's *Das Jahr 1683 und der folgende grosse Türkenkrieg bis zum Frieden von Carlowitz, 1690* (Graz 1882) is still useful.

The Spanish Succession; The concluding section of John Lynch, *Spain under the Habsburgs* (2 vols, Oxford 1966, 1969), gives a good summary of Spanish affairs in the reign of Charles II. A more detailed, if less critical, study is the duque de Maura's *Vida y reinado de Carlos II* (3 vols, Madrid 1942). French diplomacy is covered in A. Legrelle, *La diplomatie française et la succession d'Espagne* (6 vols, Braine-le-Comte 1895–99); the Austrian side in Arnold Gaedeke, *Die Politik Österreichs in der spanischen Erbfolgefrage* (2 vols, Leipzig 1877).

Austria and France; The Habsburg monarchy has long served French (and British) historians as a convenient whipping-boy. An interesting corrective to this perspective is Pierre Goubert's *Louis XIV and Twenty Million Frenchmen* (New York and London 1972). Heinrich Ritter von Srbik's *Wien und Versailles 1692–1697, zur Geschichte von Strassburg, Elsass und Lothringen* (Munich 1944) suggests something of the complexity and subtlety of Habsburg and Bourbon interests on the Rhine. Unfortunately there is nothing on Leopold I to compare with Ragnhild M. Hatton's 'Louis XIV and His Fellow Monarchs' in John C. Rule (ed.), *Louis XIV and the Craft of Kingship* (Columbus, Ohio, 1969).

Notes to the Text

Chapter I

1 [Eucharius Gottlieb Rinck], *Leopolds des Grossen Rom. Kaysers wunderwürdiges Leben und Thaten* (Leipzig 1709), another version of the same work: (Cologne 1713). Nana Eisenberg, 'Studien zur Historiographie über Kaiser Leopold I', *MIÖG*, Vol. 51 (1937) 359–413. Alphons Lhotsky, *Österreichische Historiographie*, (Vienna 1962) 93ff. The definitive work on contemporary historical writing is Anna Coreth, *Österreichische Geschichtsschreibung in der Barockzeit, 1620–1740* (Vienna 1950) see especially pp. 68–78.

2 Adam Wandruszka, *The House of Habsburg* (London 1964) 7. See also Grete Mecenseffy, 'Habsburger im 17. Jahrhundert. Die Beziehungen der Höfe von Wien und Madrid während des dreissig-jährigen Krieges', *AÖG*, Vol. 121 (1955).

3 On the Reformation in Austria see G. Loesche, *Geschichte des Protestantismus im vormaligen und im heutigen Österreich* (Vienna 1930); and Grete Mecenseffy, *Geschichte des Protestantismus in Österreich* (Graz 1956). Hugo Hantsch, *Geschichte Österreichs* (4th edit., 2 vols, Graz 1959) I, 251f.

4 V.-L. Tapié, *The Rise and Fall of the Habsburg Monarchy* (New York 1971) 84ff.; and Erich Zöllner, *Geschichte Österreichs* (2nd ed., Vienna 1961) 211–221. Tapié summarizes much of the recent work by Czech historians.

5 Anna Coreth, *Pietas Austriaca, Ursprung und Entwicklung Barocker Frömmigkeit in Österreich* (Vienna 1959): see particularly the introduction: *Die Pietas als Herrschertugend.*

6 *Ibid.*, 10. In the seventeenth century much was made of the scriptural passage (Proverbs VIII:15) *Per me reges regnant et legum conditores iusta decernunt* (By me kings reign, and rulers decree what is just.)

7 *Ibid.*, 17–30. The rituals surrounding the Eucharist were especially significant in both Spain and Austria in this period. *Corpus Christi* became the great church holiday of the religious year, and Latin epigrammers found many ways to play with the word EVCHARISTIA: HIC AVSTRIA, HEC AVSTRIA, and so forth.

Chapter II

1 Victor-L. Tapié, *The Rise and Fall of the Habsburg Monarchy* (trans. by Stephen Hardman, New York 1971) 119f., 137f. notes 4 and 5. The debate over the consequences of the war is still unsettled, the statistical evidence easy to challenge. It is likely that many locally produced surveys of depopulation were exaggerated, while at the same time the areas hit hardest by the crisis produced very incomplete accounts at best.

2 Quantitative analysis of Austrian social and economic development is only now producing sufficient material to give us a closer look at the structure of Austrian society and its economy in the seventeenth century. A very recent work edited by Heimold Helcz-

manovski for the Austrian Central
Statistical Office, *Beiträge zur Bevölke-*
rungs- und Sozialgeschichte Österreichs
(Vienna/Munich 1973) contains two
important studies on this period: Kurt
Klein, 'Die Bevölkerung Österreichs
vom Beginn des 16. bis zur Mitte des
18. Jahrhunderts' and Michael Mit-
terauer, 'Zur Familienstruktur in
ländlichen Gebieten Österreichs im 17.
Jahrhundert'.

3 Franz Fischer, 'Die blaue Sensen,
Sozial und Wirtschaftsgeschichte der
Sensenschmiedezunft zu Kirchdorf-
Michaeldorf bis zur Mitte des 18.
Jahrhunderts', FGÖ, Vol. IX (1966).

4 For a good general picture of the
complexity of agricultural and mineral
production in Austria see Erich Zöllner, *Geschichte Österreichs* (Vienna
1961) 275–287.

5 William McNeill, *Europe's Steppe*
Frontier, 1500–1800 (Chicago 1964).
McNeill suggests some interesting
reasons for Habsburg success in
organizing the large part of this still
open frontier. It is useful to remember
that in south-eastern Europe, at least,
the success of the Austrian monarchy
should be judged by its effectiveness in
competition with the Turks, the Poles
and the Russians, not in comparison
with the French administrative model.

6 L. Gross, *Die Geschichte der deutschen*
Reichshofkanzlei, 1559–1806 (Vienna
1933).

7 For the Tyrolean succession see
Hugo Hantsch, *Geschichte Österreichs*
(3rd edn., Graz 1962) II, 23–25.

8 The standard reference for the central
governmental organization is Thomas
Fellner and Heinrich Kretschmayr,
Die Österreichische Zentralverwaltung,
Vol. I Pt. I (Vienna 1907), which
provides a historical outline of the
administration from Maximilian I to
1749, with very useful chronological
lists of the men who held the leading
positions in the system.

9 *Ibid.*, 53–57. The privy conference
probably developed out of sensitive
discussions about foreign affairs, which
were always the '*geheimsten Sachen*',
and could be discussed freely only
among a very few trusted advisers.

Chapter III

1 A sixth child was born to Ferdinand
III and his third wife, Eleanora
Gonzaga of Mantua, on 30 December
1654: Maria Anna, who married
Johann Wilhelm of Pfalz-Neuburg in
1678 and died in 1691.

2 Georg Mentz, *Johann Philipp von*
Schönborn Kurfürst von Mainz (2 vols.,
Jena 1896, 1899) 1, 70ff.

3 Joseph Fiedler (ed.) *Die Relationen*
der Botschafter Venedigs über Deutschland
und Österreich im 17. Jahrhundert (FRA,
vols. XXVI and XXVII, Vienna
1867) 1, 5f.

4 Rinck, *Leopold des Grossen* 76–77,
81–83.

5 ÖNB Albertina, Musiksammlung.
Over a hundred of Leopold's compositions survive, many of them as
complete scores for performance. A
recent recording by the Musical
Heritage Society, 'Music of the
Habsburg Emperors' (MHS 737),
devotes one side to the delightful
incidental music Leopold composed
for theatrical performances at the
court.

6 Much of Leopold Wilhelm's collection was dispersed after his death,
many of the finest of the Flemish
works finding their way into scattered
European collections. The superb
Brueghels now in the Kunsthistorisches
Museum in Vienna were kept by the
family, however, and indicate the
magnificent scale on which he collected.

7 A good case could be made that
Leopold was a strongly Oedipal
personality, though intimate details of
his childhood are few and often
unreliable. It is a fact that when his
father died Leopold noted the event
in his 'Cracow Calendar' with cold
dispassion, recording merely the hour
of the Emperor's death and his precise
age. Erwin Sicher, *Leopold I of Austria:*
A Reappraisal, Dissertation, University of Southern California, 1970
(University Microfilms 70-25062).

8 Samuel J. Miller and John P. Spiel-
man, *Cristóbal de Rojas y Spínola,*
Cameralist and Irenecist (1626–1695),
Transactions of the American Phil-

osophical Society, New Series Vol. 52 Pt. 5 (Philadelphia 1962).

9 Grete Mecenseffy, 'Im Dienste Dreier Habsburger, Leben und Wirken des Fürsten Weikhard Auersperg (1615–1677)', AÖG, Vol. 114 Pt. 2 (Vienna, 1938).

10 Eduard Holzmair, 'Geld und Münze unter Kaiser Leopold I', MIÖG, Vol. 60 (1962) 238–250.

11 Alfred Francis Pribram, 'Die Niederösterreichische Stände und die Krone in der Zeit Kaiser Leopold I', MIÖG, Vol. 14 (1893) 589–652. Unfortunately there are few equally detailed studies of other provinces to complete the picture, but the situation was probably similar throughout the hereditary lands, perhaps somewhat less confused in better-managed Bohemia, worse if anything in Hungary.

Chapter IV

1 Gunther E. Rothenberg, *The Austrian Military Border in Croatia, 1522–1747* (Urbana, Illinois, 1960).

2 Turkish trade in Christian slaves remained an important element in the Ottoman economy. Generally it was women who were taken, the men were usually killed if they were caught in a raid. At one point toward the end of the century there were so many Christian women flooding the slave markets of Constantinople that dealers feared the price level would collapse in a glutted market. See Erich Zöllner, *Geschichte Österreichs*, 276.

3 In his recent dissertation Erwin Sicher argues this point, and the interpretation seems to fit the evidence, though Leopold found bickering distasteful and often took what measures he could to avoid being personally involved in squabbles.

4 Alfred Francis Pribram and Moritz Landwehr von Pragenau, *Die Privatbriefe Kaiser Leopold I an den Grafen F. E. Pötting, 1662–1673*, FRA, Vols. 56, 57 (Vienna 1903, 1904): see volume I, introduction and reports for 1662–63.

5 For a good discussion of the relations between Austria and Turkey in this period see Thomas M. Barker, *Double Eagle and Crescent* (Albany 1967).

6 H. Forst, 'Die deutschen Reichstruppen im Türkenkriege 1664', MIÖG, Supplementary Volume 6 (Vienna 1901) 634–648.

7 Georg Wagner, 'Der angebliche kaiserliche "Türkentribut" nach der Schlacht von Mogersdorf 1664' MIÖG, Vol. 72 (Vienna 1964) 409–441. Wagner argues that the payments stipulated in the treaty of Vasvár were not a tribute, but an 'exchange of gifts' with the Turks.

8 Quoted by O. Redlich, *Weltmacht des Barock*, 192–193, note 4. See also Pribram and von Pragenau, *Privatbriefe*, I, 83, note 2.

Chapter V

1 On Louis XIV see the admirable biography by John B. Wolf, *Louis XIV* (New York 1968) and John C. Rule (ed.), *Louis XIV and the Craft of Kingship* (Columbus, Ohio 1969). In the latter work, particularly see John C. Rule's article 'Louis XIV, Roi-Bureaucrate' and Ragnhild M. Hatton, 'Louis XIV and his Fellow Monarchs'.

2 G. Mentz, *Johann Philipp von Schönborn*, 111, note 3; S. Miller and J. Spielman, *Cristóbal de Rojas y Spínola*, 21: Rojas was induced to broach the subject discreetly in Madrid while he was there in 1663 ostensibly negotiating commercial agreements.

3 Leopold to von Pötting, 18 February 1665: 'bin ich entschlossen kein primo ministro oder valido zu haben': Pribram and von Pragenau, *Privatbriefe*, I, 105.

4 See Andreas Liess, *Wiener Barockmusik* (Vienna 1946), for a general account of the theatrical and musical life of Vienna, and more specifically for the festivities of 1666 to 1668, Marc Antonio Cesti, *Il pomo d'oro*, in *Denkmäler der Tonkunst in Österreich* (Graz 1959).

5 ÖNB, Musiksammlung, 16885. Leopold I: 'Aliquos cantilenarum modi inserti operi dramatico "il pomo d'oro"'.

6 The text of the treaty is in Arsène Legrelle, *La diplomatie Française et la succession d'Espagne* (2nd ed., 6 vols, Braine-le-Comte 1895–99) I, 518.

7 Leopold to von Pötting, 14 December 1669. Leopold warned von Pötting that there would be much noise made about the affair, for he refused to discuss the matter with Auersperg – 'y no cumple mi serbitio que se able mucho de los motibos, que tube para ello . . .': Pribram and von Pragenau, *Privatbriefe*, II, 56.

8 Oswald Redlich, 'Das Tagebuch Esias Pufendorfs, schwedischen Residenten am Kaiserhofe von 1671 bis 1674', MIÖG, Vol. 37 (Vienna 1916) 575. When there was complaint about Leopold's favours to Hocher, a mere bourgeois, Leopold was reported to have said that he 'had enough nobles, and could create as many as he wanted, but talented and experienced men like Dr. Hocher are rare and neither he nor the Empire should be robbed of their service'.

9 Redlich, *Weltmacht des Barock*, 108.

10 *Ibid.*, 109f. See also Redlich's edition of Pufendorf's journals and the relation of 1672 cited in note 8 above.

Chapter VI

1 See Thomas von Bogyay, *Grundzüge der Geschichte Ungarns* (Darmstadt 1967) 105–118; W. McNeill, *Europe's Steppe Frontier* (Chicago 1964) 147f.; C. A. Macartney, *Hungary, A Short History* (Edinburgh 1962) 85f.

2 Herbert Hassinger, 'Die erste Wiener Orientalische Handelscompagnie, 1667–1683', *Vierteljahrheft für Sozial und Wirtschaftsgeschichte*, Vol. 35 (1942) 1–53.

3 Oswald Redlich, *Weltmacht des Barock*, 202f. This account relies heavily on Redlich for the details, if not always for the interpretation of the Hungarian troubles.

4 Although there were no Hungarians on the panel, at least one of its members, Dr Christof Abele, who had also served on the preliminary inquiry, knew the Hungarian law and cited it in his *votum* in favour of the death penalty

against Nádasdy. Johann Graf Mailáth, *Geschichte des österreichischen Kaiserstaates* (5 vols, Hamburg 1834–50) IV, 93.

5 Leopold to von Pötting, 2 December 1671: 'Ich hab es nit gern getan, allein ne Hungari possunt credere Germanis omnia condonari, illos solum plecti': Pribram and von Pragenau, *Privatbriefe*, II, 202.

6 O. Redlich, 'Das Tagebuch Esias Pufendorfs . . .', MIÖG, Vol. 37, p. 588.

7 *Ibid.*

8 See M. Bucsay, *Geschichte des Protestantismus in Ungarn* (Stuttgart 1959).

9 O. Redlich, *Weltmacht des Barock*, 222; also 'Das Tagebuch von Esias Pufendorf . . .' 590, 591. Emmerich Sinelli at one point expressed the wish that he, rather than 'those others', had been sent to Hungary.

10 ÖNB, Musiksammlung, 16054: Leopold I, *Missa pro defunctis*, Anno 1673. Although the exact date is not certain, it seems likely that Leopold found consolation in composing the music of this touching requiem.

11 A. F. Pribram, 'Ein Habsburg-Stuartisches Heiratsprojekt', MIÖG, Vol. 29 (1908) 423–466.

Chapter VII

1 Stories circulated that Leopold had been poisoned; an Italian adventurer named Borri claimed to have cured him. Mailáth concluded that Borri's story was a fabrication. The nature of Leopold's illness remains a mystery: Mailáth, *Geschichte des österreichischen Kaiserstaates*, IV, 98ff.

2 Although Leopold punctiliously observed public mourning, he did occasionally allow himself private indulgence. In March 1666 when *Fasching* (the pre-lenten carnival) was subdued by court mourning, he wrote to von Pötting: 'doch haben wir etliche Festl in camera gehabt, dann es hilft dem Todten doch nicht wann man traurig ist . . .': Pribram and von Pragenau, *Privatbriefe*, I, 210.

3 Leopold's only mention of this incident to von Pötting, with whom he

usually shared everything he regarded as important, is in a letter of 9 September 1671 in which he mentions his satisfaction at the cordiality shown him by the city fathers at the consecration of the church built on the site of the old synagogue: *ibid.*, II, 185. See Carl Weiss, *Geschichte der Stadt Wien* (2 vols, 2nd edn., Vienna 1882–83) II, 228ff. The disturbances in the European Jewish communities arising out of the messianic movement of Sabbatai Sevi, who converted to Islam in 1666, may also have played a role in the decision.

4 The best source on Lobkowitz remains Adam Wolf, *Fürst Wenzel Lobkowitz, erster geheimer Rath Kaiser Leopold I, 1609–1677* (Vienna 1869). On Lisola's part in these events see Alfred Francis Pribram, *Franz Paul Freiherr von Lisola, 1613–1674, und die Politik seiner Zeit* (Leipzig 1894).

5 O. Redlich, *Weltmacht des Barock*, 139.

6 The most vivid contemporary picture of Hocher is in Esias Pufendorf's journal and dispatches. See O. Redlich, 'Das Tagebuch Esias Pufendorf . . .', 574–576.

7 Montecuccoli was a scholar as well as a practitioner of war, having written three books on the art: *Tratato di guerra* (1641), *Dell'arte militare* (1653), and *Della guerra col Turco in Ungheria* (1670). He was a complex personality; according to Pufendorf, a man who remained poor in spite of many opportunities to enrich himself.

8 O. Redlich, *Weltmacht des Barock*, 155–156.

Chapter VIII

1 Several versions of histories of the Hungarian rebellions appeared in France and the Dutch Republic between 1680 and 1739: *Histoire des troubles d'Hongrie* (6 vols, Paris 1680), *Histoire des revolutions d'Hongrie* (6 vols, The Hague 1739). Both contain *mémoires* by one Niclos Bethlen; the latter includes purported *mémoires* of Ferenc II Rákóczy, covering events down to 1711. Ever since the propaganda and pamphlet controversies of

the seventeenth century this period has been a battlefield for national prejudices. A thorough and impartial study of Hungary is still badly needed, particularly for the period 1671–1703.

2 See I. Huditá, *Histoire des relations diplomatiques entre France et la Transylvanie au XVIIème siècle* (Paris 1927).

3 S. Miller and J. Spielman, *Cristóbal de Rojas y Spínola*, 33–41.

4 Thomas M. Barker, *Double Eagle and Crescent* (Albany 1967) 103f. The legend of 'Du lieber Augustin' comes from the plague year in Vienna: a drunken minstrel, having passed out from drink, found himself thrown onto a heap of corpses; regaining consciousness, he began to play his little bagpipe to attract attention to the fact that he was still alive.

5 The complaints of the peasants presented to Leopold in Prague on 22 November 1679 and the *Robotpatent* are reprinted in Günther Franz, *Quellen zur Geschichte des Bauernstandes in der Neuzeit* (Darmstadt 1963) 157–165.

6 O. Redlich, *Weltmacht des Barock*, 230f.

7 Fellner and Kretschmayr, *Österreichische Zentralverwaltung*, 89–91.

8 *Ibid.*

Chapter IX

1 T. Barker, *Double Eagle and Crescent*, 136f. and 400 note 17.

2 The major work on French diplomacy in Constantinople is Kurt Koehler, *Die orientalische Politik Ludwigs XIV.: ihr Verhältnis zum Türkenkrieg von 1683* (Leipzig 1907). Equally valuable for the international background is Onno Klopp, *Das Jahr 1683 und der folgende grosse Türkenkrieg bis zum Frieden von Carlowitz, 1699* (Graz 1882).

3 The best work on Poland under Sobieski is Otto Forst de Battaglia, *Jan Sobieski: König von Polen* (Einsiedeln-Zurich 1946). A summary of this superb political biography is in Forst de Battaglia's chapter 24 of the *Cambridge History of Poland*.

4 See A. N. Kurat, 'The Ottoman Empire under Mehmed IV' in the *New Cambridge Modern History*, V, 500–518. For a good analysis of various historical views of the Ottoman empire in this period see T. Barker, *Double Eagle and Crescent*, 55–63.
5 Some of these units were recruited and maintained by the palatine and the Catholic magnates to defend their own estates from the *Kuruc*.
6 Reinhold Lorenz, 'Reisen des Kaisers Leopold I. und des Kurfürsten Max Emmanuel im Türkenjahr 1683', MIÖG, Vol. 52 (1938), and R. Miller, 'Die Hofreisen Kaiser Leopold I', MIÖG, Vol. 55 (1967). One of the most circumstantial reports from the days before the siege is that of the Hessian envoy Justus Passer, edited by Ludwig Vauer: 'Bericht des hessendarmstädtischen Gesandten Justus Eberhard Passer an die Landgräfin Elisabeth Dorothea über die Vorgänge am kaiserlichen Hofe und in Wien von 1680–1683', AÖG, Vol. 37 (1867).
7 T. Barker, *Double Eagle and Crescent*, 244–245. Barker estimates that some 60,000 people fled Vienna and its environs, almost certainly an exaggerated figure, since the population within the walls could hardly have been more than half again that large. The refugees were mostly officials, nobles, diplomats and the economic elite of the city who had the means of fleeing with their retinues of servants.

Chapter X

1 O. Redlich, *Weltmacht des Barock*, 332.
2 For the military operations during the siege, see T. Barker, *Double Eagle and Crescent*, Chapter 8.
3 Paul Wentzcke, *Feldherr des Kaisers; Leben und Taten Herzog Karls V. von Lothringen* (Leipzig 1943), a scholarly study with much useful detail under the propagandistic surface.
4 T. Barker, *Dougle Eagle and Crescent*, 306. See also 427, note 71, for a careful analysis of Polish strength. Given the distance he had to cover in a short

time, Sobieski could hardly have brought large masses of infantry; he wisely chose to push ahead with his cavalry and such other units as could find wagon transport.
5 Richard F. Kreutel, translator and editor, *Kara Mustafa vor Wien, Das türkische Tagebuch der Belagerung Wiens 1683, verfasst vom Zeremonienmeister der Hohen Pforte*: Vol. I of the series *Osmanische Geschichtsschreiber* (Graz 1955) 107.
6 *Ibid.*, 110. The author of the Turkish journal puts the time of the vizier's decision to break off the engagement and flee at 'an hour and a half before sunset'. He notes later that the vizier lost his way in the dark before he reached the Raab.
7 T. Barker, *Double Eagle and Crescent*, 341, and 432–433, note 19.
8 *Ibid.*, 341f., and O. Redlich, *Weltmacht des Barock*, 263f.
9 T. Barker, *Double Eagle and Crescent*, 363–364; O. Redlich, *Weltmacht des Barock*, 266; Walter Stürminger. *Bibliographie und Ikonographie der Türkenbelagerungen Wiens 1529 und 1683* (Vienna-Graz 1955) 63. The fate of Kara Mustafa's head is a matter of some dispute. When Belgrade fell to the Austrians a few years after the siege, a skull, purported to be the vizier's, was sent to Vienna. The grisly relic is still displayed in the municipal museum. Barker's account, which I follow here, seems the most likely one, for the Sublime Porte still expected its agents to provide evidence that they had faithfully carried out the sultan's orders.

Chapter XI

1 AGS: Estado, 3925. Manuel de Lira's reply to the papal appeal for peace, dated 9 May 1683. See also O. Redlich, *Weltmacht des Barock*, 271.
2 AGS: Estado, 3924. Consultas del consejo del estado, 2 and 30 December 1683. The Spanish council was clearly frustrated by its apparent impotence in the face of French power, obsessed with keeping the Netherlands out of Louis' grasp. The councillors wavered in

their faith in the Empire's ability to help them, but concluded that they would have to go to war even without allies.

3 O. Redlich, *Weltmacht des Barock*, 275.

4 F. Schevill, *The Great Elector* (Chicago 1947). For the diplomacy see Ferdinand Fehling, *Die europäische Politik des Grossen Kurfürsten 1667–1688* (Leipzig 1910).

5 Friedrich Kleyser, *Der Flugschriftenkampf gegen Ludwig XIV zur Zeit des pfälzischen Krieges* (Berlin 1935). O. Redlich, *Weltmacht des Barock*, 271, note 3 surveys nineteenth-century judgments on Leopold's decision, most of them unfavourable.

6 Onno Klopp edited the correspondence between Leopold and Marco d'Aviano: *Corrispondenza epistolare tra Leopoldo I imperatore ed il P. Marco d'Aviano Capuccino* (Graz 1888). Next to the letters to von Pötting edited by Pribram and von Pragenau, this is the most important collection of Leopold's personal correspondence available in print. Scholars have been working on some other parts of Leopold's private correspondence, but the Emperor's impossible handwriting has made the task all but hopeless.

7 O. Redlich, *Weltmacht des Barock*, 285.

8 *Ibid.*, 286f.

Chapter XII

1 Otto Brunner, 'Österreich und die Walachei während des Türkenkrieges von 1683–1699', MIÖG, Vol. 44 (1930), 265ff.

2 There were many officers in the Brandenburg army who shared the strong anti-French views of the electoral prince Friedrich.

3 O. Redlich, *Weltmacht des Barock*, 289f. For a full account of these negotiations see A. F. Pribram, *Österreich und Brandenburg 1685–1686* (Innsbruck 1884).

4 Reports of this audience are vague. See O. Redlich, *Weltmacht des Barock*, 298, and Leopold's letter to Marco d'Aviano dated 4 June 1686: Klopp, *Corrispondenza*, 103.

5 For details of the siege of Buda and the campaign against Suleiman's relief force see O. Redlich, *Weltmacht des Barock*, 198–205.

Chapter XIII

1 Among the Turkish prisoners captured in 1688 was one Osman Aga of Temesvár, whose sensationalized autobiography of his years of captivity offers many revealing details about the war zone in these years: Richard F. Kreutel and Otto Spies (editors and translators), *Der Gefangene der Giauren*, Vol. 4 in the Series *Osmanische Geschichtsschreiber* (Graz 1962)

2 O. Redlich, *Weltmacht des Barock*, 415.

3 Given the nearly unanimously unfavourable portraits of Caraffa, it is difficult to understand why Leopold appointed him in the first place, unless he shared Caraffa's hatred for the Magyars and only later discovered how dangerous the man was. See Denis Sinor, *History of Hungary* (London 1959) 214; V.-L. Tapié, *The Rise and Fall of the Habsburg Monarchy*, 146–149.

4 Caraffa hinted in his early reports that the conspiracy had flourished because the Emperor had been too lenient and moderate in dealing with the malcontents: Mailáth, *Geschichte des Österreichischen Kaiserstaates*, IV, 226.

5 On the work of the commissions and the diet of 1687–88 the best account is still O. Redlich, *Weltmacht des Barock*, 419–435.

6 The coronation oath as finally recorded is excerpted in C. A. Macartney, *The Habsburg and Hohenzollern Dynasties in the Seventeenth and Eighteenth Centuries* (New York 1970) 85f.

7 The crucial question of interpretation of laws was left vague. Joseph's coronation oath included a statement that 'the king and the assembled estates were to agree on the interpretation and application of the laws': *ibid.*, 82.

8 Denis Sinor, *History of Hungary*, 214–215.

9 V.-L. Tapié, _The Rise and Fall of the Habsburg Monarchy_, 150–155, gives a brief summary of their ideas.
10 Quoted in O. Redlich, _Weltmacht des Barock_, 415.
11 In this the commission presumably drew upon Leopold's _Robotpatent_ of 1680 for Bohemia. See above, p. 187.

Chapter XIV

1 Richard Place, 'The Self-Deception of the Strong, France on the Eve of the War of the League of Augsburg', _French Historical Studies_, Vol. 4 No. 4 (1970) 459–473.
2 O. Klopp, _Corrispondenza_, 179f.
3 O. Redlich, _Weltmacht des Barock_, 332–333. Leopold's own confessor probably had little to say in this matter, for Leopold habitually tried to separate public issues from his personal sins in the privacy of the confessional.
4 O. Klopp, _Corrispondenza_, 191.
5 HHSA England. Hofkorrespondenz, 1689–1690.
6 Leopold profited by 100,000 Ducats in granting Victor Amadeus II the right to style himself 'Royal Highness'. Leibniz, who was in Vienna at the time, noted in a letter to Sophia of Hanover that the money was called 'miracle money' coming as it did at the moment of greatest need: Onno Klopp, _Das Jahr 1683_, 466.
7 Max Braubach, _Prinz Eugen von Savoyen_ (5 vols, Vienna 1963–65) I, 160f.
8 Onno Klopp, _Der Fall des Hauses Stuart und Succession des Hauses Hannover in Grossbritannien und Irland im Zusammenhange der europäischen Angelegenheiten von 1660–1714_ (14 vols, Vienna 1875–88): see vols V and VI on Hanoverian policy in the 1680s and on the ninth electorate.
9 O. Redlich, _Weltmacht des Barock_, 348.

Chapter XV

1 Quoted in Max Braubach, _Prinz Eugen_, I, 197, 408 note 332.
2 Pierre Goubert, _Louis XIV and Twenty Million Frenchmen_, translated by Anne Carter from the French version of 1966 (New York 1970, London 1972).
3 The story of these secret negotiations has been told in great detail by Heinrich Ritter von Srbik, _Wien und Versailles, 1692–1697_ (Munich 1944).
4 The new Viennese nuncio, Tanara, who was a Pole by birth, corresponded with the French ambassador in Warsaw, d'Esneval. The Hanoverian delegates negotiating their duke's elevation to the electoral dignity offered another avenue for transmitting secret correspondence with France. More dramatic yet was the work of adventurers and double agents like the 'comte de Sanis', a Persian by birth, and the inveterate traveller, writer and jewel dealer Jean-Baptiste Tavernier: see Srbik, _Wien und Versailles_, 45–83.
5 O. Redlich, _Weltmacht des Barock_, 371.
6 _Ibid._, 437–438. Otto Brunner, 'Österreich und die Walachei während des Türkenkrieges von 1683–1699', MIÖG, Vol. 44 (1930) 265–323 gives a detailed survey of Vienna's relations with one of the key Balkan principalities caught in the midst of the conflict between two imperial powers and three warring religions.
7 Leopold did not wait for confirmation of the news. In fact Eugene's commission had been drawn up some days before it was clear that Friedrich August would win the election. See Max Braubach, _Prinz Eugen_, I, 244–247.
8 For a detailed account of the battle see _Feldzüge_, II, 144–154.
9 O. Redlich, _Weltmacht des Barock_, 479.

Chapter XVI

1 The best study of the depressing reign of Charles II is the Duque de Maura, _Vida y reinado de Carlos II_ (2nd. edn. 2 vols, Madrid 1954). See also Adalbert, Prinz von Bayern, _Das Ende der Habsburger in Spanien_ (2 vols, Munich 1929) and Ludwig Pfandl, _Karl II_ (in Spanish translation _Carlos II_, Madrid 1947). There is a

good, if brief, survey of the period in John Lynch, *Spain under the Habsburgs* (2 vols, Oxford 1966–69), II, 229–280.
2 Quoted in O. Redlich, *Weltmacht des Barock*, 380. Apparently the Austrians were as surprised as the French by the alacrity with which the Spaniards greeted the Bavarian candidacy, though there was as yet no agreement to establish Max Emmanuel in the Spanish Netherlands.
3 O. Klopp, *Corrispondenza*, 321. Leopold was clearly disappointed by the will, but could still draw satisfaction from the fact that it excluded France, while the Bavarian succession offered future marital prospects that might reunite the crown to the dynasty.
4 For a detailed account of these sessions in the privy conference see Arnold Gaedeke, *Die Politik Österreichs in der Spanischen Erbfolgefrage* (2 vols, Leipzig 1877).

Chapter XVII

1 Pierre Goubert, *Louis XIV and Twenty Million Frenchmen*, offers some striking evidence of Leopold's contemporary popularity.
2 On Austrian baroque architecture see Ann T. Leitich, *Vienna Gloriosa, Weltstadt des Barock* (Vienna 1963) and Fred Hennings, *Das Barocke Wien* (2 vols., Vienna 1965).
3 'Rat der Greisen': O. Redlich, *Das Werden einer Grossmacht, Österreich von 1700 bis 1740* (3rd. edn, Baden bei Wien 1938) 11.
4 Wilhelm Bauer, 'Der "Ehren-Ruff Teutschlands" von Wagner von Wagenfels', MIÖG, Vol. 41 (1926) 257–272.
5 Arnold Berney, 'Die Hochzeit Josephs I', MIÖG, Vol. 42 (1927) 64–83.
6 Villars wrote Louis XIV that 'all who have close acquaintance with the Emperor say they have never seen this prince so disturbed': quoted in Max Braubach, *Prinz Eugen*, I, 305.
7 HHSA 45. England, Weisungen. Leopold to Goess, 29 January 1701: '... wir auf dem toto nicht zu beharen

begehren; wir stehen aber sehr an ob davon in der allianz etwas zu melden, der zeit rathsamb seye.'
8 For the role of the allied demand for 'cautionary towns' in the breakdown of the negotiations see R. M. Hatton, 'Louis XIV and His Fellow Monarchs', *Louis XIV and the Craft of Kingship* (ed. John C. Rule, Columbus, Ohio, 1969) 172–73 and authorities there cited.
9 HHSA 45. England, Weisungen. Leopold to Wratislaw, 9 March 1701: The Emperor will be content with 'der Niederlanden und der in Italien zur Cron Spanien gehörig gewesenen Länder.'

Chapter XVIII

1 For the troubles plaguing Eugene in Italy, see *Feldzüge*, Vols III and IV; also Max Braubach, *Prinz Eugen*, I, 331f.
2 O. Redlich, *Das Werden einer Grossmacht*, 11; Max Braubach, *Prinz Eugen*, I, 353–358.
3 M. Grunwald, *Samuel Oppenheimer und sein Kreis* (Vienna 1953).
4 Eugene to Guido Starhemberg, 27 June 1703. *Feldzüge*, V, Appendix, 83.
5 Printed in English translation in C. A. Macartney, *The Habsburg and Hohenzollern Dynasties*, 87–88.
6 The main source for French plans is F. E. de Vault and J. J. G. Pelet, *Mémoires militaires relatifs à la succession d'Espagne sous Louis XIV* (11 vols, Paris 1835–62).
7 Quoted in Redlich, *Das Werden einer Grossmacht*, 25. For a detailed account of the uprisings and their military consequences see *Feldzüge*, V, 463–499.
8 Bela Köpeczi, *La France et la Hongrie au début du XVIIIᵉ siècle; Étude d' histoire des relations diplomatiques et d'histoire des idées* (Budapest 1971).
9 *Feldzüge*, VI, 524.

Chapter XIX

1 Ferdinand Menčik, 'Die letzten Tage Kaiser Leopolds I', MIÖG, Vol. 19 (1898), 518–520.

2 Fellner and Kretschmayr, *Zentral-verwaltung*, 275ff. There was no change in the court chamber (Gundaker Starhemberg), the war council (prince Eugene of Savoy), the aulic council (count Oettingen), or in the Imperial chancellery (count Schönborn had taken office as vice-chancellor in February 1705). Bucellini was replaced by Seilern in the Austrian chancellery on 3 June but Seilern had been doing most of the chancellor's work for some time. Prince Salm replaced Harrach as grand chamberlain on 15 June; the Bohemian chancellor count Wrbna was replaced by count Wenzel Kinsky on 6 June 1705, but

Leopold had already assured Kinsky of this office by an edict of 29 May 1704.
3 For the spectacular funeral monuments proposed to mourn Leopold, see ÖNB Bildarchiv, Albertina, ALB 55.046-049.
4 For an exaggerated version of this portrayal, see Victor S. Mamatey, *Rise of the Habsburg Empire 1526–1815* (New York, 1971), 68.
5 Anna Coreth, *Pietas Austriaca*, 7, suggests that it was the new orders – Jesuits, Capuchins, Carmelites and Piarists – who built 'the direct spiritual bridge between the dynasty and the people'.

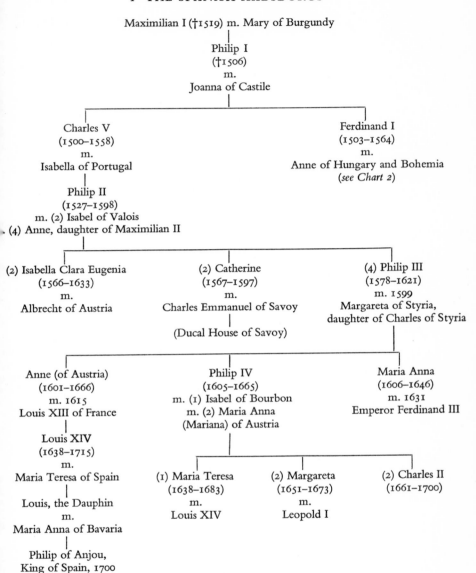

Maximilian I (†1519) m. Mary of Burgundy

Philip I
(†1506)
m.
Joanna of Castile

Charles V
(1500–1558)
m.
Isabella of Portugal

Ferdinand I
(1503–1564)
m.
Anne of Hungary and Bohemia
(*see Chart 2*)

Philip II
(1527–1598)
m. (2) Isabel of Valois
(4) Anne, daughter of Maximilian II

(2) Isabella Clara Eugenia
(1566–1633)
m.
Albrecht of Austria

(2) Catherine
(1567–1597)
m.
Charles Emmanuel of Savoy

(Ducal House of Savoy)

(4) Philip III
(1578–1621)
m. 1599
Margareta of Styria,
daughter of Charles of Styria

Anne (of Austria)
(1601–1666)
m. 1615
Louis XIII of France

Philip IV
(1605–1665)
m. (1) Isabel of Bourbon
m. (2) Maria Anna
(Mariana) of Austria

Maria Anna
(1606–1646)
m. 1631
Emperor Ferdinand III

Louis XIV
(1638–1715)
m.
Maria Teresa of Spain

Louis, the Dauphin
m.
Maria Anna of Bavaria

Philip of Anjou,
King of Spain, 1700

(1) Maria Teresa
(1638–1683)
m.
Louis XIV

(2) Margareta
(1651–1673)
m.
Leopold I

(2) Charles II
(1661–1700)

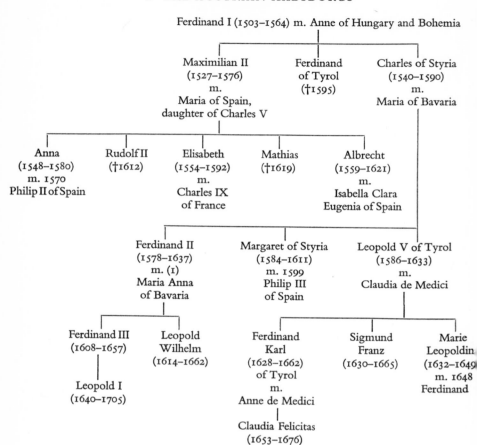

Ferdinand I (1503–1564) m. Anne of Hungary and Bohemia

Maximilian II (1527–1576) m. Maria of Spain, daughter of Charles V

Ferdinand of Tyrol (†1595)

Charles of Styria (1540–1590) m. Maria of Bavaria

Anna (1548–1580) m. 1570 Philip II of Spain

Rudolf II (†1612)

Elisabeth (1554–1592) m. Charles IX of France

Mathias (†1619)

Albrecht (1559–1621) m. Isabella Clara Eugenia of Spain

Ferdinand II (1578–1637) m. (1) Maria Anna of Bavaria

Margaret of Styria (1584–1611) m. 1599 Philip III of Spain

Leopold V of Tyrol (1586–1633) m. Claudia de Medici

Ferdinand III (1608–1657)

Leopold Wilhelm (1614–1662)

Ferdinand Karl (1628–1662) of Tyrol m. Anne de Medici

Sigmund Franz (1630–1665)

Marie Leopoldin (1632–1649) m. 1648 Ferdinand

Leopold I (1640–1705)

Claudia Felicitas (1653–1676)

3 THE FAMILY OF LEOPOLD I

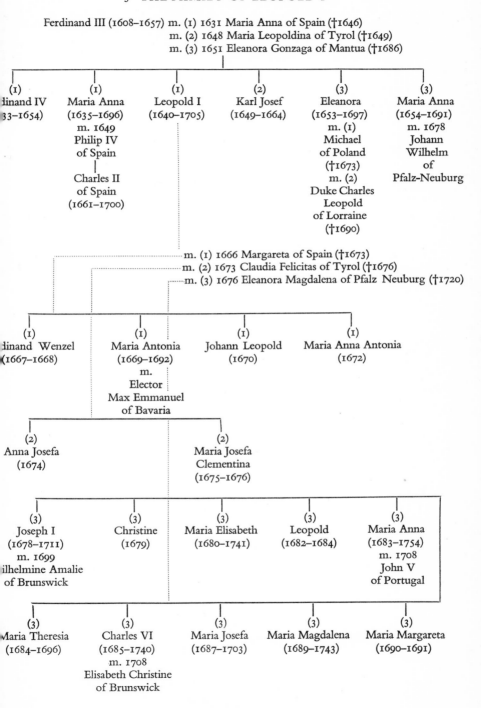

Ferdinand III (1608–1657) m. (1) 1631 Maria Anna of Spain (†1646)
m. (2) 1648 Maria Leopoldina of Tyrol (†1649)
m. (3) 1651 Eleanora Gonzaga of Mantua (†1686)

(1) ...dinand IV ...3–1654)	(1) Maria Anna (1635–1696) m. 1649 Philip IV of Spain Charles II of Spain (1661–1700)	(1) Leopold I (1640–1705)	(2) Karl Josef (1649–1664)	(3) Eleanora (1653–1697) m. (1) Michael of Poland (†1673) m. (2) Duke Charles Leopold of Lorraine (†1690)	(3) Maria Anna (1654–1691) m. 1678 Johann Wilhelm of Pfalz-Neuburg

m. (1) 1666 Margareta of Spain (†1673)
m. (2) 1673 Claudia Felicitas of Tyrol (†1676)
m. (3) 1676 Eleanora Magdalena of Pfalz Neuburg (†1720)

(1) ...dinand Wenzel (1667–1668)	(1) Maria Antonia (1669–1692) m. Elector Max Emmanuel of Bavaria	(1) Johann Leopold (1670)	(1) Maria Anna Antonia (1672)

(2) Anna Josefa (1674)	(2) Maria Josefa Clementina (1675–1676)

(3) Joseph I (1678–1711) m. 1699 ...ilhelmine Amalie of Brunswick	(3) Christine (1679)	(3) Maria Elisabeth (1680–1741)	(3) Leopold (1682–1684)	(3) Maria Anna (1683–1754) m. 1708 John V of Portugal

(3) ...Maria Theresia (1684–1696)	(3) Charles VI (1685–1740) m. 1708 Elisabeth Christine of Brunswick	(3) Maria Josefa (1687–1703)	(3) Maria Magdalena (1689–1743)	(3) Maria Margareta (1690–1691)

Leopold I's dominions in relation to his neighbours (1699).

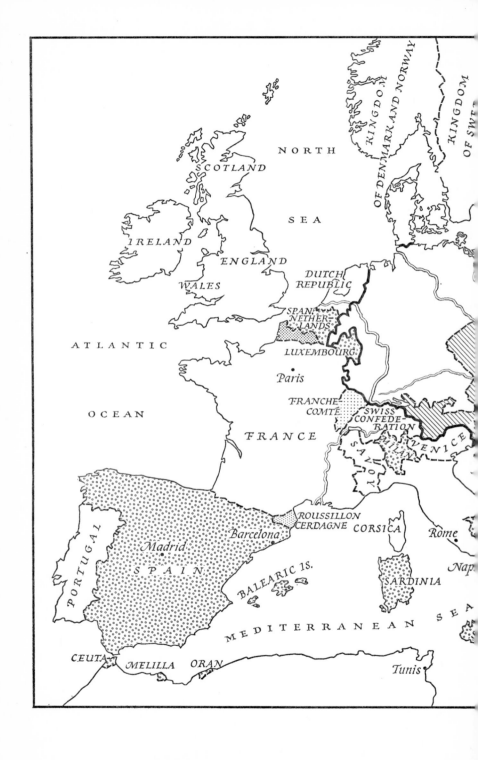

AUSTRIAN AND SPANISH HABSBURG POSSESSIONS IN
EUROPE 1658~1700

Austrian Habsburg possessions
Gains from Ottomans 1699
Spanish Habsburg possessions
Loss to France 1659 (Roussillon, north Cerdagne)
Loss to France in Spanish Netherlands 1659 & 1668
Loss to France in 1678 (Franche-Comté)
Effective border of Holy Roman Empire of German Nation ——

FINLAND

ESTONIA

LIVONIA

COURLAND

POLISH-

LITHUANIAN

COMMONWEALTH

RUSSIA

KHANATE
OF
CRIMEA

MOLDAVIA

Bude-Pest
HUNGARY

WALLACHIA

BLACK SEA

Belgrade

OTTOMAN

Constantinople

EMPIRE

CRETE

| 100 | 200 | 300 | 400 Mls |
| 100 | 200 | 300 | 400 | 500 | Kms |

List of Illustrations

27 Eleanora Magdalena of Pfalz-Neuburg; print by J. Gole. Österreichische Nationalbibliothek

28 Emperor Joseph I; bust by anonymous Austrian sculptor, c. 1695. Kunsthistorisches Museum

29 Emperor Charles VI; bust by anonymous Austrian sculptor, c. 1695. Kunsthistorisches Museum.

30 First project for palace of Schönbrunn; engraving by J. A. Delsenbach after drawing by J. B. Fischer von Erlach. Österreichische Nationalbibliothek

31 Leopold I in Spanish dress; print by Caspar Luyken. Österreichische Nationalbibliothek

32 Father Emmerich Sinelli; anonymous portrait, 1680. Photo Österreichische Nationalbibliothek.

33 Title page of Ph. W. von Hörwigk's *Österreich über Alles*, 1684. Österreichische Nationalbibliothek.

34 S. Oppenheimer; print by J. A. Pfeffel. Österreichische Nationalbibliothek

35 The burning of Heidelberg, 1693; contemporary print. Österreichische Nationalbibliothek

36 Elector George Ludwig of Hanover, after 1714 King George I of England; print by I. C. Weigel. British Museum

37 Battle of Blenheim, 13 August 1704; medal by M. Brunner. Kunsthistorisches Museum

38 Prince Wenzel Lobkowitz; print by J. Borckwig, c. 1670. Österreichische Nationalbibliothek

39 Count Georg Ludw von Sinzendorf; print after drawing by Jan de Herr Österreichische Nationalbibliothek

40 Count Franz Ulri Kinsky; print by H. H. Quiter. Österreichische N tionalbibliothek

41 Count Johann Wenz Wratislaw von Mitrowit contemporary print. Österreichische Nationalbibliothek

42 Cardinal Kolonitsch; co temporary print. Österreichische Nationalbibliothek

43 Joseph as king of Hu gary, 1687; contemporary print. Österreichische Natio albibliothek

44 Leopold I lying in stat 1705; contemporary prir Österreichische Nationalbibliothek

Index